CAMBRIDGE NATIONAL LEVEL 1 / LEVEL 2

Enterprise and Marketing

Student Book

Mark Tippins, Karen Tullett
& Julie Whatford

CAMBRIDGE
UNIVERSITY PRESS

University Printing House, Cambridge CB2 8BS, United Kingdom

One Liberty Plaza, 20th Floor, New York, NY 10006, USA

477 Williamstown Road, Port Melbourne, VIC 3207, Australia

314–321, 3rd Floor, Plot 3, Splendor Forum, Jasola District Centre, New Delhi – 110025, India

103 Penang Road, #05–06/07, Visioncrest Commercial, Singapore 23846

Cambridge University Press is part of the University of Cambridge.

It furthers the University's mission by disseminating knowledge in the pursuit of education, learning and research at the highest international levels of excellence.

www.cambridge.org
Information on this title: www.cambridge.org/9781009106474

First published 2022

20 19 18 17 16 15 14 13 12 11 10 9 8 7 6 5 4 3 2 1

Printed in Italy by L.E.G.O. S.p.A.

A catalogue record for this publication is available from the British Library

ISBN 978-1-00910647-4 Paperback with Digital Access (2 Years)
ISBN 978-1-00910279-7 Digital Student Book (2 Years)
ISBN 978-1-00910280-3 Year site license

Additional resources for this publication at www.cambridge.org/9781009106474

Cambridge University Press has no responsibility for the persistence or accuracy of URLs for external or third-party internet websites referred to in this publication, and does not guarantee that any content on such websites is, or will remain, accurate or appropriate. Information regarding prices, travel timetables, and other factual information given in this work is correct at the time of first printing but Cambridge University Press does not guarantee the accuracy of such information thereafter.

The teaching content of this resource is endorsed by OCR for use with specification Level 1/Level 2 Cambridge National in Enterprise and Marketing (120 GLH)

All references to assessment, including assessment preparation and practice questions of any format/style, are the publisher's interpretation of the specification and are not endorsed by OCR.

This resource was designed for use with the version of the specification available at the time of publication. However, as specifications are updated over time, there may be contradictions between the resource and the specification, therefore please use the information on the latest specification and Sample Assessment Materials at all times when ensuring students are fully prepared for their assessments.
Endorsement indicates that a resource is suitable to support delivery of an OCR specification, but it does not mean that the endorsed resource is the only suitable resource to support delivery, or that it is required or necessary to achieve the qualification.
OCR recommends that teachers consider using a range of teaching and learning resources based on their own professional judgement for their students' needs. OCR has not paid for the production of this resource, nor does OCR receive any royalties from its sale. For more information about the endorsement process, please visit the OCR website.

....

....

Contents

Acknowledgements

The authors and publishers acknowledge the following sources of copyright material and are grateful for the permissions granted. While every effort has been made, it has not always been possible to identify the sources of all the material used, or to trace all copyright holders. If any omissions are brought to our notice, we will be happy to include the appropriate acknowledgements on reprinting. Thanks to the following for permission to reproduce images:

Cover Maskot/GI *Inside* **R067** Tolga Akmen/GI; Shapecharge/GI; Ian Gavan/GI; Johannes Eisele/GI; Pool/GI; Rachel Luna/GI; Leon Neal/GI; FatCamera/GI; Lilly Roadstones/GI; Andresr/GI; David Levenson/GI; BJI/GI; Douglas Stratton/GI; Thianchai Sitthikongsak/GI; Isabel Pavia/GI; Vera_Petrunina/GI; Lingqi Xie/GI; Jeff Greenberg/GI; Dan Kitwood/GI; Education Images/GI; Kris Connor/GI; Netrun78/GI; David Cole/Alamy Stock Photo; SOPA Images/GI; Adriana Iacob/Shutterstock; Linda Bestwick/Shutterstock; Simon Marcus Taplin/GI; Juan Zapata/GI; Leren Lu/GI; Martin Barraud/GI; Kwanchai Lerttanapunyaporn/GI; Krblokhin/GI; Picture Post/GI; Mike Kemp/GI; Fig. 1.36 by permission of MellowMill; Pekic/GI; 10'000 Hours/GI; Karl Tapales/GI; Clive Brunskill/GI; Oleksandr Hruts/GI; Oleksandr Hruts/GI; Isabel Infantes/GI; Naomi Baker/GI; tupangato/GI; Angelafoto/GI; Images By Tang Ming Tung/GI; JessicaGirvan/Shutterstock; Whitemay/GI; Image Source/GI; Coldsnowstorm/GI; Nathan Stirk/GI; Joe Raedle/GI; Matthew Horwood/GI; Mike Kemp/GI; NurPhoto/GI (x2); Mark Bassett/Alamy Stock Photo; A Stockphoto/GI; StefaNikolic/GI; Westend61/GI; MachineHeadz/GI; Nathan Stirk/GI; Sot/GI; Krisanapong Detraphiphat/GI; **R068** Viaframe/GI; Sarinyapinngam/GI; Jeff Greenberg/GI; MMassel/GI; wdstock/GI; Kiyoshi Hijiki/GI; Jeff Greenberg/GI; Andia/GI; Mgstudyo/GI; JohnnyGreig/GI; Jonathan Knowles/GI; Robert Carner/GI; SOPA Images/GI; Rachel Murray/GI; Westend61/GI; Tetra Images/GI; Jeremy Moeller/GI; NYS444/GI; Sergeyryzhov/GI; Morten Falch Sortlan/GI; Image Source/GI; Imran Kadir Photography/GI; Valentinrussanov/GI; Mariia Kozub/GI; SOPA Images/GI; Jung Yeon-JE/GI; Mediaphotos/GI; Justin Sullivan/GI; Westend61/GI (x2); Peter Dazeley/GI; Stefano Bianchetti/GI; Ollie Millington/GI; Kiyoshi Hijiki/GI; NICOLAS ASFOURI/GI; Matt Cardy/GI; **R069** Alexander Spatari/GI; Cavan Images/GI; SOPA Images/GI; South China Morning Post/GI; SOPA Images/GI; John Keeble/GI; Emmanuel Dunand/GI; Andrew Fox/GI; Pawel Liber/GI; Future Publishing/GI; Matthew Horwood/GI; D3sign/GI; Indranil Mukherjee/GI; Aldara Zarraoa/GI; Ian Forsyth/GI; Aleaimage/GI; Luis Alvarez/GI; Skynesher/GI; Flashpop/GI; Laflor/GI; Gregory Costanzo/GI; Timothy A. Clary/GI; Alvarez/GI

Key: GI–Getty images

About your Cambridge National Enterprise and Marketing course and qualification

Launching a new product or service onto the market can be an exciting challenge. The Cambridge National Enterprise and Marketing course will help you learn the vital skills necessary for success in business. You will learn how to find out about the needs and wants of your potential customers through market research, and how to use this information to plan and target promotions at the right people. You will learn about different types of business ownership, and how to complete financial calculations to determine whether your business idea will make a profit. You will apply your learning to design a brand identity and create a product proposal, which you will then market and pitch to an audience.

During your Enterprise and Marketing course, you will develop learning and practical skills that can be used in other life or work situations, such as skills in research, communication and presentation. Your Cambridge National in Enterprise and Marketing can help you progress on to other related study, such as further qualifications in Business.

How you will be assessed

You have to complete three mandatory units.

- R067: Enterprise and marketing concepts. You will take a written exam for this unit. The exam lasts for 1 hour 15 minutes, and is worth 70 marks (80 UMS). The exam is set and marked by OCR.

- R068: Design a business proposal. You will be given a set assignment with 6 practical tasks, which is worth 60 marks (60 UMS).

- R069: Market and pitch a business proposal. You will be given a set assignment with 5 practical tasks, which is worth 60 marks (60 UMS).

How to use this book

Throughout this book, you will notice lots of different features that will help your learning. These are explained below.

These features at the start of each unit give you guidance on the topic area, what you will learn and how you will be assessed.

Thought-provoking questions at the start of units and topics will get you thinking about the subject.

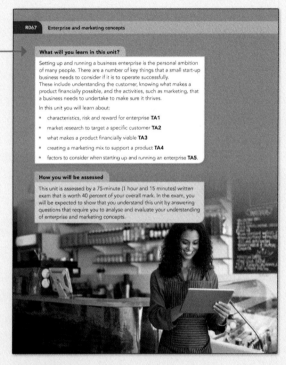

R067 **Enterprise and marketing concepts**

What will you learn in this unit?

Setting up and running a business enterprise is the personal ambition of many people. There are a number of key things that a small start-up business needs to consider if it is to operate successfully. These include understanding the customer, knowing what makes a product financially possible, and the activities, such as marketing, that a business needs to undertake to make sure it thrives.

In this unit you will learn about:

* characteristics, risk and reward for enterprise **TA1**
* market research to target a specific customer **TA2**
* what makes a product financially viable **TA3**
* creating a marketing mix to support a product **TA4**
* factors to consider when starting up and running an enterprise **TA5**.

How you will be assessed

This unit is assessed by a 75-minute (1 hour and 15 minutes) written exam that is worth 40 percent of your overall mark. In the exam, you will be expected to show that you understand this unit by answering questions that require you to analyse and evaluate your understanding of enterprise and marketing concepts.

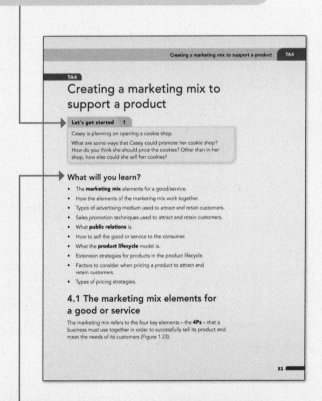

Creating a marketing mix to support a product | **TA4**

TA4

Creating a marketing mix to support a product

Let's get started **1**

Casey is planning on opening a cookie shop.

What are some ways that Casey could promote her cookie shop? How do you think she should price the cookies? Other than in her shop, how else could she sell her cookies?

What will you learn?

* The **marketing mix** elements for a good/service.
* How the elements of the marketing mix work together.
* Types of advertising medium used to attract and retain customers.
* Sales promotion techniques used to attract and retain customers.
* What **public relations** is.
* How to sell the good or service to the consumer.
* What the **product lifecycle** model is.
* Extension strategies for products in the product lifecycle.
* Factors to consider when pricing a product to attract and retain customers.
* Types of pricing strategies.

4.1 The marketing mix elements for a good or service

The marketing mix refers to the four key elements – the **4Ps** – that a business must use together in order to successfully sell its product and meet the needs of its customers (Figure 1.33).

83

Case study

Gabriel's water bottles

Gabriel runs a business that sells reusable water bottles made from recycled materials. He advertises his product range on Facebook, Twitter and Instagram. Gabriel uses a mixture of photos, videos and text to show his product range.

His posts always generate a lot of feedback from users and discussion amongst their social media friends (third parties). Gabriel finds that feedback from customers and their social media contacts is more influential than the content that he originally posts.

However, recently Gabriel received a negative review on Facebook about his water bottles, which was posted on his page by mistake. The customer meant to post it on another page. Gabriel is trying to get it removed but it is proving difficult and the post is still showing up on his page.

Check your understanding

1 Identify two benefits to Gabriel's business of advertising on social media.

2 Explain one disadvantage to Gabriel's business of advertising his water bottles via social media.

3 Explain why the feedback and posts created by third parties are more influential than those produced by Gabriel himself.

This section gives you information about what content is covered in the topic.

Case studies based on real-life situations put key concepts and practices into context. The accompanying questions check your understanding and challenge you to take your learning further.

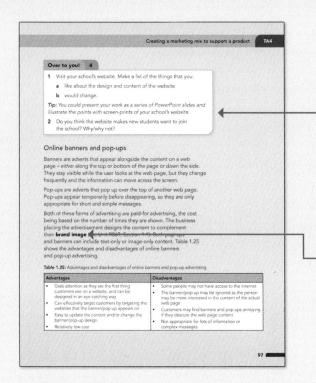

Practical activities that you can do on your own give you the opportunity to practise important skills and techniques, and to prepare for your assessments.

Over to you! activities let you apply your knowledge, and think more deeply about your course.

Key words are highlighted in the text and explained fully in the glossary, often using examples, to ensure you fully understand key terminology.

Your product proposal 2

Creative techniques

You will need to use creative techniques to come up with your initial design ideas for your assessment. You should show evidence of these in your assessment task. Some of the techniques that you could use are explained below.

Look out for the step-by-step help with your product proposal assessment.

Stretch 2

Explain how the organisers of sporting events, such as the Olympics and the football World Cup tournament, can use the product lifecycle model to plan the marketing of their sporting events.

Stretch activities and questions give you the opportunity to try more challenging questions and to extend your knowledge.

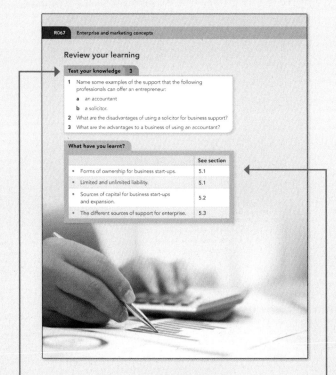

These question boxes give you regular opportunities to test your knowledge so that you feel ready for your exam or assessment.

Summary sections help you review your learning, to check you understand key concepts and can apply your learning. They also show you where to look back for more information if you need to read it again.

Support for you

Our resources in this series are designed to work together to help you with your Cambridge National course.

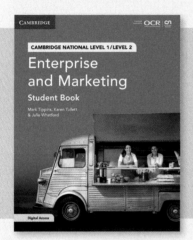

Your Student Book is where you will find the core information you need. This will help you with your knowledge and understanding of the subject. Information is arranged by unit and then by topic area, so you can easily find what you're looking for. Questions and activities will help you to apply your knowledge and understanding and to develop practical skills. You can assess your progress with the Test Your Knowledge questions. When you've completed the quiz, check your answers in the digital edition.

Your Revision Guide and Workbook supports you with the externally assessed unit of your course. The exam preparation section offers advice to help you get ready for this assessment. The revision guide section provides concise outlines of the core knowledge you need. Each page focuses on a small piece of learning to help you break your revision up into manageable chunks. The workbook section brings your revision and learning together with practice questions. Digital quizzes help you to understand the language used in your assessment and to check your knowledge and understanding of key concepts.

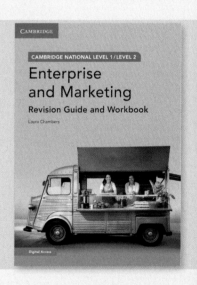

The Teacher's Resource is a rich bank of ideas to help your teacher create engaging lessons to meet the needs of your class. It contains PowerPoint slides, worksheets and audio-visual material, in addition to activity and delivery ideas that can be personalised for your lessons. Digital quizzes help test understanding and unlock the language used in assessment.

Enterprise and marketing concepts

Let's get started

If you had £500 000 to start a new business, what kind of business would you start and why? What questions would you need to ask and find answers to before investing any of your money?

What will you learn in this unit?

Setting up and running a business enterprise is the personal ambition of many people. There are a number of key things that a small start-up business needs to consider if it is to operate successfully.

These include understanding the customer, knowing what makes a product financially possible, and the activities, such as marketing, that a business needs to undertake to make sure it thrives.

In this unit you will learn about:

- characteristics, risk and reward for enterprise **TA1**

- market research to target a specific customer **TA2**

- what makes a product financially viable **TA3**

- creating a marketing mix to support a product **TA4**

- factors to consider when starting up and running an enterprise **TA5**.

How you will be assessed

This unit is assessed by a 75-minute (1 hour and 15 minutes) written exam that is worth 40 percent of your overall mark. In the exam, you will be expected to show that you understand this unit by answering questions that require you to analyse and evaluate your understanding of enterprise and marketing concepts.

TA1

Characteristics, risk and reward for enterprise

Let's get started   1

Who are the people in the photos (Figure 1.1)? What are they famous for? What do you think they have in common? Why do you think they have been successful? What personality traits do they have in common?

Figure 1.1: What do these famous people have in common?

What will you learn?

- The **characteristics** of successful **entrepreneurs**.
- Potential **rewards** of risk-taking.
- Potential drawbacks of risk-taking.

What an entrepreneur is

Entrepreneurs are all around you. They are people who start and operate a **business** that satisfies the needs of customers. Businesses offer **goods** and **services** that customers are willing to pay for and which should enable the business to make a **profit**.

Entrepreneurs see a **gap in the market** and start up and operate a business to fill the gap. They may fill the gap in the market by:

- designing a new good (product) or service, or

- offering a good or service to a new market (e.g. opening a café on a high street that has no café), or

- improving or updating a good or service that they already offer.

Entrepreneurs often stumble upon a great business idea by chance when they are least expecting it and at any age. Many well-known entrepreneurs, such as Richard Branson and Mark Zuckerberg, started their entrepreneurial journey when they were teenagers. Entrepreneurs make things happen and are very motivated.

Case study

Enterprising Eavis – Founder of Europe's biggest music festival

Michael Eavis is a dairy farmer and the founder of the Glastonbury Festival (Figure 1.2). After seeing the rock band Led Zeppelin headline at a nearby open-air concert in 1970, he was inspired to create his own music festival.

As a farmer, Michael Eavis owns a lot of land and he decided to open his fields to 1500 people later that year. The first festival, which was a pop, blues and folk music festival, took place in September 1970. A second festival took place in the summer of 1971.

Figure 1.2: Can you name any bands that have performed on the Pyramid Stage at the Glastonbury Festival?

Although the early festivals were well attended, the organisers suffered huge financial losses. However, Michael Eavis used his entrepreneurial characteristics to turn the idea into the hugely profitable Glastonbury music festival that millions of people worldwide now enjoy.

Several **charities** benefit from the festival which is now considered to be the largest music festival in the world. In the early days, very few people would have imagined that Eavis's idea would be the huge event that it is today, more than 50 years later.

Continued

Check your understanding

1   What inspired Michael Eavis to organise the first Glastonbury Festival?

2   Explain possible reasons why the early festivals suffered huge financial losses.

3   Assess the reasons why Michael Eavis donates some of the money he makes from the festival to charities and other good causes.

1.1 Characteristics of successful entrepreneurs

Every day lots of people set up new businesses. However, some businesses do not survive the first 12 months of trading, and fewer still are operating after three years or more. Those businesses that do survive and succeed are headed by successful entrepreneurs.

The personal characteristics of an entrepreneur can influence the likely success of a small **start-up business**. Figure 1.3 shows that successful entrepreneurs generally have certain specific characteristics.

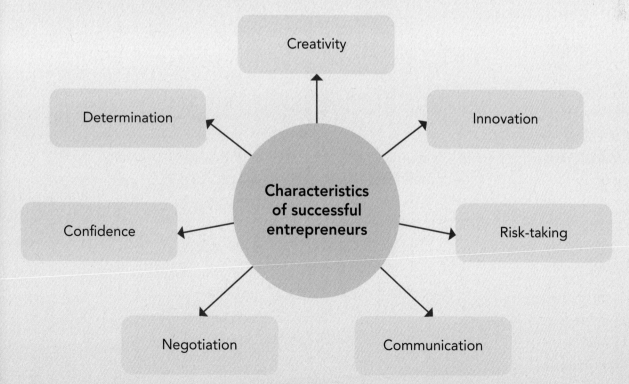

Figure 1.3: Successful entrepreneurs generally have certain specific characteristics

Creativity

Creativity involves using your imagination and original ideas to create or invent something or to find a new solution to a problem.

Successful entrepreneurs need creativity to:

- develop a product or service that is different to others already available

- invent a brand-new good/service

- adapt an existing business idea.

New and creative ideas may come to an entrepreneur by chance or by:

- thinking about a problem in different ways

- creating a mind map of their thoughts

- 'thinking outside the box'.

Innovation

Innovation is a creative process. It is often about turning a new idea into a product or service. Innovation can help an entrepreneur to create a new or different product/service.

However, innovation isn't just about creating a new business idea or product. It can also be about improving:

- existing goods and services

- business processes to make the business more productive and efficient.

Often entrepreneurs have limited resources, such as people and money, and they need to complete tasks in an innovative way. For example, a business might have limited finances so they cannot afford to pay for an expensive **advertising** campaign for a new product. The entrepreneur therefore has to be innovative and find free or low-cost ways to advertise the product.

Risk-taking

Entrepreneurs have to be willing to take **risks** when they set up a new business. In return, there is the potential for large rewards such as becoming wealthy if the business is successful and **self-satisfaction** from being their 'own boss' and achieving their dreams.

There is always the risk that a business will fail or the product or service will not succeed. Also, running a business alone may be more challenging and lonely than the entrepreneur first thought. They may suffer ill health or stress due to the long hours that they need to work. Often entrepreneurs have given up other jobs or careers in order to set up their new enterprise, so there is a lot at stake as the new business may be their only source of **income**.

Communication

Good communication skills – both verbal and written – are essential for entrepreneurs as they need to share their product and business ideas with others clearly. Throughout the process of creating and developing new products, entrepreneurs have to communicate with lots of different people, such as:

- lenders, if they need finance

- future customers for **feedback** on their ideas and products

- suppliers to avoid any **manufacturing** or production issues.

It is important for entrepreneurs to communicate their business idea clearly and in a way that excites investors and lenders for example. This will help the investors and lenders to understand and believe in the potential of the new business venture.

Figure 1.4: Why does an entrepreneur need to communicate their business idea clearly and with enthusiasm?

Negotiation

Often people have different ideas or **objectives**. **Negotiation** is where individuals (or parties) have a discussion with the aim of reaching an agreement. Each party may need to be willing to compromise and change their ideas or objectives in order to reach an agreement. To move forward with their business idea, entrepreneurs often have to negotiate with lenders, manufacturers and shops. For example, they may need to negotiate:

- additional funding from the bank
- the best price for manufacturing the product
- the date that a product can be delivered to a customer
- the price that a shop will pay for the product.

As a result of the negotiations, the entrepreneur may have to amend their plans or scale back on the product or service. For example, an entrepreneur may approach a shop to sell their new product. As it is a new product, the shop may not wish to stock it initially, but they may agree to stock it for a one-month trial period to assess customer demand.

Confidence

It can be lonely setting up a small business on your own, but entrepreneurs are self-confident and positive people who believe in their ideas. Successful entrepreneurs have the confidence to take risks and approach others to turn their business idea into a reality. They must:

- believe in the potential success of their business idea
- be able to encourage others to share their confidence.

Determination

Not everything goes to plan when setting up a new small business. There are often setbacks and rejections along the way. For instance, a lender may decline an entrepreneur's loan application if they feel the idea is too risky.

Successful entrepreneurs are able to overcome obstacles and make things happen. They have the determination to carry on despite rejections and to try alternative options.

Many entrepreneurs spend their evenings or weekends planning their new business idea whilst working in a full-time job. It is not until the business opens or reaches a certain size that they can afford to leave their other employment. It is often hard work to become successful, so an entrepreneur must be determined to see things through.

Over to you! 1

Could you be a successful entrepreneur?

Complete the table below by rating your own characteristics. Look back at the characteristics of successful entrepreneurs (Section 1.1) to remind yourself about each one. A score of 1 means that you need to develop the characteristic further whilst 5 indicates that this characteristic is a strength.

For any characteristics where you gave yourself a low rating, what actions could you take to improve them so that they do not hinder the success of your business?

Table 1.1: Characteristics of successful entrepreneurs

Characteristic	1	2	3	4	5
Creativity					
Innovation					
Risk-taking					
Communication					
Negotiation					
Confidence					
Determination					

Case study

Shalia's homemade delights

Shalia has always enjoyed cooking, especially baking cakes, for family and friends. After being made redundant from her full-time office job she decided to use her redundancy money to set up a website selling homemade cakes.

After six months of trading, Shalia did not sell enough cakes to make a profit. As she was relying on the business to pay her bills, she knew she could not afford to continue this way.

Shalia's friend, Suki, works as a carer and supports older people to live independently in their own homes. One day, following a conversation with Suki about the older people relying on frozen meals from the supermarket, Shalia had an idea to develop her business. She decided that rather than just focusing on cakes, she could provide ready-made, healthy and nutritious meals for older people. She added the new range of ready-made meals to her website and within two months she started to make a profit.

Figure 1.5: How did Shalia come up with her business idea?

Check your understanding

1 Identify three characteristics that Shalia has which led to her being a successful entrepreneur.

2 For each of the three characteristics, explain how they helped Shalia to make her business a success.

3 Analyse how Shalia filled a gap in the market.

1.2 Potential rewards of risk-taking

Let's get started   2

What benefits do you think entrepreneurs get from running a business? Think about someone you know, or a famous person, who runs a small business. Create a list showing how they benefit from running the business.

When setting up a new business all entrepreneurs take risks, but in return they stand to benefit from the potentially large rewards.

Generally, the greater the risk, the larger the potential rewards, but also the more they have to lose if things do not work out. For example, some entrepreneurs give up stable full-time jobs to set up a new business. That means not only can they spend all of their time setting up the business, but they will also benefit financially if the business is successful. However, they will not have a job to return to if the business does not succeed.

Rewards can be financial, but many are non-financial and linked to improved quality of life or personal ambitions.

Financial

The main aim of most entrepreneurs and businesses is to make a profit. Not only do entrepreneurs need to make a profit to live off (if they have given up their main job) but they also need profits to invest money back into the business to make it grow.

Profit is also a motivating factor for many entrepreneurs. Depending on the success of the business the entrepreneur may make a lot of money and become wealthy. If they work for themselves, they will benefit from a large share of the profit and enjoy a more luxurious lifestyle.

Independence

One common reason why an entrepreneur sets up a small business is to work for themselves (i.e. to be independent) rather than working for someone else. There are benefits of working for themselves:

- Many entrepreneurs want to be able to make their own creative decisions and not have to answer to anyone else. This means that they bear the risk of the decisions, but they also gain the credit for the business's success.

- They can set their own working hours and have a more flexible work schedule.

- They can choose the kind of work that they do.

Self-satisfaction

Setting up and running a small business can be extremely self-satisfying for the entrepreneur. Setting up a small business is often a life-long ambition.

Fulfilling that ambition can bring self-satisfaction and a sense of achievement. It may also be self-satisfying to set up a business to fill a gap in the market identified by the entrepreneur and which could also help others or the environment. Figure 1.6 shows aspects of entrepreneurship that can bring self-satisfaction.

Figure 1.6: Some aspects of running a small business can bring self-satisfaction and a sense of achievement

Making a difference or change

Some entrepreneurs set up a business to make a difference to others and/or change something that does not meet customers' needs. Sometimes the entrepreneur has personally experienced a need for a product/service that does not exist, so they have created something to fill the gap in the market. This benefits them as well as others. Other ways in which an entrepreneur's business could make a difference include by:

- being more environmentally friendly/**sustainable**
- supporting entrepreneurship in schools
- helping people to live a healthier life with more exercise.

Over to you! 2

1 Making a difference can be an important reward for a new entrepreneur. What type of difference would be most important to you if you were to set up a business, and why?

Stretch

2 Research real-life examples of entrepreneurs who have made a difference. How have they made a difference?

Case study

The Dyson bagless vacuum cleaner

In the 1970s James Dyson (Figure 1.7), the founder of Dyson, had the idea of designing a new vacuum cleaner because he was frustrated with the lack of suction and performance of the one that he was using. As the dust bag and filters became clogged up it was losing suction. He was confident that he could design a vacuum cleaner that would not lose suction, and so he invented the first bagless vacuum.

Figure 1.7: James Dyson initially sold his new vacuum cleaners in Japan before they became popular in the UK

He worked on his idea for a number of years before he created his first bagless vacuum cleaner. Initially it was not a success in the UK, so he sold it in Japan where it became successful and won a design award in 1991. As none of the major manufacturers in the UK were interested in his product, he set up his own factory in the UK.

As a result of a successful TV advertising campaign in the UK, customers realised that if they bought a Dyson, they would no longer have to change the dust bags or buy replacement bags. By 1995, it had become the top-selling vacuum cleaner in the UK.

Continued

Check your understanding

1   Identify one reward that James Dyson gained when he first set up the business.

2   Explain two personal characteristics that helped James Dyson to become a successful entrepreneur.

3   Analyse why James Dyson had to work on his initial idea for a number of years before he created his first successful product design.

Test your knowledge   1

1   Identify some of the potential rewards for an entrepreneur.

2   Henry set up a small business venture that produces and sells reusable cloth bags at music festivals to reduce plastic waste. Identify which potential reward is most relevant for Henry's business and explain why.

3   'The larger the risk, the greater the potential reward.' Explain what this means in relation to entrepreneurs.

1.3 Potential drawbacks of risk-taking

When taking a risk there is always the chance that things may go wrong. A large percentage of new businesses fail. A report by the Office for National Statistics (ONS) in 2019 showed that only 43 percent of UK businesses were still trading five years after they were started.

The risks that an entrepreneur takes may affect their:

* financial situation
* health and **well-being**
* **work–life balance**
* personal relationships.

Financial

Not all businesses are **financially viable** – they might run out of money or not make a profit. Despite thorough planning, hard work and **market research** some business ideas fail. An entrepreneur may lose all of the money they used to set up the business and/or find themselves in debt, owing large sums to lenders and suppliers. This is a serious risk if in order to set up the business the entrepreneur has given up a paid job, borrowed large sums of money or used all of their savings.

Health and well-being

Risk-taking is part of setting up a successful enterprise, but taking risks can be stressful and put entrepreneurs under a lot of pressure. Some people are not natural risk takers, which can lead to worry, stress and anxiety.

Stress has been linked to poor **physical health** and **mental health**. Entrepreneurs must ensure that they take care of both their health and well-being.

Many entrepreneurs work alone, so they may not get an opportunity to talk to somebody about their problems. That may increase their levels of stress and anxiety. Often entrepreneurs continue to work when they are unwell, as there is nobody to run the business in their absence. This may hinder a prompt and full recovery to good health, which can have longer-term effects on both their health and their business.

Work–life balance

Work–life balance refers to the balance between the amount of time spent working and the amount of time spent on non-work activities. Setting up a small business is hard work and requires a huge time commitment. There is often lots to do and nobody else to do it. An entrepreneur may therefore need to work long hours, especially at the start. They may end up working seven days a week to make the business a success. Working long hours leaves little time for hobbies and relaxation. Entrepreneurs may have a poor work–life balance, with work taking up all of their time. This can affect their health and well-being.

Figure 1.8: If an entrepreneur has an unhealthy work–life balance, how might this affect the success of their business?

Over to you! 3

It can be tempting to work very long hours when starting a new business as there are so many jobs to do. Imagine your friend has recently set up a new business and you are concerned that they are working too many hours.

Research work–life balance tips online. Using the advice that you find, design a leaflet or infographic aimed at your friend and other entrepreneurs to promote a better work–life balance.

Personal relationships

The stress and long working hours when starting a small business can bring out the worst in someone's character and leave them feeling physically and emotionally tired. This can have a huge impact on an entrepreneur's personal life.

If an entrepreneur devotes significant time to their business, it will leave them with little time to spend with their children, family and friends, who may become resentful. They may lose touch with family and friends.

Entrepreneurs who are single may not have time to meet people and build new relationships and friendships. For those who are married or in a relationship, it can put the relationship under a lot of strain. This may lead to the breakdown of a marriage or relationship.

Over to you! 4

Read the scenarios below. For each one, decide which of the four potential drawbacks of risk-taking (financial; health and well-being; work–life balance; personal relationships) it would best fit under.

1   Stella owns and runs a successful restaurant. She suffers back pain as a result of carrying heavy supplies for her restaurant.

2   Gary is a tech entrepreneur who started his computer games business six months ago. He rarely sees his children during the week as he leaves the house before they wake up and returns home after they have gone to bed in the evening.

Continued

3   Dev has been a keen tennis player since childhood, but he has started his own property development business and now he struggles to find time to play tennis.

4   Carol invested her personal savings to set up her window cleaning business. However, during the winter months she can only work reduced hours due to shorter daylight hours, which has resulted in her business making a **loss**. She has no savings left to repair her car.

Review your learning

Test your knowledge   2

Nadiya has recently given up her full-time job in finance to set up an Indian street food business. She has two young children under the age of six. In her free time, she enjoys making clothes and going for long walks. She sells her products at local markets and also caters for large events, such as weddings and parties.

1   Identify two aspects of entrepreneurship that can bring self-satisfaction.

2   Describe two potential drawbacks that Nadiya might face from taking risks.

3   Explain two entrepreneurial characteristics that Nadiya needs in order to run her business successfully.

What have you learnt?

	See section
• Characteristics of successful entrepreneurs.	1.1
• Potential rewards of risk-taking.	1.2
• Potential drawbacks of risk-taking.	1.3

TA2

Market research to target a specific customer

Let's get started   1

You've decided to leave your full-time job to open a street food van at your local market.

Figure 1.9: What market research would you need to do before opening a street food van?

What do you need to find out before deciding on whether to open the street food van? Write five questions that you may need answers to.

What will you learn?

- The purpose of market research.
- Primary and secondary market research methods and sources.
- Types of **data**.
- Types of market segmentation.
- The benefits of market segmentation to a business.

2.1 The purpose of market research

A business carries out market research activities to obtain information about the market in which it operates and customers' views, needs and wants.

Market research involves collecting, presenting and analysing information about the business's customers, **competitors** and market trends. It is typically carried out before developing a new product, adapting an existing product, deciding on a price change, or creating a new **promotion**.

It is essential to understand whether there is sufficient demand for the goods and services (i.e. the product) that the business currently offers or is planning to offer and what customers think about a product. This will avoid wasting money when developing new ideas. A new product will not be successful if nobody wants to buy it. Figure 1.10 summarises the purposes of market research.

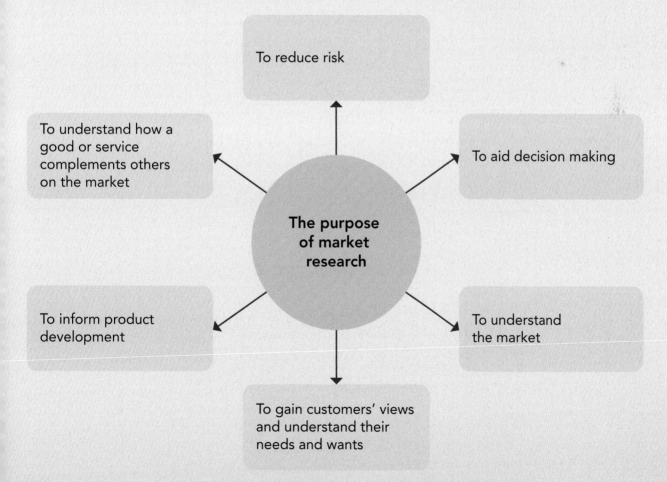

Figure 1.10: What is the purpose of market research?

Over to you!   1

Louis owns a pizza restaurant. All pizzas are made to order using recipes that he creates. Louis is proud to offer a menu that is different from those offered by his competitors. He regularly updates his menu by adding new flavours of pizza.

Four weeks ago he launched a new 'sweet and savoury' flavour which included a strawberry jam base with Stilton cheese and jalapeño topping, which he thought was delicious. Unfortunately orders for the pizza have been very disappointing and Louis has received complaints from three regular customers about this product. Louis now regrets not carrying out market research before he wasted time and money launching the new product.

1   Describe the mistake Louis made when introducing a new product to his pizza restaurant.

2   Explain how market research could have supported Louis to successfully launch a new pizza flavour.

3   Analyse two ways that Louis' business has been negatively affected as a result of not carrying out market research.

To reduce risk

Entrepreneurs face big risks when setting up a new business or developing a new product. Around 60 percent of new businesses fail in the first three years. Things may go wrong or the business may fail if it does not understand the needs of its customers.

Market research can help to reduce the risk that entrepreneurs face when setting up and running their business. It can help to ensure that their products are successful, and it reduces the risk of a product being unsuccessful.

To aid decision making

Market research can help entrepreneurs make good decisions.

An entrepreneur can use the information gained through market research to make more successful choices. Without market research, an entrepreneur doesn't have evidence to base their decisions on and may misjudge customers' wants or needs.

To understand the market

Market research allows an entrepreneur to understand the market in which their business operates. For example, the entrepreneur can use the market research to gain insight and information about market trends.

Market research can be carried out before the business starts up and at various key intervals when it is operating in order to keep abreast of developments and changes.

Market trends

The market in which the business operates will change over time. It is important that the entrepreneur understands trends in the market so that they can ensure that their products continue to meet changing customer needs and wants. The market may change due to:

- new competitors

- product developments

- changing customer views, needs and wants as a result of fashion trends and media coverage.

The market for technology products, such as mobile phones, changes rapidly. Companies such as Apple and Samsung, for example, need to carry out market research on an ongoing basis. This helps with new product development and it provides information about the products offered by competitors. New products are being developed continually in the mobile phone market in order to keep up with market trends.

To gain customers' views and understand their needs/wants

Entrepreneurs must understand the views, needs and wants of the **target market** (potential customers) at which they are aiming their products. By understanding their customers, a business can meet the customers' expectations, and the entrepreneur/business can increase the likelihood that their product will be successful.

The entrepreneur/business can break the target market down by characteristics, such as age, gender and income (see Section 2.5 on **market segmentation**). This will help them to understand the **customer profile** within the target market. They will also be able to identify whether customer numbers are increasing or reducing and what their interests and buying habits are.

They can use this information to help develop a product that best suits the needs and wants of the target market. It will also help them to decide how and where to promote the product.

To inform product development

Findings and data from market research can help entrepreneurs to:

- find out what customers think of a new product idea before spending money on developing and launching it

- make the right product development decisions so that the product is better suited to customers' needs. For example, the entrepreneur could add a new **function** or feature to a product following market research feedback, or add a new service to existing services.

To understand how a good or service complements others on the market

Market research also involves finding out information about other businesses (competitors) that offer similar products, such as:

- what products they offer

- what price they charge

- what their **market share** is.

This information allows an entrepreneur or business to analyse and compare their products to those offered by competitors and to make decisions about how to make their own business and products more appealing. Successful businesses usually offer products that are different from or better value than those sold by their competitors. It is important for a new business to know whether customers are loyal to a competitor and why, so that the business can try to attract those customers to its products.

Case study

Researching the market

Craig and Zeena Davies are the owners of CZ Designs – a business that makes and sells mobile phone cases. The business offers over 100 different designs and is continually developing new ones. Craig and Zeena employ a designer to create their chosen designs, and that costs approximately £200 per design.

Zeena is responsible for marketing. As each design is so costly to make, before asking the designer to create it, Zeena carries out market research with the target market to discover the target market's thoughts on each new design idea. Her research also considers how CZ's new design may complement others offered by competitors. As 60 percent of design ideas are abandoned following feedback from the target market, Craig and Zeena feel that market research is essential to the success of their business.

Check your understanding

1 Define the term 'target market'.

2 Explain two purposes of the market research carried out by Craig and Zeena.

3 Carrying out market research can be time-consuming. Do you feel that it is a worthwhile activity for CZ Designs? Justify your answer.

Market research is not a one-off activity that happens when starting a new business. It needs to be carried out regularly to ensure that the business and its products remain desirable to customers. The market and customers are continually changing. Entrepreneurs must keep up to date with changes so that they can develop new products and improve existing ones.

Test your knowledge　　1

1 Identify some situations when an entrepreneur needs to carry out market research.

2 Explain a way that market research can help to inform product development.

3 Why is it important to understand how a product complements others on the market?

2.2 Primary market research methods

Let's get started   2

Now that you know the questions you need to ask about starting your street food business, how might you go about collecting the information?

Primary market research methods gather new data that has not been collected before. It is usually collected directly by the business or entrepreneur and can be tailored to the specific product or industry. Primary market research can be carried out physically (e.g. face-to-face, in person) or digitally (e.g. online or face-to-face virtually via an app) – see Figure 1.11.

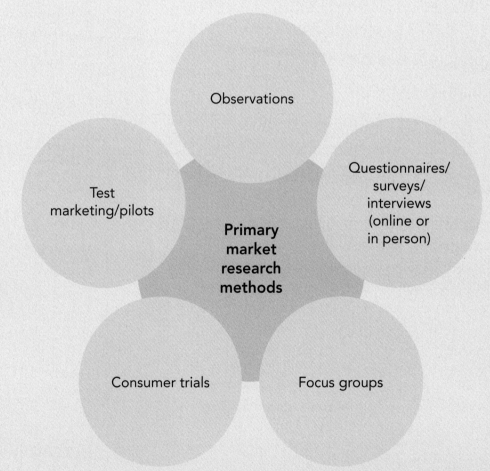

Figure 1.11: Primary market research methods gather new data that has not been collected before

Observations

An entrepreneur can observe the behaviour of people/customers and/or locations.

Observations of people

Observations involve watching and recording the behaviour of people at a particular time or place. Observing customers can be challenging as it may be difficult to see their ordinary behaviour if they know they are being watched. To overcome this issue some businesses now observe customer behaviour using CCTV footage. They make customers aware of the recording when they enter the store or building. Supermarkets often observe how customers move around the store and use this information to improve the store layout to encourage customers to spend more.

Figure 1.12: Supermarkets observe how customers move around the store in order to plan the best layout for each store

Observations of a specific location

Before deciding on an appropriate location for a new shop, entrepreneurs will spend time in the area at different times of day to observe the **footfall**. This will enable them to decide whether the location is likely to be busy enough to attract a sufficient number of customers. The entrepreneur will also wish to check that the location will be suitable for the business – for instance, is the building large enough and does it complement the business image so that it will attract the desired customer group.

Table 1.2 lists some of the advantages and disadvantages of observation.

Table 1.2: Advantages and disadvantages of observation

Advantages	Disadvantages
• Easy to carry out • Can see what people actually do rather than what they say they do • Gives detailed insight into customer behaviours	• Time-consuming to carry out an observation on a large number of people and/or multiple locations • Only considers what is happening and not why it is happening • Consumers may not be happy about someone watching them without their permission • Observation notes may be less easy to analyse than numerical/structured data • People may not behave naturally if they know they are being observed • The time of the observation may not actually reflect the general level of activity within a location

Questionnaires, surveys and interviews

These are all popular research methods and involve asking a set of questions, which individuals answer.

- A **questionnaire** involves asking people a set of written questions to find out their opinions. It usually has a choice of answers. It can be done by email, online, face-to-face, over the telephone or by post. It is the main tool used to carry out surveys.

- A **survey** is the process of collecting, collating and analysing all of the data from the questionnaire responses, i.e. the questionnaire is used as part of the survey to collect data. Surveys can be done:

  - **in person** – either on the street or at an agreed place and time

  - **online** – using Google Forms for example, or an online survey tool such as SurveyMonkey

  - **by telephone** – a researcher phones the participant at an agreed time

  - **by post** – a paper copy of the questionnaire is sent to individuals by post.

- An **interview** is a structured verbal conversation, based on a pre-written list of questions. An interviewer (e.g. the entrepreneur) asks the interviewee (e.g. the customer) questions. The interview may be with just one interviewee or a group of interviewees. To get more information and to gain a better understanding of the reasons for their answers, the interviewer may ask the interviewee additional, more detailed questions. The structure of the interview can vary. In some cases, all interviewees may be asked the same questions. In other cases, the interviewer may vary the questions depending on the interviewee's replies to earlier questions. An interview can be done in person, online or by telephone.

Open and closed questions

Questionnaires, surveys and interviews are made up of two types of questions:

- **Open questions** encourage people to offer their own response. People can give their views or reasons for their answers. For example: 'What is the most important feature of our product?'

- **Closed questions** are those where the answer is limited to specific options, such as 'yes' or 'no', e.g. 'Do you like our product?' Interviewees cannot give reasons for their answers.

Table 1.3 shows some of the advantages and disadvantages of questionnaires, surveys and interviews.

Table 1.3: Advantages and disadvantages of questionnaires, surveys and interviews

Advantages	Disadvantages
- Can ask specific questions to a large group of people - Data may be easy to analyse - Can be carried out in various formats, e.g. email, online, face-to-face to meet all needs - If questions are chosen/planned carefully, the information that is collected will be relevant and up to date - Online surveys are cost-effective as they don't require someone to carry out the interview - Can provide a wide range of data	- **Respondents** may not answer all the questions if there are a lot of questions - Respondents may not want to take part, especially if the questions are about sensitive topics, there are a lot of questions or if they don't want to be disturbed - Some people may rush through the questions and not provide accurate answers or may not respond at all - Can be costly and time-consuming to carry out on large numbers - Questionnaires, surveys and interviews that involve small numbers may not generate data that is representative of *all* customers - Face-to-face questionnaires, surveys and interviews can be time-consuming as each interviewer can only interview up to a few people at a time

Over to you!   2

To improve students' exam results, your school is thinking about reducing the school holidays by four weeks each year. Students will have to attend school during these four weeks for additional lessons.

1   Design a questionnaire with ten questions to collect students' views on introducing four weeks of extra lessons each year. Is the idea welcomed by students? Include a mix of open and closed questions.

2   Analyse the data from your questionnaire and create some graphs to illustrate your results.

Stretch

3   Explain whether your questionnaire provides sufficient data for the school to reach a conclusion.

4   Would you recommend that the school carries out any other type of market research? If so, what would you recommend?

Focus groups

A **focus group** involves interviewing a small group of carefully chosen people. The interview can take place online or in person. The focus group discusses their views on specific products or topics and gives their honest opinions.

The person running the focus group (known as the **facilitator**) will often ask open questions to start a group discussion. The facilitator's role is to take notes on the content of the group's discussion. Group members are encouraged to speak freely as if the facilitator is not in the room. The facilitator will only step in if the conversation goes off topic or if they want to get more detailed opinions. The group discussion is important as it helps the facilitator gain in-depth information. Sometimes participants are given refreshments, a small payment or a free product/voucher to thank them for giving up their time and to provide an incentive to support the market research. Table 1.4 shows some of the advantages and disadvantages of focus groups.

Table 1.4: Advantages and disadvantages of focus groups

Advantages	Disadvantages
• The facilitator can probe/question participants to gain a deeper understanding of an issue or customers' needs and collect detailed information • Participants can debate and discuss points in detail • The facilitator can explain the questions if participants do not understand them	• Can be expensive and time-consuming to organise • Face-to-face focus groups may be challenging to organise, e.g. a venue needs to be booked in advance • May only involve a relatively small number of participants so data is not representative of all customers • Some participants may dominate discussions, so not everyone contributes

Case study

Fareedah's Designs focus group

Fareedah's Designs is a small shop selling zero-waste and responsibly sourced products. The owner, Fareedah, is thinking of launching some new Fairtrade clothing and decides to organise a focus group to obtain customers' views. Fareedah invites eight regular customers to the focus group held at a small meeting room in a local hotel. She orders refreshments for the meeting and offers all attendees a £30 Fareedah's Designs gift voucher to thank them for their time.

Figure 1.13: Focus groups can provide information about the types of products customers are likely to buy

Continued

Fareedah starts the meeting by showing the attendees examples of the new garments and asks for feedback. She asks them if they would buy each item and how much they would pay. The attendees can feel the material and try on the garments. She also asks them questions about other products that she is thinking of stocking.

Two of the attendees dominate the meeting and four quieter individuals hardly say anything. Fareedah steps in a couple of times to keep the conversation focused on the topics that she needs to cover. Occasionally she has to ask the attendees further questions to get them to explain their answers in more detail. Fareedah obtains a lot of information from the focus group. She can use it to help her get ready to sell the clothing in the shop and to decide how to develop the range of products she offers in the future.

Check your understanding

1   Identify two advantages of Fareedah arranging a focus group for her market research.

2   Explain why Fareedah offered the customers refreshments and gave them a gift voucher for attending the focus group.

3   Analyse two disadvantages of using a focus group as a method of gathering Fareedah's primary market research.

Stretch

4   What could Fareedah have done to ensure that she got the opinions of everyone in the focus group?

Consumer trials

A consumer trial tests a new product. A small number of customers try a product, often before a business launches it. The product being trialled is either sent to the customer to use at home or customers are stopped in the street or in a store and invited to test it. Consumer trials are used to judge consumers' reactions to new products. For example, food producers often set up a stall in a supermarket, shopping centre or train station and hand out free samples for customers to try and feedback on whether they like the product. Table 1.5 shows some of the advantages and disadvantages of consumer trials.

Figure 1.14: What are the advantages and disadvantages of a consumer trial?

Table 1.5: Advantages and disadvantages of consumer trials

Advantages	Disadvantages
• Feedback is received from people who have actually used the product • Consumers who have tried the product for free may like the product and become loyal customers • Reliable and honest feedback about the specific product is often provided	• Can be expensive – giving away a product for free • There is a risk that some customers may not provide honest feedback • Competitors may get to see the full product before it is launched • When there are numerous different opinions, it can be difficult to analyse the data into set categories

Test marketing and pilots

Launching a new product can be very expensive. To test whether customers will buy a product a business may sell it for a short trial period or to a small part of the target market. If customer reaction and sales are positive, the business may sell it on a permanent basis or make it available to the whole market.

Alternatively, if a business is planning to sell the product nationwide, they may set up a trial selling it in one region of the UK initially. The business will make a decision about launching the product across the whole country based on the reaction of customers in this region. Table 1.6 shows some of the advantages and disadvantages of test marketing.

Table 1.6: Advantages and disadvantages of test marketing

Advantages	Disadvantages
• Customers may like the product that is being trialled and become loyal customers • Research data and feedback are based on a 'real' product rather than a product that has not yet been created • Specific customers/areas can be targeted • It reduces the financial risk to the business as launching a product nationwide is costly • It often provides reliable and honest feedback about the specific product	• Can be expensive – even a small-scale launch is costly • Competitors may hear about the trial and copy the new product. They may even launch their own version of the product first • Results are only based on a small group of customers who may not be representative of the whole population

Carrying out primary market research – physical or digital

Primary market research can be carried out using physical or digital methods:

• **Observations** – the entrepreneur may drive to a location and watch the footfall in the area (physical) or they could observe the footfall remotely from CCTV footage or a live webcam (digital).

- Questionnaires/surveys/interviews – people may be asked to complete a printed copy of a questionnaire by hand or answer interview questions face-to-face in the same room/location as the interviewer (physical). Alternatively the questionnaire could be completed electronically using a web-based form such as Google forms or an email attachment (digital). Interviews can also be carried out online using apps such as Skype, Zoom or Microsoft Teams (digital).

- Focus groups – the group may meet face-to-face in the same physical room/location (physical) or online using apps such as Skype, Zoom or Microsoft Teams (digital) so that members can participate in the focus group despite being in different locations (or even different countries).

- Consumer trials – the customer may meet the entrepreneur in a shop or in the street and may be given a sample of the product to test (physical) or may be asked to test a service or app online (digital).

Test your knowledge   2

1   What are some primary market research methods?

2   What is the difference between a questionnaire and an interview?

3   What are some of the advantages and disadvantages of test marketing when developing a new product?

2.3 Secondary market research sources

Secondary market research involves analysing data sources that have already been collected by another researcher, such as a market report, statistics or an article in a newspaper or magazine. Secondary market research sources may be available in printed form or digitally on the internet (Figure 1.15).

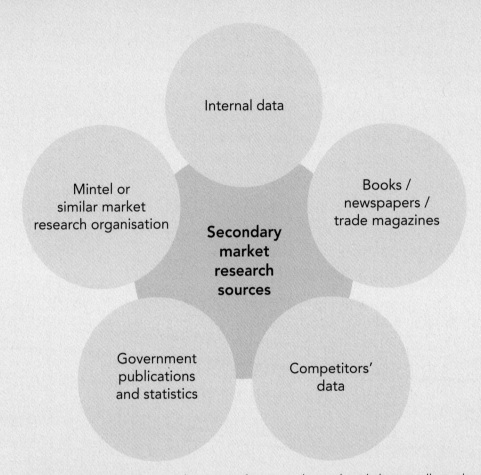

Figure 1.15: Secondary market research sources have already been collected

Internal data

Internal data is information or data that a business stores within the business, such as sales data from products it has already sold or the **costs** of **raw materials** in its current product. This data is a useful source of market research information when making decisions about new products. Table 1.7 shows some of the advantages and disadvantages of internal data.

Table 1.7: Advantages and disadvantages of internal data

Advantages	Disadvantages
• Easy to access and available free of charge • Relates to the specific business • Can offer insight into what happened in the past, which may indicate future trends	• Only relates to the specific organisation – the data does not add anything new to the knowledge already possessed by the business or entrepreneur • Past events may not be a reliable indication of the future • Data may be out of date or incomplete • Data may not be relevant if launching a brand-new product

Books, newspapers and trade magazines

Books, newspapers and trade magazines may be accessed in printed form or electronically – either freely via the internet or via a secure link with password access.

- Books are a useful source of factual information. However, information may change after the book has been published.

- Newspapers often have a business section that contains up-to-date, national and international stories on business and current affairs. They can help an entrepreneur to understand what is happening in the world around them, for instance how the **economy** is performing and what the latest trends are.

- Trade magazines are specialist publications that focus on news about a particular industry. They may be printed or online, and they contain information aimed at industry professionals. They may also contain historical information and data. Trade magazines can be particularly helpful if a business is planning a product targeted at other businesses (rather than the general public/individuals).

Table 1.8 shows some of the advantages and disadvantages of books, newspapers and trade magazines.

Figure 1.16: Newspapers can help an entrepreneur to understand what is happening in the world around them

Table 1.8: Advantages and disadvantages of books, newspapers and trade magazines

Advantages	Disadvantages
• Easy to access and generally fairly low cost • Trade magazines usually focus on a specific industry	• The information may be too general and not relevant • The information in books may be out of date as information may change after the book has been published • May be **biased** or inaccurate

Over to you!   3

You are thinking of setting up a fashion clothing shop in your local town. This is your first shop so your friend suggests that you should look at fashion magazines and the business pages of national newspapers as part of your market research.

1   Identify the names of three national newspapers and three fashion magazines that you could use.

2   Find two examples of information that you could use from the:

   a   national newspapers

   b   fashion magazines.

3   Explain why each type of information will help you to set up a successful business.

Tip: Remember that you can look at the online versions of national newspapers and fashion magazines.

Competitors' data

Understanding the strengths and weaknesses of rival businesses can help a new business to compete more successfully. Competitors may have been trading for several years, and finding out how they operate can help a new business to avoid making the mistakes they made. Useful information about competitors, such as published financial **accounts**, price lists and advertising campaigns, can be found on the competitor's website and in annual reports and product brochures. Table 1.9 shows some of the advantages and disadvantages of looking at competitors' data.

Table 1.9: Advantages and disadvantages of looking at competitors' data

Advantages	Disadvantages
• Information is freely available • Competitors operate in the same industry so the data is relevant • It provides a useful insight into the organisation that the business is competing against • Many businesses publish key financial information publicly, such as past sales and profit figures	• Competitors are unlikely to release key data that a competitor can use • The data may be out of date or inaccurate • The competitor's products and business may be very different, e.g. different business size or type of ownership (see Section 5.1). This will limit the usefulness of the data

Government publications and statistics

Government data is an excellent source of secondary market research data. The government regularly carries out surveys, polls and research and provides official statistics data free of charge. The Office for National Statistics (ONS) is the government department responsible for collecting and publishing the government statistics on people's spending, income, trends and employment. In 2021, the ONS produced and published data from the UK Census. Table 1.10 shows some of the advantages and disadvantages of government publications and statistics.

Table 1.10: Advantages and disadvantages of government publications and statistics

Advantages	Disadvantages
• Official statistics are likely to be accurate and reliable • A lot of data is available covering a wide range of topics • They are normally free to access • They are easy to access online	• There is a vast amount of data available so it may take a long time to find the information required • Some data could be biased to support the government's viewpoint • Data may be out of date, e.g. the UK Census is only done once every ten years

Case study

Census 2021

Every ten years all adults in the UK complete a census questionnaire to help the government to plan public services, such as health care, education and transport.

The census asks questions about the property they live in, their employment and health. The questionnaire is completed online but a hard copy version is available.

If a household does not complete the census the residents can be fined up to £1000 to encourage everyone to answer. The quality of the results would be spoilt without the participation of all households.

The results are published by the government and can be helpful for anyone setting up a new business. For instance, someone looking to set up a mobile car repair business can see how many people in a specific area own a car.

Figure 1.17: The census is a reliable source of secondary market research

Continued

The last census was carried out in March 2021 and the next one will be in 2031. The data collected by the census can be viewed online.

Check your understanding

1 Why does the government fine people who refuse to complete the census?

2 Explain why the government also offers a hard copy version of the questionnaire.

3 Find the March 2021 Census online and look at the information collected. Evaluate why it might be helpful to someone planning to set up a men's barbers in your area. Give some examples of data that may be particularly relevant.

Market research reports

There are many professional market research organisations, such as Mintel and Keynote. They carry out market research on specific industries and products. These organisations publish reports containing information on a particular topic or sector which can offer detailed insight. However, as it was collected for a specific purpose, the information may not be relevant. And because it is collected by professional organisations, it can be expensive to purchase the data. Table 1.11 shows some of the advantages and disadvantages of market research reports.

Table 1.11: Advantages and disadvantages of market research reports

Advantages	Disadvantages
• The information is collected by a professional market research organisation so is likely to be accurate • The data may be very specialised and offers a detailed insight into an industry	• Can be very expensive • Some statistics may only be available to members who pay a subscription • As it is published for a specific purpose, it may not be useful • Information may be out of date

Using secondary market research sources – physical or digital

Secondary market research sources may be internal or external, physical or digital:

• **Internal data** – this data may be stored in hard copy, e.g. documents in a filing cabinet or papers filed in a folder (physical), or could be stored in a spreadsheet or intranet (digital).

External sources include:

- **Books/newspapers/trade magazines** – most publications are available in a printed format (physical) or electronically as an eBook, via the title's website or can be downloaded to an app (digital).

- **Competitors' data** – this data may be stored in hard copy, e.g. documents in a filing cabinet (physical), or could be available to view/download from the competitor's website (digital).

- **Government publications and statistics** – the information may be presented in print form as a booklet or table (physical) or available to view/download from the government department's website (digital).

- **Mintel or similar** – some reports may be available to view in printed format (physical) or available to view/download from the market research company's website (digital).

Choosing the most appropriate type of market research

Table 1.12 shows that there are advantages and disadvantages with both primary and secondary market research. The entrepreneur's market research aims, **budget** and timescale will determine their choice of primary or secondary market research methods. Often entrepreneurs investigate secondary market research first and then use primary market research to complement it.

Table 1.12: Advantages and disadvantages of primary and secondary market research

	Advantages	Disadvantages
Primary market research	<ul><li>Relevant and tailored to the needs of the specific business</li><li>Provides detailed information which is specific to your needs and type of business (e.g. customer opinions)</li><li>Up-to-date information</li><li>Information is not available to other organisations, which may lead to a competitive advantage</li><li>As the entrepreneur or business designs and carries out the data collection methods, the research will produce reliable and **unbiased** data</li></ul>	<ul><li>Often the data is time-consuming to collect</li><li>It can be expensive if visiting different locations to collect data</li><li>It can be challenging to reach the target market and encourage them to participate</li></ul>

Table 1.12: Continued

	Advantages	Disadvantages
Secondary market research	• Often a more cost-effective option than primary data, and may even be free • A wide range of information is quickly available, especially online • The raw data may already be collated and analysed (e.g. graphs already produced) • Research carried out by the government or a professional market research organisation gives a large sample size	• The research and data may be out of date • The research will have been created for another user and purpose, so may not be specific to the needs of the business • As the data was collected by another organisation, it may not be accurate or reliable • The information is available to everyone, so competitors will also have access to it

Test your knowledge   3

1   Why is a competitor unlikely to show its sales and profit data to someone who is planning a new business?

2   Why might information in newspaper articles be helpful to someone planning to set up a new furniture shop?

3   Name some of the benefits of looking at secondary market research sources before planning any primary research.

2.4 Types of data

Let's get started   3

Market research activities collect data. What sort of data may be collected by primary and secondary market research?

Think about some different market research methods and sources – do they all collect the same data? Is the data only numerical?

Market research activities may collect two different types of data – **quantitative** or **qualitative data**. The data can be collected internally within the business (e.g. internal sales data) or externally outside of the business (e.g. from interviews with potential customers or looking at government statistics).

Quantitative data

Quantitative data is numerical data that can be measured, such as facts, percentages and numbers. For example, 25 percent of customers prefer Product B, or the business served 250 customers last week. Quantitative data is usually easier to analyse than qualitative data and can be presented as graphs, charts and tables.

Quantitative data can be collected from a number of primary and secondary market research methods/sources. It is quick to analyse and gives a visual representation of the data that is easy to understand. However, it does not allow a business to understand customers' opinions and thoughts.

Qualitative data

Qualitative data consists of opinions and judgements that express a person's views, attitudes and beliefs. This type of data does not contain numbers.

Qualitative data can be collected using a range of methods. These include focus groups and interviews where individuals are asked to explain their opinions and views about a product or situation. It can help entrepreneurs to gain a more detailed insight into the views of customers. However, it is more costly to collect than quantitative data as the information is not in a numerical format so it can be more time-consuming to analyse.

Test your knowledge   4

1 What are some examples of market research data that has been collated internally?

2 Why might qualitative data help an entrepreneur to gain a more detailed insight into the views of customers?

3 What are some benefits of quantitative market research data?

Stretch

An entrepreneur is looking to set up a personal training business in a small town. They have downloaded some government statistics which provide data about the make-up of the local population (e.g. percentage of the population in each age group and percentage of the population that visit a gym regularly).

Continued

Unfortunately, the secondary data does not offer any information about how many people use a personal trainer. Also, it does not provide people's views and opinions about using a personal trainer.

4   What further market research would you recommend?

5   Explain how the results from primary and secondary market research, and quantitative and qualitative data will complement each other to enhance the entrepreneur's knowledge.

2.5 Types of market segmentation

Let's get started   **4**

What type of customer might the following products be aimed at? Describe the target market.

- BMW car
- Barbie 3-in-1 Dream Camper
- A cordless screwdriver

Why have the companies that produce these products targeted specific types of customers? Why don't these products appeal to everyone?

Once a business or entrepreneur has undertaken market research, they will better understand who their potential customers are. Market segmentation is the process of dividing the market for a specific product into different groups or **segments** to better target the potential customers it has identified. For example, car manufacturers target specific models at different market segments linked to customer lifestyle, such as:

- SUVs or off-road vehicles for those customers who enjoy taking their automobiles off-road or using them in difficult driving conditions

- hybrid or electric cars for those who are concerned about the impact of cars on the environment

- compact city cars and practical family hatchbacks for those who are most concerned about the size of their car.

The business can offer different products to meet the different needs of each segment effectively (e.g. with various features, benefits, prices and levels of quality). The segment that the business or entrepreneur aims their product at is called the target market.

Only a very few products, such as Coca-Cola, are aimed at the **mass market**. Coca-Cola appeals to customers of all ages, genders and backgrounds. Generally, if an entrepreneur or business does not segment a market, they will face the following challenges:

- The product will not appeal to any customer effectively as it will leave some needs and wants unfulfilled. This will limit the product's success as there will be other competitor products that meet all of the customers' needs and wants.

- It is challenging to make effective decisions about marketing and promotion without a clear target market.

- Ineffective marketing and advertising are a waste of time, resources and money.

By understanding the characteristics of the market segment at which their product is targeted, an entrepreneur can create and develop something that best meets the segment's needs. The entrepreneur can adapt the product to appeal to the characteristics of the target market segment.

To be financially viable, the entrepreneur must ensure that the chosen market segment includes enough customers to be profitable. It can be challenging to choose which segment of the market to target, as there can be so many categories. It is therefore important to focus consistently on one segment in order to have the best chance of meeting the specific customer needs and wants.

When segmenting the market, an entrepreneur also needs to be careful not to stereotype customers. Just because someone is of a specific age or gender it does not mean that they will not be interested in the product. For example, an equal number of men and women play computer games.

There are different ways in which the overall market may be divided. Popular methods of market segmentation are shown in Figure 1.18.

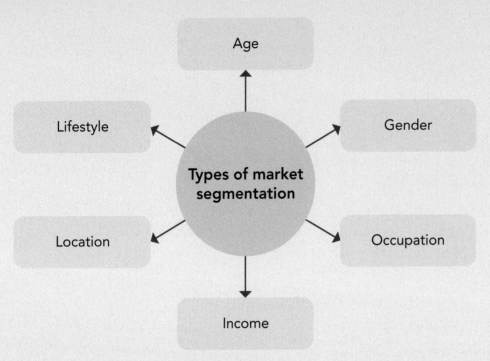

Figure 1.18: How is a market segmented?

Age

The market for many products is divided according to age, because customer needs and wants often change with age. For example, different types of holiday are aimed at specific age groups, such as Vibe by Jet2holidays which is aimed at millennials (25–40 year olds), and Saga Holidays tours and cruises which are aimed at the over 50s.

Case study

LEGO

LEGO building bricks were first manufactured in 1949 and have been a popular product ever since (Figure 1.19). The company regularly launches new edition LEGO sets to keep the product fresh and interesting for customers of all ages. It segments its product range by age and targets different products at different age groups. There are simple models for younger children and more complex models for older children. For example:

Figure 1.19: LEGO product ranges are segmented by age to appeal to different age groups, including adults

Continued

- LEGO DUPLO – for 18 months to 5 years
- LEGO Juniors – for ages 4 to 7 years
- LEGO City and Friends – for ages 5 to 12 years
- LEGO Ninjago and Creator – for ages 7 to 16 years
- LEGO Technic – for ages 8 to 16 years.

While its main target customers are children aged up to 16 years, another very important target market is adult fans of LEGO (known as AFOL). LEGO has introduced high-performance vehicles in the LEGO Creator Expert range and LEGO Star Wars buildable helmets for this particular market.

Check your understanding

1   Explain the term 'market segmentation'.

2   Explain how LEGO adapts its products to appeal to different age groups.

3   Analyse one benefit to LEGO of segmenting the market by age.

Gender

Some products are aimed more at females and some are aimed more at males. For example, there are magazines targeted specifically at men and others targeted specifically at women. Shoe and clothes designers create different styles, designs and sizes for male and female customers. Other unisex products may be aimed at both genders equally. Recently, there has been a growing trend towards unisex hair and beauty products, with gender-neutral packaging, branding and product names.

Case study

Segmenting the magazine market

There are thousands of magazine titles available every week – all aimed at different types of reader. For example:

Age: Some magazines, such as *National Geographic Kids Magazine* and *Minecraft World*, are aimed at children whereas others such as *Cosmopolitan* and *GQ* are read mostly by 16–35 year olds. *Good Housekeeping* and *Country Living* are aimed at readers in their 40s.

Gender: *Woman's Own* and *Grazia* are aimed at females and *Men's Health* and *Sorted* are aimed at males.

Specific interests: *Mountain Biking UK Magazine* and *Cage and Aviary Birds Magazine* target readers with those specific interests.

Check your understanding

1 Identify two benefits of market segmentation to the publishers of magazines.

2 Explain two other examples of the types of market segmentation used in the magazine market.

3 Analyse two ways that market segmentation might influence the methods of marketing magazines.

Figure 1.20: There are thousands of magazine titles, all aimed at different market segments

Occupation

The job that someone does may affect the types of products that they are likely to purchase. For example, commercial vans are targeted at certain occupations and businesses, such as plumbers or builders who need to transport tools and equipment as part of their job.

Income

Income level affects what someone is able to afford and therefore the types of product that they might choose to buy. Businesses are aware of this and therefore offer products targeted at people with different incomes. Many supermarkets offer a range of products, from affordable own-brand 'essential' and 'value' products targeted at customers on a lower income to 'premium' or 'finest' own-brand products aimed at customers with a higher income. By doing this, they offer a range of products that suits all levels of income.

Figure 1.21: Supermarkets offer product ranges aimed at customers with different incomes

Location

Some markets are segmented according to where customers live. For example, some products target customers who live in a rural area whereas other products may target customers who live in the city. For example, garden products are more likely to be in demand by those living outside of city centres where gardens are more common.

Product ranges are often adapted according to the country in which they are sold in order to cater to different customer tastes, cultural differences or climates. For example, McDonald's is well known for its segmentation to cater for local differences; there is the Maharaja Mac in India, which does not contain beef, and the Ebi Burger in Hong Kong, which includes a breaded shrimp patty. Many businesses offer products within a specific geographic area surrounding their location as it is not cost-effective to travel significant distances to serve customers. For example, a plumber may decide to only visit customers' homes within a 20-mile radius of their business.

Lifestyle

Lifestyle includes people's activities, interests and hobbies which are influenced by their opinions and habits. An individual's lifestyle often influences the types of product they buy, and businesses often target customers with a specific lifestyle. For example, there has been an increase in the number of people following a vegan diet due to increasing environmental awareness and the desire for a healthy lifestyle. As a result, supermarkets have increased their ranges of vegan products.

As more people are working from home, there has been a growing demand for certain products, such as home office furniture and videoconferencing apps and exercise apps. Businesses need to keep up to date with changing lifestyle trends.

Over to you!   4

The market for shampoo is segmented, and products are targeted at customers with different hair types. For example, those with coloured or dyed hair, children's hair and those with specific conditions such as thinning hair. The products contain specific ingredients to meet each particular need. They are promoted to attract the individual type of customer.

1   Carry out some research into the market for shampoo and identify four different market segments within the shampoo market.

2   State two or three examples of products targeted at each of the four market segments. How do the shampoo manufacturers target individuals in the market segment to encourage them to buy?

3   Present your findings as a mind map.

2.6 The benefits of market segmentation to a business

Carefully segmenting the market can offer several benefits to a business. Table 1.13 summarises the main benefits.

Table 1.13: The benefits of segmenting a market

Ensures specific customer needs are matched and met	• By focusing on the wants and needs of a specific market segment it is easier for a business to meet specific customer needs. • The business can design specific products that satisfy the requirements of the target market.
Potential for increased profits/ profitability	• The more that a product meets the needs of the customer, the more likely customers are to buy it, which can lead to increased sales. • Profits will also increase as the business can effectively target its product promotions at its target market segment rather than promoting to the whole market. This is known as targeted marketing. • It may also be able to charge a higher price to a loyal market segment.
Enables targeted marketing	• A business can aim its products and promotions, such as advertising, at the people who are most likely to be its target customers.
Increased customer retention	• Customers are likely to remain loyal to a business if it continues to meet their needs. They are likely to return to a business if they were satisfied with a past purchase, which leads to increased customer retention. • Retaining customers is very important as it is often challenging to attract new customers to buy a product, especially if they are already loyal to a competitor's product.
Potential for an increase in market share	• As the business will meet the needs of specific types of customers more effectively, it should enjoy increased sales. • As a result, market segmentation may lead to an increase in the market share that a particular business has. The more sales that it is able to generate at the expense of competitors, the greater the share of the market that it will gain.

Review your learning

Test your knowledge   5

1 What is a challenge that an entrepreneur may face if they do not segment the market?

2 Explain some ways of segmenting the market for chocolate.

3 What are some benefits of market segmentation to a business?

What have you learnt?

	See section
• The purpose of market research.	2.1
• Primary market research methods.	2.2
• Secondary market research sources.	2.3
• Types of data.	2.4
• Types of market segmentation.	2.5
• The benefits of market segmentation to a business.	2.6

TA3

What makes a product financially viable?

Let's get started   1

Laura owns a toy business that produces traditional teddy bears. Why might an entrepreneur, such as Laura, have to think about each of the following costs?

- **Wages**
- Raw materials
- Electricity
- Rent

Figure 1.22: Why might entrepreneurs have to think about costs?

What will you learn?

- The costs of producing a product.
- Revenue generated by sales of the product.
- How to calculate profit/loss.
- Use of break-even as an aid to decision making.
- Importance of **cash**.

3.1 The costs of producing a product

Costs are the money that a business has to pay out to run the business. That is, they are expenses that a business has to incur in order to produce and sell its goods and services. Costs include purchasing materials and equipment, rent, wages, electricity and advertising. There are two types of cost that a business will incur:

- **fixed costs**
- **variable costs**.

Fixed costs

Fixed costs are costs that do not change no matter how many products or services (units) the business sells. Fixed costs stay the same even when the output of the business changes. The costs are the same regardless of whether the business produces 50 units or 150 units.

Examples of fixed costs include:

- advertising for the goods and services
- **insurance** of the factory building and the factory contents, such as stock
- interest charged on loans by lenders
- rent of the factory, shop or office premises
- **salaries** paid to employees
- **utilities** such as gas and electricity.

A salary is a payment given to an employee for work done. It is a fixed cost because the amount paid does not vary according to hours worked or the amount of output produced. A salary is usually given as a total amount per year, which is divided into twelve equal payments. Employees who receive a salary are usually paid monthly.

Utilities are services, such as electricity, gas, water, telephone and broadband. The cost of these utilities does not generally change according to the level of output so this cost is usually considered to be a fixed cost.

When a business takes out a loan it has to repay the capital borrowed plus interest on the amount. The repayment of the capital is part of the business's liabilities and not a cost. However, the interest charged by the lender is a cost. The interest is considered a fixed cost because it does not vary with output. Most businesses pay the same amount of interest every month.

The business still has to pay fixed costs, such as rent, even when it is closed and is not producing any products or providing any services.

Figure 1.23 shows that fixed costs are represented by a straight line on a graph as they do not change with output.

Fixed costs can be expressed:

- for an overall **level of output** (total fixed cost)

- per individual product or unit of output (fixed cost per unit).

Although fixed costs stay the same no matter the level of output, they are unlikely to stay the same over time. For example, the rent paid on a shop or factory building may increase (or decrease) over time. Even though the amount of rent might change, it is considered a fixed cost because it must be paid no matter the level of output.

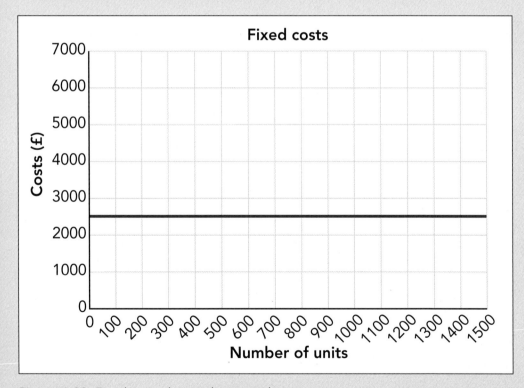

Figure 1.23: Fixed costs do not change with output

Fixed costs for a time period

Fixed costs are often expressed as a value for a specific time period, e.g. £900 rent each month or £3500 advertising annually. Often the time period needs to be changed to obtain information for a different period (see Worked example 1).

Worked example   1

Ken pays £75 interest per month on a business loan.

To calculate the value of this cost per year the monthly figure must be multiplied by 12 as there are 12 months in a year:

£75 loan interest per month × 12 months =

£900 loan interest per year

Worked example   2

Ken pays £6500 for gas to run his business each year.

To calculate the value of this cost per week the annual figure must be divided by 52 as there are 52 weeks in a year:

£6500 gas per year ÷ 52 weeks =

£125 gas per week

Fixed cost per unit

The fixed costs can be shared amongst the number of units produced during the time period to calculate the fixed cost per unit.

Worked example   3

Ken's fixed costs total £6000 per month. During July Ken makes 300 units.

To calculate the value of the fixed cost per unit the monthly figure must be divided by the number of units made during the month, i.e. 300 units:

£6000 ÷ 300 units =

£20 fixed cost per unit

Variable costs

Variable costs vary with changes in the level of output. If a business is producing fewer products, then it will have to buy fewer raw materials to make the products. The amount that a business has to pay for these costs will increase or decrease as the number of units it is producing increases or decreases.

Examples of variable costs include:

- raw materials/components used to produce the product
- packaging to present the finished product for sale, such as the outer wrapper on a packet of biscuits
- wages paid to employees, such as those paid by the hour or per unit of output produced.

Some employees are paid wages that increase/decrease as the employee works more/fewer hours and/or produces more/fewer units of output. As few employees work the same number of hours and/or produce the same number of units each week or month the amount of payment is likely to change, which is why wages are a variable cost. Wages are different from a salary as the amount paid will change each time. Wages are usually paid weekly or monthly.

Figure 1.24 shows that variable costs are directly dependent on the level of output. So if, for example, a business produces half the number of cartons of fruit juice, then its variable costs will halve. Whereas, if it produces double the number of cartons of fruit juice, its variable costs will also double. Variable costs can be calculated using the following formula:

variable costs = variable cost per unit × output

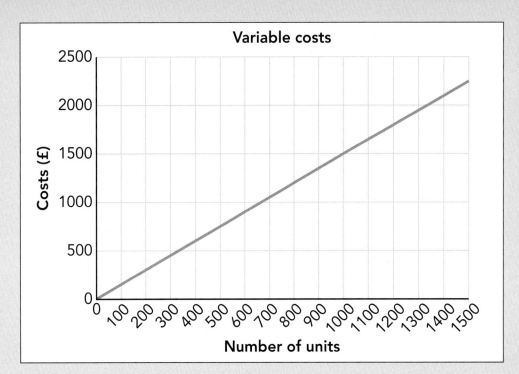

Figure 1.24: Variable costs are directly dependent on the level of output

Variable costs can be expressed:

- per individual product or unit of output (variable cost per unit)
- for an overall level of output (total variable cost).

Variable cost per unit

Sometimes entrepreneurs might need to rearrange a formula to find another figure. For example, they might need to know the variable cost per unit as shown in Worked example 4.

Worked example   4

Ken pays £450 variable costs to produce 30 units. He can use the following variable cost formula to calculate the variable cost per unit:

variable costs = variable cost per unit × output

The formula can be rearranged:

$$\text{variable cost per unit} = \frac{\text{variable costs}}{\text{output}}$$

$$\text{variable cost per unit} = \frac{£450}{30}$$

variable cost per unit = £15

Variable cost for a level of output or period of time

Where variable costs are expressed for an overall level of output (total variable cost) the figure may be shown as the total variable cost for a specific time period, e.g. £6000 on components per month or £20 000 wages annually. Often the time period needs to be changed to obtain information about a different period (see Worked example 5).

Worked example　5

Ken pays £90 for packaging during an average week.

To calculate the value of this cost per year, the weekly figure must be multiplied by 52 as there are 52 weeks in a year.

(For this example, note that it is assumed that Ken's business output is constant throughout the year, i.e. the output does not change each week.)

　£90 packaging per week × 52 weeks =

£4680 packaging per year

Worked example　6

Ken pays his employee £18 000 in wages over the year.

To calculate the value of this cost per month the annual figure must be divided by 12 as there are 12 months in a year.

(For this example, note that it is assumed that Ken's employee works the same number of hours each month, i.e. the amount of wages paid does not change each month.)

　£18 000 wages per year ÷ 12 months =

£1500 wages per month on average

Case study

Counting the cost of production

Thomas owns a small business that produces trainers made from recycled materials. He has recently designed a range of vegan-friendly products that will be launched this summer. The synthetic material used to make these products does not contain animal products.

Thomas operates the business from a factory that he rents and he employs six production employees who are supervised by a team leader. The production employees are paid an hourly wage and the team leader receives a salary. Thomas sells the products online and sends the products to customers' homes.

Figure 1.25: Recycled materials can be used for all sorts of things!

Check your understanding

1   Identify two fixed costs that Thomas's business incurs.

2   Identify three variable costs that Thomas's business has to pay.

3   Using an example from Thomas's business, explain how one of the variable costs changes.

Total costs

Total costs are all of the costs that a business incurs. They are calculated by adding together the fixed costs and the variable costs as shown in Figure 1.26. The formula for total costs is:

> **total costs = fixed costs + variable costs**

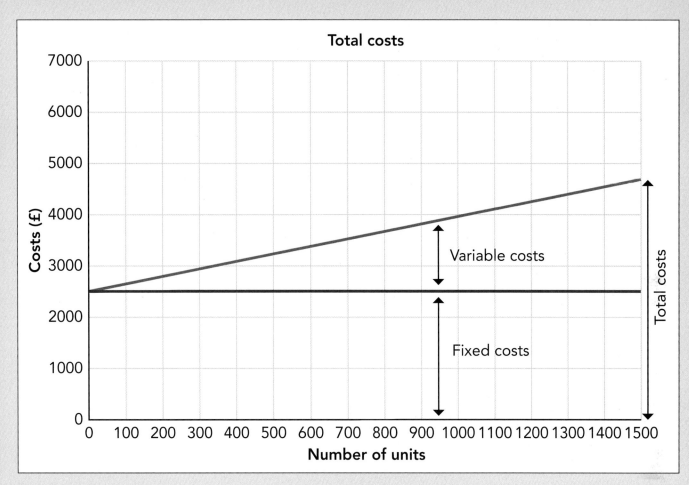

Figure 1.26: Total costs are all of the costs that a business incurs

Total costs can be expressed:

- for an overall level of output (total cost)
- per individual product or unit of output (total cost per unit).

Total cost for a level of output

The total costs can be expressed for a specific number of units produced, i.e. the level of output. For instance, if the fixed costs for a business during April are £5000 and the variable costs are £8000, the total cost for the 800 units made during April will be £13 000.

Total cost per unit

The total costs can be expressed as a value per individual product or unit of output. When working out the total cost per unit, it is important to ensure that you use the fixed cost per unit and variable cost per unit.

Worked example   **7**

Ken's total costs during December are £15 000. He makes 500 units during the month.

The total cost per unit is found by dividing the total cost by the number of units produced (i.e. 500).

    £15 000 total cost for December ÷ 500 =

£30 total cost per unit

Over to you!   **1**

Henri owns a sandwich shop and incurs the following costs to operate the business:

- Rent of the shop: £1000 per month
- Average cost of raw materials per sandwich: £0.80
- Packaging: £0.30 per sandwich
- Insurance: £1500 per year
- Advertising: £2300 per year

Henri estimates that he sells 8500 sandwiches each year.

Calculate the following:

a   annual fixed costs for Henri's business

b   variable cost per unit (i.e. per sandwich)

c   total cost for Henri's business over the course of a year.

3.2 Revenue generated by sales of the product

Let's get started   **2**

The following anagrams are two terms that entrepreneurs commonly use.

    UNREEVE   **FIRPOT**

Can you work out what the terms are? What do you think the terms mean? Do they differ, and if so, how?

Revenue is the money that a business receives from selling its goods or services. It is calculated using the following formula:

> **total revenue = selling price per unit × number sold**

Worked example   8

For example, if a fruit shop sells six oranges at 45p each and four apples at 35p each, the total revenue will be:

£0.45 (selling price per unit) × 6 (quantity sold) = **£2.70**

£0.35 (selling price per unit) × 4 (quantity sold) = **£1.40**

total revenue = £2.70 (oranges) + £1.40 (apples) = £4.10

Sometimes entrepreneurs need to rearrange the revenue formula. For example, they may know how much revenue they have made from selling a specific number of units so they can use this information to find out the selling price per unit.

Worked example   9

Ken sells a product within his business. He has made £750 of revenue from selling 30 units (products). He can use the revenue formula to work out the selling price per unit:

total revenue = selling price per unit × number sold

The formula can be rearranged:

$$\text{selling price per unit} = \frac{\text{total revenue}}{\text{number sold}}$$

$$\text{selling price per unit} = \frac{£750}{30}$$

selling price per unit = £25

Often the revenue is expressed for a specific time period, which may need to be changed to obtain information for a different period (see Worked example 10).

Worked example 10

Ken's business generates £500 of sales revenue during an average week.

To calculate the revenue generated per year the weekly figure must be multiplied by 52 as there are 52 weeks in a year.

(For this example, note that it is assumed that Ken's revenue is constant throughout the year.)

£500 revenue per week × 52 weeks =

£26 000 revenue per year

Worked example 11

Sally earns £24 000 revenue during her first year of trading.

To calculate the revenue earned during an average month the annual figure must be divided by 12 as there are 12 months in a year.

(For this example, note that it is assumed that Sally's business generates a constant revenue each month.)

£24 000 revenue per year ÷ 12 months =

£2000 revenue per month on average

3.3 How to calculate profit and loss

Profit is the amount of money that a business or entrepreneur makes after paying all the costs. Profit is a measure of a business's success. Many entrepreneurs set up a business in the hope of making a profit – it is a key objective of any business. It is therefore important to be able to calculate profit. Most businesses will not survive long if they do not make a profit (i.e. they make a loss). Making a loss is the opposite of making a profit. To make a profit a business's revenue must be more than its total costs.

Profit (or loss) can be expressed:

- for an overall level of output

> **profit = total revenue − total costs**

- per individual product or unit of output

> **profit per unit = revenue per unit − total costs per unit**

Sometimes an entrepreneur might need to rearrange the profit formula to find other figures such as total revenue or total costs.

Worked example   12

Ken makes £500 profit from his business during the month of June. He wants to calculate the total costs for the month of June based on revenue of £1760 that month.

    profit = total revenue − total costs

The formula can be rearranged:

    total costs = total revenue − profit

    total costs = £1760 − £500

total costs = £1260

Over to you!   2

Henri predicts that he will sell 550 sandwiches per month. Use the information from Over to you! 1 to answer the following questions.

Calculate the:

a   total variable costs per month for Henri's sandwich shop

b   average selling price of one of Henri's sandwiches if the total revenue he makes during an average month is £1375

c   estimated profit/loss for Henri's business over the coming year.

1. Identify some examples of variable costs.
2. Identify some examples of fixed costs.
3. How would you calculate profit/loss per unit?
4. Define the term 'revenue'. Explain how a furniture shop generates revenue.

3.4 Use of break-even as an aid to decision making

Let's get started   **3**

Your friend has made a list of all the fixed costs that they have to pay to run their small business.

- Insurance
- Newspaper advertising
- Rent
- Wages
- Electricity

What problems can you identify with the list? Explain what is wrong with the list of fixed costs and why.

No business will survive for long if it makes a loss. In order for a new business to survive, it has to be able to **break even**.

Break-even is the point at which the business is making neither a profit nor a loss. The total revenue from sales is equal to the total costs. Although the business will not make a profit, at least all of its costs are covered by the revenue.

Break-even: total revenue = total costs

An entrepreneur can work out the number of products that they need to produce and sell in order to break even. This is known as the **break-even quantity**, or the **break-even point**.

Calculating break-even using a formula

The formula for calculating the number of units to break even is:

$$\text{break-even quantity (in units)} = \frac{\text{fixed costs}}{\text{selling price per unit} - \text{variable cost per unit}}$$

When calculating the break-even point sometimes the answer will not be a whole number, and it will include decimal places. In this situation the number should be rounded up (not down) to ensure that total costs are completely covered.

Often entrepreneurs use the break-even point as the minimum level of sales/output to aim for. It becomes a sales/output target for the business.

Break-even calculations are normally carried out using figures from **forecasts** or estimates about the future. The forecasted costs and revenue may be based on:

* past figures

* what the entrepreneur predicts they will be in the future.

Rearranging the break-even formula

Sometimes an entrepreneur has to rearrange the break-even formula to find the fixed costs, the selling price per unit or the variable cost per unit.

Worked example   13

Ken needs to work out the fixed costs for his business. He knows that he needs to sell 800 units to break even. The selling price is £25 per unit and variable costs are £15 per unit. The break-even formula can be used to calculate the fixed costs.

$$\text{break-even quantity (in units)} = \frac{\text{fixed costs}}{\text{selling price per unit} - \text{variable cost per unit}}$$

The formula can be rearranged:

fixed costs = break-even quantity (in units) × (selling price per unit − variable cost per unit)

fixed costs = 800 units × (£25 − £15)

fixed costs = 800 units × £10

fixed costs = £8000

Worked example   14

Seth needs to work out the selling price for his product. He knows that he needs to sell 2000 units to break even. The fixed costs are £5000 and variable costs are £7.50 per unit. The break-even formula can be used to calculate the selling price.

$$\text{break-even quantity (in units)} = \frac{\text{fixed costs}}{\text{selling price per unit} - \text{variable cost per unit}}$$

The formula can be rearranged:

$$\text{selling price} = \text{variable cost per unit} + \left(\frac{\text{fixed costs}}{\text{break-even quantity}}\right)$$

selling price = £7.50 + (£5000 ÷ 2000)

selling price = £7.50 + £2.50

selling price = £10.00 per unit

Over to you!   3

Driven by the environmental impact of disposable coffee cups, Vincent has decided to produce a range of re-usable plastic coffee cups which have insulating features to keep drinks warm for longer.

Vincent's fixed costs are £7500 per year and his variable costs are £1.90 per cup. Vincent sells the coffee cups for £4.90 each.

1   Calculate the number of coffee cups that Vincent must sell to break even.

2   Explain whether Vincent will make a profit or a loss if he sells 3000 cups over the course of a year.

3   Explain one action that Vincent could take to reduce the break-even point.

Over to you!   4

Nabil makes bobble hats and he is going to set up a market stall selling them. He will rent a market pitch from the local council. He estimates that the fixed costs of running the stall will be £600 per week. The variable costs (i.e. the costs of materials to make the hats and packaging) total £2.50 per hat. Nabil charges £7.50 per hat.

Continued

1   Use the information provided to complete Table 1.14.

Table 1.14: Nabil's sales of bobble hats

Number of bobble hats sold per week	Total revenue (£)	Fixed costs per week (£)	Variable costs (£)	Total costs per week (£)
0	0	600	0	600
20		600		800
40				
60				
80				
100				
120				
140				
160				
180				
200				

a   Identify the number of bobble hats that Nabil must sell to break even.

b   Using the figures within your table, state the profit or loss that Nabil will make if he sells:

   i   60 bobble hats per week   ii   140 bobble hats per week.

c   Nabil decides to increase the selling price from £7.50 to £10.00 per hat. All other costs remain unchanged.

   i   Use the break-even formula to calculate how many bobble hats Nabil will need to sell after he increases the selling price.

   ii   Explain the impact of the price increase on the break-even point.

d   Explain two ways that Nabil can estimate the cost and revenue information to help him to calculate the break-even quantity.

Identifying break-even point from a break-even graph

In addition to calculating break-even using the formula, an entrepreneur can use a break-even graph (Figure 1.27) to identify the break-even quantity. On a graph, the break-even quantity is represented by the break-even point. A break-even graph has three lines:

- The **fixed costs line** is a straight horizontal line because fixed costs do not change as the level of output increases or decreases.

- The **total costs line** starts at the same point as the fixed cost line because even at a level of zero output, fixed costs are incurred. Remember that total costs are the fixed costs plus the variable costs.

- Finally, the **total revenue line** starts at zero and goes up diagonally as the number of units increases. Revenue will increase as the business produces and sells more products.

The **break-even point** is where the total costs and total revenue lines cross on the graph. It is the revenue that the business needs to cover all of its costs and break even. The break-even point can be identified from the horizontal axis.

The break-even graph in Figure 1.27 shows that the entrepreneur needs to sell 400 units to break even. The area of the graph shaded blue shows that the entrepreneur will make a loss if they sell between 0 and 399 units of the product. However, if the entrepreneur sells over 400 units, they will make a profit, as illustrated by the area of the graph that is shaded orange.

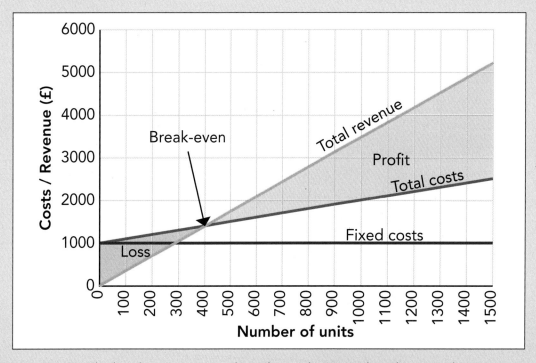

Figure 1.27: The break-even point is where the total costs and total revenue lines cross

Stretch

Hassan started a small business a year ago selling beanie hats online via a website that he created. A break-even graph for his online business is shown in Figure 1.28.

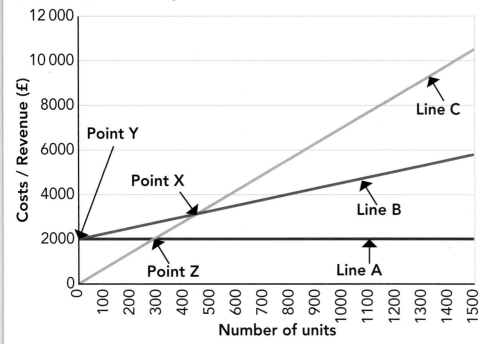

Figure 1.28: What are the various points and lines on the break-even graph called?

1 Using Figure 1.28, state the name of:

   a   Line A   **b**   Line B   **c**   Line C

2 Hassan is unsure of the break-even point. Identify which of the three points (X, Y and Z) is the break-even point.

How entrepreneurs use break-even information

Break-even information is useful for helping entrepreneurs to make decisions about their business. Break-even information tells the entrepreneur the number of units that they must sell to cover all of the production costs and make a profit. If they do not sell that number of units, they will make a loss.

It also allows them to look at different scenarios, such as changing the price or number of units that they produce, to see the effect on the break-even point. This is sometimes referred to as 'what if' scenario planning.

Break-even information can be used by an entrepreneur to:

- work out how many units they need to sell to make a profit

- support an application for a bank loan or to get investment from an investor. Before risking their money/investment, bank managers and investors will want to assess how likely it is that a business will make a profit. A break-even graph is needed in a business plan and it shows that the entrepreneur knows how many units they need to sell to avoid making a loss

- identify any costs that the business needs to reduce. The break-even graph can be changed to show the impact of reducing a specific cost. For example, the business could use less packaging per product, which will reduce the variable cost per unit. Figure 1.29 illustrates how an increase in the fixed costs (fixed costs 2) of a business will increase total costs (total costs 2) and this will increase the break-even point. The business will need to sell a greater number of units (1200 units instead of 1000 units) to cover the increased fixed costs to break even

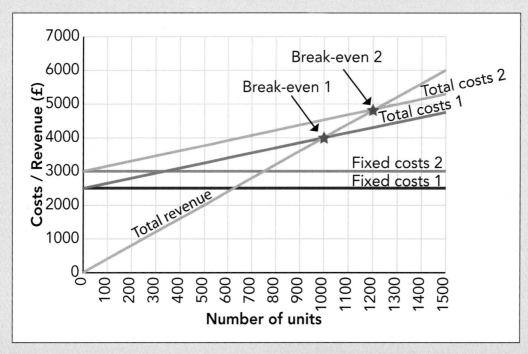

Figure 1.29: What impact will increased fixed costs have on the break-even point?

- decide what price to charge for a product. The price that the business charges will have a direct effect on the total revenue it generates and therefore the break-even point. For example, an entrepreneur has to pay £8000 in fixed costs each month to run her business and the variable cost per unit is £15. If she charges £25 per unit for her product, she needs to sell 800 units to break even. However, if she increases the price to £35 per unit she will only need to sell 400 units to break even (assuming all costs remain unchanged). The price increase means that the entrepreneur does not need to sell as many items to break even.

Case study

The price is right!

Gennaro owns an ice cream stall located in a busy seaside town. His weekly fixed costs are £1000. The variable costs are £1.00 per ice cream, and his selling price is £3.50. Based on these figures, Gennaro needs to sell 400 ice creams each week to break even.

Gennaro discovers that a local café sells similar ice creams at a price of £4.50 each. Gennaro therefore decides to increase his prices to £4.50 per ice cream. If the total costs do not change, the number of ice creams that Gennaro needs to sell each week to break even will reduce, as shown in Figure 1.30.

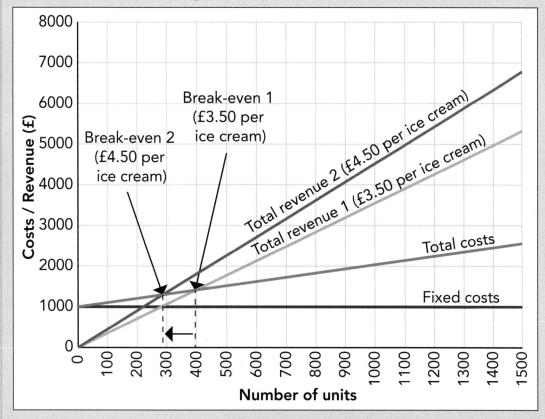

Figure 1.30: What impact will the increase in the ice cream price have on the break-even point?

Continued

Due to the price increase, Gennaro now needs to sell approximately 285 ice creams to break even rather than 400 ice creams.

Check your understanding

1 Identify two examples of variable costs for Gennaro's business.

2 Explain two implications of the price rise on Gennaro's business.

3 Recommend whether Gennaro should increase the price of his ice creams. Justify your decision.

Test your knowledge   2

Break-even calculations and graphs are based on forecasted, or estimated, data.

1 What is a risk of making important business decisions (such as choosing what selling price to charge) using forecasted data?

2 What are some factors that could lead to forecasted data being inaccurate?

3 AB Salons is a chain of hairdressing and beauty salons. Using the break-even graph in Figure 1.31, state the amount of fixed costs that it has to pay.

4 Using the break-even graph, state the approximate number of customers that AB Salons requires to break even.

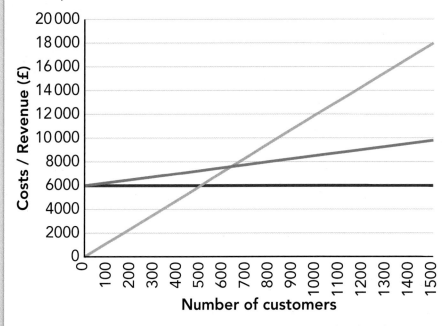

Figure 1.31: How many customers does AB Salons need to break even?

Continued

5   Explain two actions that the manager of AB Salons could take to reduce the number of customers that they need to break even. You should explain why each action will reduce the break-even quantity.

3.5 Importance of cash

Let's get started   4

A local business is struggling to pay its bills because it does not have the cash when the bills arrive.

Why might the business not have enough cash to pay the bills? Think of as many reasons as you can.

All businesses need an appropriate amount of cash in order to operate. Cash is:

* the money kept in the business's bank account that is readily available to pay any debts and expenses

* actual notes and coins in a till or cash box.

The main source of cash flowing into a business is revenue from selling goods and services. Cash flows out of the business when it pays costs, such as wages and salaries for employees and payments to suppliers. To ensure it has enough cash, a business must make sure that the amount of cash flowing in is greater than the amount flowing out of the business. For example, it needs to make sure that it receives prompt payment for the goods that it sells (i.e. it receives the cash quickly), and that it only pays costs after it has received enough cash into the business.

Managing cash flows is challenging as the figures change continually. However, it is extremely important as it is a common reason why a lot of start-up businesses fail.

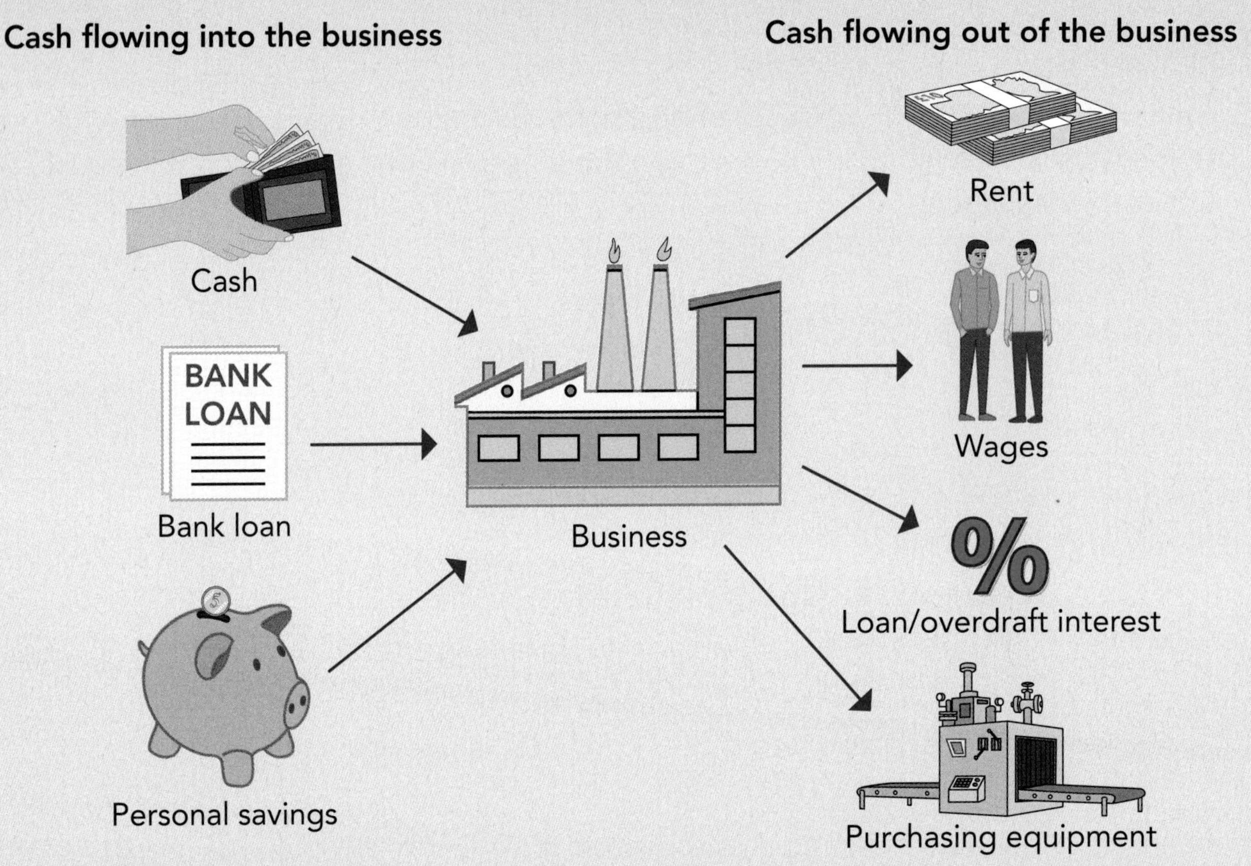

Cash flowing into the business

Cash flowing out of the business

Cash

Bank loan

Personal savings

Business

Rent

Wages

%
Loan/overdraft interest

Purchasing equipment

Figure 1.32: Cash flows into and out of a business

The difference between cash and profit

Cash is very different from profit. Profit is calculated by subtracting the money a business has spent (e.g. costs) from its total revenue. Cash is the amount of money a business has available to pay its bills. Even if a business makes a good profit it might be short of cash.

For example, a large customer may be late paying for goods they have purchased. Alternatively, a business may hold a lot of cash but make no profit. For example, a business may hold a large cash balance, but this cash could be for supporting the future expansion of the business or for buying more equipment.

How much cash to hold is a challenging decision for an entrepreneur. They need to hold enough to be able to pay the bills, but not too much as it could be better used to support the future development of the business.

Why a business needs cash

Without cash a business is unlikely to survive for long as it will be unable to pay its debts and expenses. If it does not pay its debts and expenses, the individuals and businesses it owes money to will take action to recover the debt, which may lead to the closure of the business.

For example, if a business does not have enough cash to pay its electricity bill, the electricity supplier will refuse to supply electricity to the business and may eventually cut off the supply altogether. As the business will not be able to operate its machines or light rooms without electricity, it will have to stop trading. Cash is therefore extremely important as it enables a business to pay its debts and expenses so that it can continue to operate and trade.

Review your learning

Test your knowledge   3

Perfect Panini is a mobile catering business owned by Modesto. It sells panini sandwiches near a college site. As part of a loan application, Modesto has to calculate various financial forecasts for a business plan.

Modesto has forecasted the following information:

Table 1.15: Forecasts for Perfect Panini

Average price of a panini	£4.00
Average number of panini sandwiches sold per week	150
Cost of bread per panini	£0.28
Cost of fillings per panini	£0.15
Fuel for the catering van per week	£200
Insurance per week	£30
Other fixed costs per week	£50

1   Calculate the total fixed costs that Modesto has to pay each week.

2   Calculate the variable cost per unit.

3   Calculate the total sales revenue that Modesto's business generates during an average week.

Continued

4 Calculate the profit/loss that Modesto's business makes during an average week.

5 Calculate the break-even quantity for Modesto's business.

6 Explain what would happen to Modesto's break-even point if he reduced the price to £3.80 per panini sandwich.

7 Explain why Modesto must keep sufficient cash within the business at all times.

What have you learnt?

	See section
• The costs of producing a product.	3.1
• Revenue generated by sales of the product.	3.2
• How to calculate profit/loss.	3.3
• Use of break-even as an aid to decision making.	3.4
• Importance of cash.	3.5

TA4

Creating a marketing mix to support a product

Casey is planning on opening a cookie shop.

What are some ways that Casey could promote her cookie shop? How do you think she should price the cookies? Other than in her shop, how else could she sell her cookies?

What will you learn?

- The **marketing mix** elements for a good/service.
- How the elements of the marketing mix work together.
- Types of advertising medium used to attract and retain customers.
- Sales promotion techniques used to attract and retain customers.
- What **public relations** is.
- How to sell the good or service to the consumer.
- What the **product lifecycle** model is.
- Extension strategies for products in the product lifecycle.
- Factors to consider when pricing a product to attract and retain customers.
- Types of pricing strategies.

4.1 The marketing mix elements for a good or service

The marketing mix refers to the four key elements – the **4Ps** – that a business must use together in order to successfully sell its product and meet the needs of its customers (Figure 1.33).

Figure 1.33: What are the elements of the marketing mix?

To be successful the elements of the marketing mix need to work together, as each element (or ingredient) impacts on the others. A business must therefore create a well-balanced marketing mix of the 4Ps. That means selling the right product, in the right place, at the right price and supported by the right promotion.

Over to you!   1

1 For a smartphone of your choice:

   a Describe the four elements of the marketing mix:

      i   Product   iii   Place

      ii   Price   iv   Promotion.

   b Identify the factors that you think an entrepreneur should consider under each of the four headings.

   c Describe why you think that decisions regarding each of the elements may influence the success of the product.

Continued

Stretch

2   Now, think about the four elements of the marketing mix for a handcrafted item of jewellery, such as a luxury necklace.

    a   Identify the factors that you think the entrepreneur should consider under each of the 4Ps.

    b   Compare your answers to those for the smartphone. List the similarities and differences between the elements of the marketing mixes.

      i   Why is a different marketing mix required for each product?

      ii   Do all elements of the marketing mix stay the same forever?

      iii   Why might the elements change over time?

      iv   Can you give examples of factors that may lead to a change?

4.2 How the elements of the marketing mix work together

Creating a well-balanced marketing mix is essential. A business needs to look at each of the elements of the marketing mix (product, price, place, promotion – the 4Ps) with the target market in mind.

Any decisions about one element will affect decisions relating to the other elements. For example, the marketing mix will not be effective if a business decides to:

- charge a high price for a basic product, and

- sell that product in a shop that specialises in economy products, and

- promote the product using simple leaflets that it has designed and printed itself in the office.

The product will not be successful because the price is not in line with the other elements of the marketing mix, which are related to a basic product. So customers may feel that it is not worth paying a high price for a basic product. To meet the needs of the target market segment, all of the elements (all of the 4Ps) must be aimed at the same target market, for example premium or economy.

The marketing mix for a product will vary from business to business. It may change over time if a business decides to alter its image or aim its product at a different target market. For example:

- When a business first launches a product, promotion may be a very important element of the marketing mix in order to make customers aware of the product's existence.

- When a product has been available for a number of years, and the business launches a new product, it may need to focus on the price element of the marketing mix. By reducing the price of the original product, it may still appeal to customers and the business will maintain its level of sales.

Case study

Lucozade – Changing the marketing mix

Lucozade was originally marketed as a drink to 'aid recovery' by restoring energy during/after a period of illness or after a busy day at work as shown by the advert from the 1950s (Figure 1.34).

In the 1980s, Lucozade decided to sell it as a sports energy drink, so the company had to change all of the elements of the marketing mix. The marketing team at Lucozade made this change to prevent sales of the drink declining.

Changes to the marketing mix

The company:

- used leading athletes to promote the product in an advertising campaign

- updated the packaging to give it a more modern and 'active' image

- started selling the product:

  - in a new plastic bottle (rather than a glass bottle)

  - in a range of different sized stores and sports centre vending machines so customers could buy it after playing sport

- changed the price so that it was affordable for the target market.

Figure 1.34: Lucozade has changed from being marketed as a drink to restore energy to a sports energy drink

Continued

The changes to the marketing mix were highly successful and the drink is now a very popular sports drinks within the UK.

Check your understanding

1   Why did Lucozade decide to change its marketing mix?

2   Explain how each of the elements of the 'new' Lucozade marketing mix made it appeal to those looking to buy a sports energy drink.

3   Why was the change in Lucozade's packaging design an important part of the marketing mix?

Test your knowledge   1

1   Can you name the elements of the marketing mix?

2   Explain how the four elements of the marketing mix for an economy cola drink differ from those for a premium-brand cola drink.

3   Why is it important that the four elements of the marketing mix are well balanced? What might happen if one element is not in line with the others?

4   Explain some of the reasons why the marketing mix for a product may need to change over time.

4.3 Types of advertising medium used to attract and retain customers

Let's get started   2

Choose a well-known brand, such as Nike, Tesco or McDonald's. How do they advertise their products? Think of as many different ways as you can.

Many entrepreneurs choose to advertise their product(s) as part of their promotion plans. Advertising can help to attract customers and also inform them about the features and benefits of the product, which will persuade them to purchase it.

When choosing an advertising medium, a business/entrepreneur must consider:

- the needs and profile of customers within the target market segment
- whether the advertising will appeal to the target market segment
- how to reach the target market segment so that they will see the advertising
- the cost – so that it keeps within budget but still has the greatest impact.

Advertising mediums may be:

- **non-digital** – more 'traditional' ways of advertising, such as leaflets and newspapers, that do not rely on digital technology
- **digital** – using digital technology and the internet.

Non-digital advertising mediums

Leaflets

A leaflet is a printed medium containing information and advertising. Leaflets contain easy-to-read information and visual images such as photos and graphics. They are relatively low cost.

Leaflets are often used by businesses to target customers within a local area, by posting them through letterboxes and handing them out in the street. They can also be inserted into magazines/newspapers or put in a display in a store or at an event. For example, a new gym might use leaflets to promote their memberships or classes to people in the local area. Table 1.16 shows some of the advantages and disadvantages of leaflets.

Table 1.16: Advantages and disadvantages of leaflets

Advantages	Disadvantages
<ul><li>Effectively target customers in a local area</li><li>Visually appealing and easy to read</li><li>Can include photos, graphics and lots of information</li><li>Relatively cheap to produce</li><li>Can be produced in colour or in black and white to reduce costs</li></ul>	<ul><li>The customer may throw the leaflet away without reading it, especially if they think it is junk mail</li><li>Environmental cost of using paper</li><li>Impact is short term as leaflets are rarely kept for long</li></ul>

Over to you!   2

Look at a range of leaflets, for example those that have recently been delivered through your letter box or find some examples on the internet.

1   What is good about the leaflets? What could be improved about them?

2   A new takeaway is about to open in your local area and it wants to design a leaflet to advertise its service. What recommendations would you make so that their leaflet attracts customers? What information should it include?

Newspapers

Businesses can advertise in local or national newspapers. The cost of newspaper advertising can vary depending on the number of people that read the newspaper (readership). Generally, national newspapers that are read by a greater number of people are more expensive. For this reason, most small businesses favour local newspapers to reduce the cost of advertising and to target customers in a specific area.

The cost of newspaper advertising depends on the size of the advert, whether the advert is colour or black and white and the location of the advert within the newspaper. Some pages are more expensive to advertise on than others. For instance, adverts on the right-hand page of a newspaper are more costly as the adverts are more likely to be read and get a response. Table 1.17 shows some advantages and disadvantages of newspaper advertising.

Table 1.17: Advantages and disadvantages of newspaper advertising

Advantages	Disadvantages
• Can effectively target a specific market segment by advertising in newspapers with a particular type of readership • Can effectively target customers in a local area through local newspapers • Can use colour, headings, photos and graphics to increase the impact • The cost of advertising in local and free newspapers may be relatively low • National newspapers can have a broad reach	• Newspaper readership is generally declining • The advert content will be static (it does not move) and not interactive • Less effective for certain market segments that are less likely to read newspapers (e.g. young people) • The advert may be 'lost' if there are lots of other adverts on the same page, or people may not read the advertising pages • Can be expensive

Magazines

Magazines range from consumer magazines bought by the general public to specialist business and industry magazines. Magazines may be targeted at a specific local area or they may be available nationally. Many magazines are aimed at a specific type of reader, e.g. according to gender, special interest/hobby or age group. So, a business selling mountain bikes may choose to advertise in *Mountain Bike Rider*. With magazine advertising, an entrepreneur can effectively target customers within a specific market segment. Table 1.18 shows some advantages and disadvantages of magazine advertising.

Table 1.18: Advantages and disadvantages of magazine advertising

Advantages	Disadvantages
• Can effectively target a specific market segment according to the readership of the magazine (e.g. a sports product in a sports magazine) • Many magazines are published monthly so the advert will have a longer impact than in some other mediums • People share magazines with others, e.g. friends or family, which increases the impact of the advertisement • Can use colour, headings, photos and graphics to increase the impact	• The cost of advertising in some magazines may be very high, especially in colour • The advert may be 'lost' if there are lots of other adverts on the same page or within the same publication • Many readers skip the adverts and only read the articles • Most magazines are national so cannot target a local market • Advertising deadlines may be months before the publication

Radio

There are many commercial radio stations that have advertising breaks between programmes. Radio is an effective way to target customers in a specific local area on local commercial stations. Radio adverts can include music, speech and a catchy jingle which may strengthen the **brand**.

Advertising is usually sold in 30-second slots. Different slots throughout the day cost different amounts, with peak times being the most expensive. A business can choose what time of the day its advert is broadcast so that it is aired during programmes that the target market listen to. For example, a travel agent may choose to advertise during a commercial break in a travel show on their local radio station. Table 1.19 shows some advantages and disadvantages of radio advertising.

Table 1.19: Advantages and disadvantages of radio advertising

Advantages	Disadvantages
• Effective at targeting customers within a local area • Can use audio or a catchy jingle to increase the impact • The timing of the advert can be adjusted to best target specific listeners • Can have an immediate response if advertising offers and events	• The cost of advertising can be relatively high, especially during prime-time slots • People only hear the advert for a short amount of time so it can only include a small amount of information • Listeners may struggle to take in all the information • Many people listen to the radio whilst doing other tasks, e.g. driving, so the advert's message might be lost or ignored • The advert may need to be heard a number of times before listeners become aware of it • The product cannot be 'seen' • Can only use sound to generate impact

Posters and billboards

Posters are a visual way to advertise a product or service. They are especially popular with small businesses on a limited budget as they can be relatively cheap to produce. An eye-catching poster can be very effective if it is placed in a location visited by the target market.

Traditional billboards are static enlarged posters (i.e. they do not move). Modern billboards are digital with moving text and images. Billboards are often placed along busy roads, on the sides of buildings and in key locations, such as train stations or sport stadiums. The placement and location can be chosen to best target a specific market segment. Digital billboard adverts often rotate so that a number of adverts can be displayed in sequence. This movement increases the impact of the advertising as it better attracts the attention of passers-by. Table 1.20 shows some advantages and disadvantages of posters and billboards.

Figure 1.35: What are the advantages of billboards?

Table 1.20: Advantages and disadvantages of posters and billboards

Advantages	Disadvantages
• By selecting the location carefully, the business can effectively target a specific market • Posters are a relatively low-cost form of advertising • Very eye-catching and grab attention in public places	• Posters and traditional billboards are static • Billboards are more expensive than posters as they have to be designed professionally • Prime locations are expensive • People only see the advert for a short amount of time so the message needs to be kept simple

Cinema

Cinema screens are large and have maximum impact. Cinema advertising can be a particularly effective way of reaching a specific group of potential customers. As with radio advertising, the business can look at the types of film and the type of audience who will be attending and decide during which films to advertise. Young people (aged 15–24 years) tend to visit the cinema more than other age groups, so for businesses targeting this age group, cinema advertising is likely to be very effective.

Cinema adverts are purchased as a package containing a certain number of adverts which are aired over a period of time. Table 1.21 shows some advantages and disadvantages of cinema advertising.

Table 1.21: Advantages and disadvantages of cinema advertising

Advantages	Disadvantages
• Can target customers effectively based on the type of film • Can use audio and video to increase the impact • Very impactful on a large screen	• Expensive to produce • Many cinema goers ignore the adverts

Test your knowledge   2

1. Name some of the non-digital advertising mediums that an entrepreneur may use.

2. Explain two advantages of advertising a new leather handbag in a magazine.

3. Explain three advantages of advertising a second-hand car business in a local newspaper.

4. Explain two disadvantages of advertising a local plumbing business on local radio.

5. Analyse the advantages and disadvantages of advertising a new fast-food business in the cinema. Decide whether you think this is the best medium for the owner to use.

Digital advertising mediums

Let's get started   3

Below are three anagrams of digital advertising mediums you are likely to be aware of.

GLOBS   **ADCOPTS**   **GLOVS**

What are they? Can you explain the difference between them?

Digital advertising involves the use of the internet and social media platforms to target customers of all ages – not just younger customers.

Social media

The number of people using social media is growing all the time. Social media is used by customers of all ages around the world.

Businesses can set up social media accounts that are cheap and easy to update. A business can publish and update posts regularly with photos and videos about new products, product news and offers. Customers can then share this information with their friends (Figure 1.36).

Most other forms of advertising, such as radio or newspaper adverts, are designed and arranged by the business itself. Although social media advertising is often generated by the business, it can also be created by third parties such as customers, competitors or members of the public. For example, a customer may write a comment on their personal social media account about a product they have tried, or someone could add a comment to reply to a post written by the business.

Third-party generated posts can be helpful as complimentary comments from unbiased customers may be more credible than those posted by a business keen to sell its products. However, third-party generated posts can also create challenges as negative comments may be shared quickly and be more influential than posts created by the business. Table 1.22 outlines some of the advantages and challenges of social media content depending upon how it was created.

Figure 1.36: Social media allows businesses to publish posts about new products and offers regularly, which customers can share with friends

Table 1.22: Advantages and challenges of different social media content creators

Creator	Advantages	Challenges
Social media posts prepared by the business	• Free/cheap way of advertising • Adverts can reach customers around the globe	• Not everyone is on social media, or may only use some platforms • Can have a short timeframe • May appear biased as they are written by the business

Third-party generated social media posts	• Third-party comments may appear more credible as they appear to be from an unbiased source, so positive comments may have a more beneficial effect on sales
	• Free advertising – the business does not have to spend time or money generating these posts
	• The posts may appear on social media platforms not currently used by the business itself therefore reaching new customers
		• It can be time-consuming to identify posts created by third parties
		• Unhappy followers may post negative comments, which:
		  • are hard to delete and are visible to potential customers
		  • may include exaggerated comments
		  • can have a negative impact on the business's reputation
		• Third-party comments may appear more credible as they appear to be from an unbiased source, so negative comments can harm or even destroy a product/brand
		• Individuals may hide their true identity, e.g. a competitor may use a fake name for posts relating to a rival business

Through other forms of advertising, such as newspaper and magazine adverts, businesses often encourage potential customers to sign up and follow them on social media. As these potential customers have shown an interest in the business by signing up, the business knows that they are interested in their products, services and offers. So the business can target its social media advertising more effectively.

Businesses have to monitor their social media accounts closely. Negative or inappropriate comments and reviews can be hard to remove and can have a negative impact on the business's reputation. Table 1.23 shows some advantages and disadvantages of social media advertising.

Over to you!   3

1   The number of social media platforms is constantly growing. Make a list of all of the social media platforms that you know of.

2   Review your list and explain how a business can best use each one.

Tip: Are any of them only for posting videos, or are any of them targeted at a specific market segment?

Table 1.23: Advantages and disadvantages of social media advertising

Advantages	Disadvantages

• Can use particular social media platforms to specifically target potential customer groups
• Can use audio and video to increase the impact
• Customers can leave positive reviews/feedback and share information and offers with friends
• Customers who sign up to follow the business have an interest in the business and its product(s) or service(s)
• Free/cheap way of advertising
• Adverts can reach customers around the globe
	• Not everyone is on social media
	• Unhappy followers may post negative comments, which:
	  • are hard to delete and are visible to potential customers
	  • may include exaggerated comments
	  • can have a negative impact on the business's reputation
	• Someone needs to update, monitor and respond to social media regularly, which can be quite time-consuming

Case study

Gabriel's water bottles

Gabriel runs a business that sells reusable water bottles made from recycled materials. He advertises his product range on Facebook, Twitter and Instagram. Gabriel uses a mixture of photos, videos and text to show his product range.

His posts always generate a lot of feedback from users and discussion amongst their social media friends (third parties). Gabriel finds that feedback from customers and their social media contacts is more influential than the content that he originally posts.

However, recently Gabriel received a negative review on Facebook about his water bottles, which was posted on his page by mistake. The customer meant to post it on another page. Gabriel is trying to get it removed but it is proving difficult and the post is still showing up on his page.

Check your understanding

1 Identify two benefits to Gabriel's business of advertising on social media.

2 Explain one disadvantage to Gabriel's business of advertising his water bottles via social media.

3 Explain why the feedback and posts created by third parties are more influential than those produced by Gabriel himself.

Websites

Most businesses have their own website, which they can use to advertise and provide information about their products. A website gives a business the opportunity to showcase (display) both its existing product range and new products using text information, photos and videos. The information on the website can be updated easily to ensure that visitors have the latest details, such as price lists.

If the website has been developed correctly, search engines such as Google will list it near the top of search lists. The business will be able to track information such as the number of visitors to the website and the type of customer. This information helps the business to write suitable website content and target promotions at specific customers.

A business can also add information about its products and services and a link to its own website on other websites, such as a professional association's website, a local website directory of businesses or on social media sites. The link then directs traffic to the business's own website. Table 1.24 shows some advantages and disadvantages of website advertising.

Table 1.24: Advantages and disadvantages of website advertising

Advantages	Disadvantages
<ul><li>Can be impactful through the use of audio and video</li><li>A relatively low-cost way to advertise</li><li>Websites can be accessed from across the world so adverts can reach customers around the globe</li><li>Content can be updated easily and regularly</li><li>Accessible from anywhere at any time due to mobile phones</li><li>Can sell products via the website (online sales)</li><li>Can include links to and from websites of other businesses and organisations</li><li>Customers can post reviews, and if they are positive they can encourage other customers to purchase</li></ul>	<ul><li>Some people may not have access to the internet</li><li>A complex website may be expensive and time-consuming to set up and maintain</li><li>The business may need to employ a specialist developer to create and develop the website</li><li>Technical problems may impact negatively on the business's reputation</li><li>Need to be updated as out-of-date information may impact the business negatively</li><li>The website could be hacked and customer information could be stolen</li><li>Unhappy customers may leave negative reviews</li><li>Takes time for new websites to appear in internet search rankings</li></ul>

Over to you!   4

1   Visit your school's website. Make a list of the things that you:

   a   like about the design and content of the website

   b   would change.

Tip: You could present your work as a series of PowerPoint slides and illustrate the points with screen-prints of your school's website.

2   Do you think the website makes new students want to join the school? Why/why not?

Online banners and pop-ups

Banners are adverts that appear alongside the content on a web page – either along the top or bottom of the page or down the side. They stay visible while the user looks at the web page, but they change frequently and the information can move across the screen.

Pop-ups are adverts that pop up over the top of another web page. Pop-ups appear temporarily before disappearing, so they are only appropriate for short and simple messages.

Both of these forms of advertising are paid-for advertising, the cost being based on the number of times they are shown. The business placing the advertisement designs the content to complement their **brand image** (see Unit R069, Section 1.1). Both pop-ups and banners can include text-only or image-only content. Table 1.25 shows the advantages and disadvantages of online banners and pop-up advertising.

Table 1.25: Advantages and disadvantages of online banners and pop-up advertising

Advantages	Disadvantages
• Grab attention as they are the first thing customers see on a website, and can be designed in an eye-catching way • Can effectively target customers by targeting the websites that the banner/pop-up appears on • Easy to update the content and/or change the banner/pop-up design • Relatively low cost	• Some people may not have access to the internet • The banner/pop-up may be ignored as the person may be more interested in the content of the actual web page • Customers may find banners and pop-ups annoying if they obscure the web page content • Not appropriate for lots of information or complex messages

SMS texts

Many businesses send **SMS text messages** to customers to make them aware of current offers. One text message can be sent to all of the customers that the business has contact details for. This makes it a straightforward and simple way of advertising and allows the business to tailor the message to specific customers. Customers are usually given the option to sign up for text messages about products, offers and discounts. If they have not given their permission to the business to contact them by text message, data protection laws state that the business must not contact them that way. Businesses can track how many customers respond. Table 1.26 shows some advantages and disadvantages of SMS texts.

Table 1.26: Advantages and disadvantages of SMS texts

Advantages	Disadvantages
• As a business has customers' contact details, it can target customers more effectively • Relatively low cost • Quick to read and respond to • Can be used to highlight current offers • Can include a link to the business's website and encourage customers to visit the website	• Messages need to be short, which reduces the information a business can provide • May annoy some customers • Customers may delete the message before reading it • Only some customers will sign up for SMS texts • A customer may change their number so they no longer receive the SMS texts • A customer may opt out of receiving texts • SMS text messages are commonly used by fraudsters, which can make customers wary of clicking on links (even if the text is genuine)

Podcasts

A **podcast** is a spoken audio file on a particular topic. For example, it might be a recording of someone discussing a specific product or business. A business might use a podcast to introduce a new product and explain its features and benefits. Or an **influencer** may feature the product on one of their podcasts. Some businesses produce a series of podcasts to keep customers interested. Table 1.27 shows some advantages and disadvantages of podcasts.

Table 1.27: Advantages and disadvantages of podcasts

Advantages	Disadvantages
• Simple and fairly cheap to make using a smartphone/computer • Information can be communicated in a way that is accessible to all customers • Can use audio and video to make the content engaging • Many businesses have a loyal following of customers who download the podcast • Businesses can analyse the popularity of the podcast by looking at the number of downloads	• Producing a podcast with new content is a regular commitment • Not all customers download or listen to podcasts

Vlogs and blogs

A **blog** is written information about a product or topic that will be of interest to followers, such as a new product or an offer. A **vlog** is very similar but instead of written information it uses visual information in the form of videos. Blogs and vlogs are posted online.

Bloggers and vloggers have to produce content on a regular basis to maintain interest amongst followers. The content may be created by an influencer, or an entrepreneur in the case of a small business. If the business uses an influencer, they may have to pay them or give them free products in return for their endorsement of the product or business, especially if they are very famous. Table 1.28 shows some advantages and disadvantages of vlogs and blogs.

Table 1.28: Advantages and disadvantages of vlogs and blogs

Advantages	Disadvantages
• Many businesses have a loyal customer following that access their blogs and/or vlogs • Can be used to build a relationship between a business and its customers • Can provide detailed information about a product and its features and benefits • The content may be tailored to a topic of current interest – such as reducing single-use plastic – which is relevant to the type of product being sold • Producing a regular blog and/or vlog can make the business stand out from its rivals	• Producing a blog and/or vlog is a regular commitment and can be time-consuming • Need to be updated regularly to keep up to date with trends • Not all customers look at blogs or vlogs • Vlogs can be expensive to produce because of the cost of the equipment needed • Poorly written or inaccurate content can reflect badly on the business

Over to you! 5

Have you ever read a blog or watched a vlog?

Search online for a blog or vlog written by a small business owner, or one that promotes a new product, and read the blog/watch the vlog.

1 Identify the purpose of the blog or vlog and who wrote the content.

2 Offer three top tips for someone who wants to produce an interesting blog or vlog to promote a new healthy snack.

Tip: Include the link to the blog or vlog in your notes so that you can visit it again as part of your revision.

Test your knowledge 3

1 Name a few types of digital advertising medium that an entrepreneur may use.

2 Explain some advantages of using a website to advertise a new pet shop in your local town.

3 Sadie is preparing to open a new café and is planning an advertising campaign. Explain how Sadie could use social media and podcasts to advertise the new café.

4 Advertising should inform and persuade customers. What is the difference between 'informing' and 'persuading' customers?

5 Explain why an entrepreneur must consider the target market segment when choosing an advertising medium.

4.4 Sales promotion techniques used to attract and retain customers

Let's get started   4

Which of the following is most likely to encourage you to buy a new pair of trainers (Figures 1.37–1.39)? Explain the reason for your choice.

Figure 1.37: There is a 10 percent discount off the price of the trainers

Figure 1.38: A well-known athlete, who is sponsored by the trainer manufacturer, wears the trainers

Figure 1.39: For every pair of trainers that is purchased there is entry to a competition to win one of 50 new iPads

Sales promotions are another way of informing customers about products and attracting them to buy them. Sales promotions are not the same as advertising. They usually give customers an incentive (a reason) to buy the product, such as a discount or an opportunity to win a prize by entering a competition.

Discounts

A short-term discount is a good way of grabbing consumers' attention. Customers are always on the lookout for a bargain, and offering a discount makes the product more affordable. It will often tempt them to try something new. For example £2 off a pizza or 25 percent extra free in a packet of biscuits. While discounts may increase sales, they reduce the amount of revenue that the business generates. For this reason they should only be used for a short period of time.

They can also have a negative effect on the company's image or the brand's image (see Unit R069, Section 1.1) if customers see the discount as 'cheapening' a high-quality product. Discounts should be used with care.

Competitions

This is where customers win a prize if they buy a product or service. For example, Cadbury ran a competition whereby customers buying the brand's Creme Eggs had the chance of finding one of 200 golden Creme Eggs inside the wrapper. They could win a prize if they found one of these.

To take part in the competition, a customer has to engage with the business or the brand in some way (e.g. buying the product). Competitions are often held on social media sites with customers having the chance to win a prize if they like, comment or share a post. While paying for the prizes can sometimes be expensive, competitions can generate **market presence** and awareness, which can be invaluable when first starting a business or releasing a new product.

Buy one, get one free (BOGOF)

Buy one get one free (BOGOF) discounts are popular in supermarkets. Customers are more likely to buy products on a BOGOF than if they are discounted because they are getting something for 'free'. Customers can even be persuaded to switch from their usual brands if they are offered a free product, so customers may try a new brand of product.

However, BOGOF discounts can have a negative effect on the product's/brand's image if customers see the BOGOF as 'cheapening' the value of the product. Also, it can encourage customers to buy more than they need. With food products in particular, this can create unnecessary food waste.

Point-of-sale advertising

In shops, businesses often put small point-of-sale product displays, posters or banners at the till (the point of sale) so that customers make impulse purchases before they pay. Items such as chocolate, sweets, soft drinks and batteries are often placed on display at or near the till point or counter.

Point-of-sale promotions can be very creative and are designed to draw the customer's attention to the product on offer. They are a simple but effective way of highlighting a product. If they are placed in the wrong location or they are too small, the customer may not engage with the product as they will not see it. The cost of rolling them out nationally can be quite high.

Figure 1.40: Why do point-of-sale promotions draw customers' attention to products?

Free gifts

Free gifts are used by some businesses to encourage customers to buy a product. For example, restaurants may offer a free drink with every main meal that a customer purchases, or McDonald's offer a free toy with a Happy Meal.

To be successful, the free gift must be something that the customer values. It is an effective way of encouraging customers to try an additional product, which could lead to them buying it in the future if they like it.

Product trials

A product trial is when a product is launched to a small part of the market or when a free sample is given out to customers to try. For example a taste test in a supermarket. A free sample of a new flavour of crisps allows customers to try the product before they buy and makes them aware of the product and brand. It is also a good way of getting customer feedback on a new product before a business launches it to the wider market.

However, it can be quite costly to give away lots of free products, and there is no guarantee that the consumer will purchase the product that they tried. Also, product trials allow competitors to see a business's product before it has launched.

Loyalty schemes

Many companies, such as Costa, Boots and Nando's, offer loyalty schemes. Costa Coffee gives customers a card on which they can collect points. As the points build up, customers can spend them on food and drink at Costa. Loyalty rewards encourage customers to return to a business rather than a competitor to 'earn' points that lead to discounts, in-store coupons or free products. It is also cheaper for a business to keep a loyal customer rather than attract a new one.

Loyalty schemes are not only offered by large businesses; many small businesses also offer schemes. Independent retailers in some small towns and cities sometimes group together and operate a loyalty scheme where customers receive points when they spend in any participating retailer.

Loyalty cards also allow a business to collect useful data on customers' buying patterns and habits. It can use the information to target them with products, services and promotions. Tesco has operated its successful Clubcard loyalty scheme since the 1990s. It analyses the data collected and gives customers money-off coupons. This targeted approach increases the likelihood of extra sales but relies on a complex IT system to capture all of the information about customer buying habits, which is very expensive. Some customers may also dislike a business storing their personal data and monitoring their purchases due to fear that the information may be used inappropriately, hacked or even sold to a third-party organisation. If a large proportion of customers choose not to join the loyalty scheme it will not be effective.

As lots of companies offer loyalty schemes giving pretty much the same rewards, it is difficult to create a scheme that stands out. Loyalty schemes may not make a customer loyal to a specific retailer as often customers join multiple schemes and purchase from the retailer with the best offers each week.

Over to you!   6

1   Supermarkets use a whole range of promotional techniques. For each of the promotional techniques listed below, give an example of how a supermarket uses it.

    a   Discounts   **c**   Point-of-sale advertising

    b   BOGOF   **d**   Loyalty scheme

2   Which techniques do you feel are the most effective?

Sponsorship

Sponsorship is when a business supports an event, a television programme, a business or a person financially in return for advertising. For example, the airline Etihad Airways sponsored Manchester City Football Club for just over ten years. The communications company Three sponsors Chelsea Football Club, and M&S Food sponsors the popular television programme *Britain's Got Talent*. Many small businesses also sponsor their local sports team or a local resident raising funds for charity, such as someone running the London Marathon. The name of the sponsoring business will be on the runner's shirt.

Sponsorship does not get a business an immediate sale or engage customers in the same way as other methods of promotion. However, it raises awareness of the brand and improves market presence. It can improve the overall image of a company if it sponsors the right event, business or person. Sponsorship can be expensive.

Figure 1.41: Sponsorship raises awareness of brands

Over to you!   7

Select three promotional techniques. For each one:

a   describe the technique and how it is used

b   find real-life business examples of it, apart from those mentioned in the text

c   explain one benefit and one limitation of the method to a business.

Test your knowledge   4

1   A business is providing finance to enable a local music festival to take place. In return for the money, the business's **logo** is included on all tickets and signage on stage. Identify the sales promotion technique that the business is using.

2   Explain two limitations of a supermarket loyalty scheme as a sales promotion technique.

3   Explain two benefits to a newsagent of using point-of-sale advertising to attract and retain customers.

4.5 Public relations

Let's get started   5

Can you think of any celebrities that are linked to a particular product or brand? Do these associations with celebrities encourage you to buy the product? Why/why not?

Public relations, sometimes known as PR, is about promoting the company's reputation and building a beneficial relationship or positive image between a business and the public. Figure 1.42 shows what PR involves. Table 1.29 shows the benefits and limitations of public relations methods.

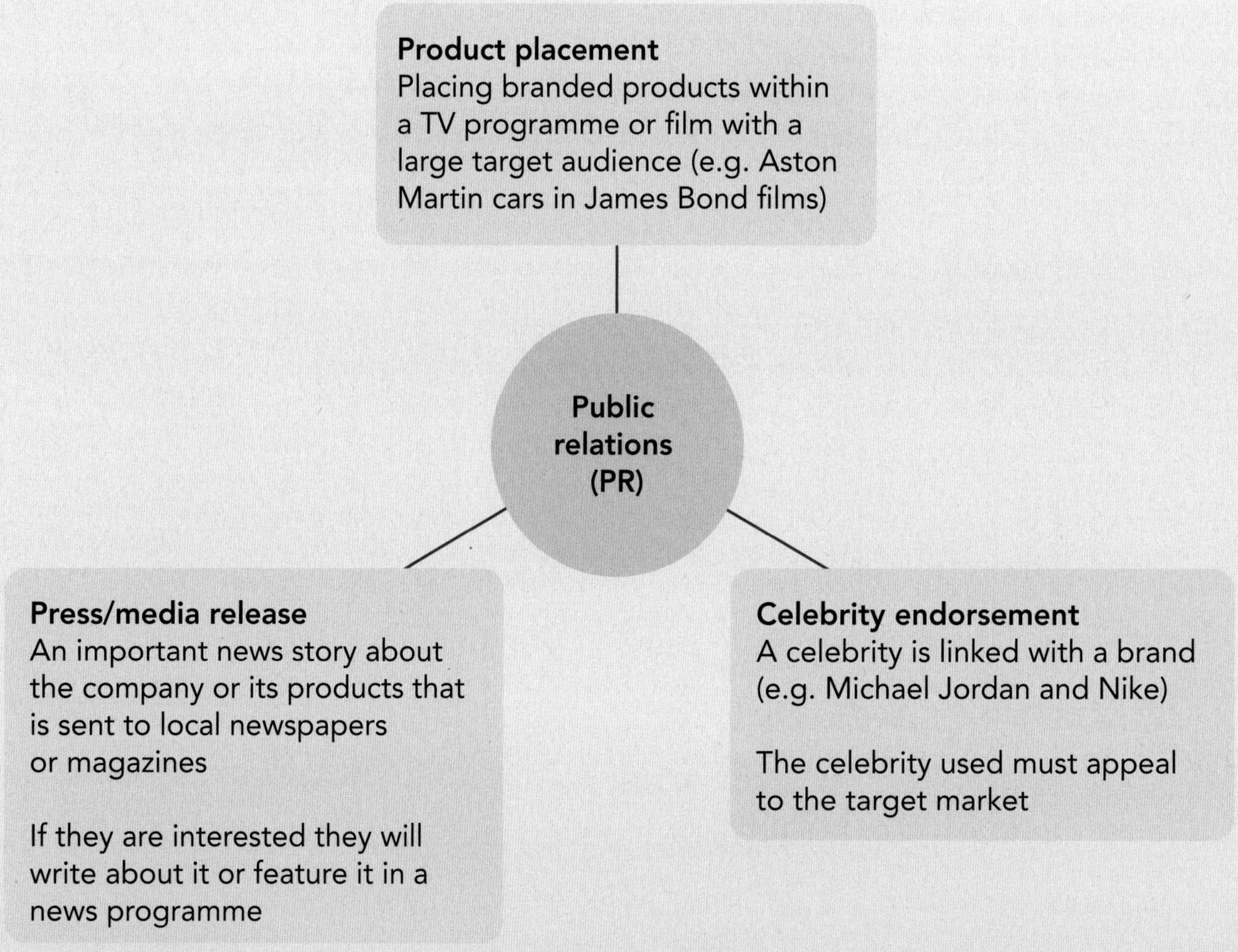

Product placement
Placing branded products within a TV programme or film with a large target audience (e.g. Aston Martin cars in James Bond films)

Public relations (PR)

Press/media release
An important news story about the company or its products that is sent to local newspapers or magazines

If they are interested they will write about it or feature it in a news programme

Celebrity endorsement
A celebrity is linked with a brand (e.g. Michael Jordan and Nike)

The celebrity used must appeal to the target market

Figure 1.42: What are the different methods used in public relations?

Many large, established businesses use public relations methods – for instance, Nike is a global brand with a large promotional budget. However, entrepreneurs starting a small enterprise, with a small promotional budget, can also use public relations methods. Small businesses will use the methods differently from a large global brand. For instance, a small business is unlikely to ask a Hollywood celebrity to support its brand, but a respected person in the local community could endorse the brand, such as through a charity fundraiser. Many small businesses regularly send press/media releases to a local newspaper or radio station to generate free coverage within the local area.

Table 1.29: The benefits and limitations of public relations methods

Public relations method	Benefits	Limitations
Product placement	• Effective because the product feels like it is part of the film/TV programme and people do not realise that the product is being promoted • If people enjoy a programme or film then their positive feelings about it translate to the product/brand • Grabs the attention of people who may be difficult to reach with more traditional promotion methods	• It is expensive to place products in popular films/programmes so small business are unlikely to be able to afford it • The film production company has overall control, so the product might not appear in a way that is beneficial for the brand/business • If there are other products within the same film/programme, they all get 'lost' and viewers do not remember them
Celebrity endorsement (can also be used as a method of branding – see Unit R069, Section 1.3)	• A celebrity name attached to a product builds trust – a celebrity would not risk their reputation on a poor-quality product • Consumers are more likely to remember the brand/business if it is linked to a celebrity • If the celebrity has a positive image, the product/business will also have a positive image	• Very expensive to get celebrity endorsement so small businesses are unlikely to be able to afford it. However, a well-known person within the local area may offer public support to a small business or its products which may be very effective • The business has no control over the behaviour of the celebrities that endorse its brand • Any negative issues regarding the celebrity may create a negative reputation for the product/business
Press/media release	• Free publicity, so it is beneficial for small businesses on a limited budget • Story/content is published by a reputable source in an engaging way • Can target a particular customer by sending the story to a specific newspaper or radio station	• The media (newspapers, radio stations, TV, etc.) receive lots of press releases from businesses, so the story must stand out • Story will not be featured if it is not interesting/unique so that it appeals to the readers/audience • The story may be misinterpreted by journalists and/or deliberately changed to make it of greater interest to readers or listeners. This could change the facts that the business wants to share

Case study

Product placement – Co-op and *Coronation Street*

Sometimes branded products are placed in a television programme or movie so that viewers can see characters or presenters using or consuming that branded product.

The *Coronation Street* set features a Co-op store. The soap's characters are often seen purchasing Co-op-branded products from the store, which raises awareness of the Co-op brand. The Co-op signage on the front of the store is also seen in outdoor scenes.

Co-op's partnership with the soap started in 2018 and was extended in 2021 for a further three years.

Check your understanding

1. State when Co-op's second partnership with the soap ends.
2. Explain one risk for the Co-op brand of the partnership with the soap.
3. Do you think Co-op should renew the product placement partnership with the soap again? Justify your answer.

Test your knowledge 5

1. What are some public relations methods that an entrepreneur may use?
2. Outline how a school may use a press/media release to promote itself to new parents.
3. What are some limitations of using celebrity endorsement when promoting a new product?

4.6 How to sell the good or service to the consumer

Let's get started 6

Think of all the different ways that you buy products.
What is your preferred method of purchasing a product? Why?

Customers need to be able to purchase goods and services conveniently if these are to be successful. Traditionally, most goods were sold through retailers in a physical shop or store, but this is changing and more people are shopping online.

Physical

Physical or 'traditional' ways of selling goods and services to consumers include:

- **shops** – the product is sold to customers through a physical shop (e.g. Superdry sells its clothing in its own shops). Other examples of shops include a local independent shop, supermarkets or department stores

- **face-to-face** – a salesperson interacts directly with the customer either in a shop, or in a **pitch**/demonstration. Services, such as hairdressers and banks, offer a face-to-face service.

Physical, or traditional ways of selling goods/services are expensive as the entrepreneur has to pay a monthly rent or mortgage cost (depending on whether they are renting or have bought the property). This can be a very large expense for the business. There also needs to be a certain number of employees within the shop at any one time to serve customers efficiently and safely.

Figure 1.43: A shop front provides a business with instant publicity

A shop front provides the business with instant publicity via the signage and window displays. Many shops are located in high streets or shopping centres alongside other shops, so they benefit from passing trade. A business can also develop a positive relationship with the customers due to the face-to-face contact that they have with them. From speaking with customers directly, an entrepreneur can clearly understand the customers' needs and wants and offer a personalised service.

Digital

Digital methods of selling products (**e-commerce**) are becoming increasingly popular and include:

- **e-commerce** – selling a good or service via a website

- **websites** – where customers can purchase goods through:

  - the business's own website (e.g. Superdry has an online shop on its own website, and most banks allow customers to manage their accounts online)

  - a third-party website, such as Amazon, that sells the product on behalf of the business

- **social media** – either through links to a business's website or the business's own social media account, such as Facebook or Twitter. The entrepreneur can share news and details of promotions via the social media account, for example details about a new product

- **marketplace sites** – e.g. Facebook marketplace allows businesses and individuals to sell new and pre-owned products and connect with a wide range of potential customers. The seller can post a full description of the good/service and a photo. Users can then send a direct message to the seller to find out more information and/or arrange to buy the product. The product can be sent to the customer via post or courier, or the customer can arrange to meet the seller and collect the item (if both parties live in the same area)

- **online auction sites** – e.g. a business can set up an eBay store to sell its products. Anyone who is interested in buying the item can put in a 'bid', which is a promise to pay a specific amount to buy the product. The seller sells the product to the person who pledges to pay the most. The product is then sent to the customer via post or courier, or the customer can arrange to meet the seller and collect the item (if both parties live in the same area). eBay can be used by private individuals or businesses. Many businesses trade just on eBay

- **downloads** – businesses providing a digital product, such as a computer game, music, or an app can make it available to customers as a digital file to download either from its own website or through a download store (e.g. the App Store or Google Play Store). Customers need to be cautious as there are many illegal download sites which can lead to the user downloading a computer virus or being hacked.

The increasing popularity of digital methods is due to a variety of reasons, including:

- changing customer buying preferences
- digital methods being often less costly as some fixed costs are reduced – for instance, having no rent to pay for shop premises
- being able to sell the product to new customer groups (type of customer and geographical location).

What is convenient for one customer to access may not be convenient for another. So businesses need to offer customers a variety of ways (or multiple channels) to purchase their products. For example, Superdry sells its clothes through:

- its high-street shops
- its own website
- third-party websites, such as Next or Very.

Over to you!   8

The costs of selling products to customers via traditional physical channels are very different to those for digital-only business.

1   Make a list of the costs that a traditional estate agency business (that operates via a branch situated on the high street) has to pay.

2   Make a second list of the costs that a digital-only estate agency business (that only operates via a website) has to pay.

3   Compare the similarities and differences between the two lists of costs.

Advantages and disadvantages of physical and digital channels

Table 1.30: Advantages and disadvantages of physical and digital channels

	Advantages	Disadvantages
Physical	• Face-to-face contact builds customer trust • Customers can see or try the product they are buying (e.g. trying on a jacket to check the fit) • Sales staff can demonstrate the features and benefits of a product (e.g. a high-specification television with surround sound)	• More expensive than selling online as businesses have to pay rent on high street shops • Customers have to travel to a shop, which takes time, and they may have problems with parking if they drive there • Opening hours can be more limited as most shops are unable to open 24 hours a day due to trading laws

Table 1.30: Continued

	Advantages	Disadvantages
Digital	• Reduces costs, such as rent and utilities, as businesses do not need physical shops. Fewer employees may be needed • Prices may be lower as the business does not have to pay rent on a physical shop • Customers can shop at any time of the day or night	• It is not as easy for the customer to speak directly to the business, e.g. if they have any queries about the product or need to make a complaint • Not all customers have access to the internet • Customers cannot touch or actually see the product or try it on before buying it • Customers sometimes have to wait a few days to receive their goods

Test your knowledge   6

1   Name some of the digital channels that a business can use to sell its products.

2   What are some reasons why there has been a decline in physical channels to sell products?

3   Explain why a supermarket uses multiple channels to sell its products.

4.7 The product lifecycle

Let's get started   7

Products come and go. CDs were once a very popular way to purchase music, but sales of CDs have now been overtaken by music downloads.

Can you think of some examples of other goods or services that were once very popular, but are now no longer available or in demand?

Tip: How do you watch films and television at home now? How did you (and your parents or grandparents) use to watch them?

Most products have a limited time span over which consumers want to buy them. The length of the time varies from product to product. Some products, such as mobile phones, have very short lives as manufacturers continually launch new phones onto the market which makes older technology less desirable with customers. Other products, such as food products, have much longer lives. For example, Heinz Baked Beanz and Coca-Cola have changed very little over the years.

The product lifecycle shows how a product moves through different stages in its lifetime and the sales that are achieved at each stage. It is useful because it allows a business to make decisions about each element of the marketing mix depending on where the product is in its lifecycle. The product lifecycle consists of five distinct phases (Figure 1.44).

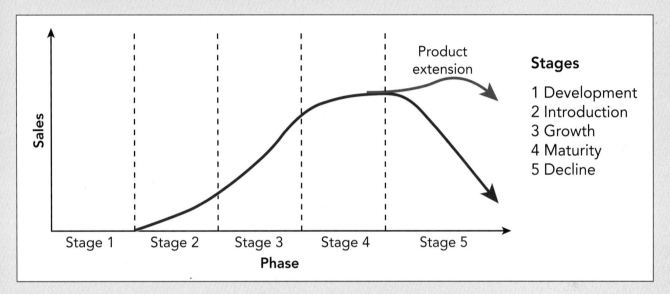

Figure 1.44: Products move through five different stages in the product lifecycle

Over to you!   9

1   At the end of the product lifecycle, the product enters the decline stage. Why might customers no longer need a product?

2   Identify some of the factors that may lead to a reduction in the sales of a product such as a mobile phone.

Development

All products need to be developed before they are sold. At the development stage, the entrepreneur/business:

- carries out market research before the product is launched to assess demand and to ensure that it is designed to meet customer needs

- creates designs and sketches of the new product (e.g. using computer-aided design (CAD) software packages)

- may test a **prototype** of the product to assess its physical attributes and performance.

During the development phase the product has not yet been launched onto the market. As the product is not available for customers to buy, no sales will be made. No sales revenue will be generated. The entrepreneur/ business is unlikely to promote it as customers will not be able to buy it. Developing new products is often very expensive, and many new product ideas are never launched onto the market.

Introduction

The product is launched onto the market but customers may not be aware of it. Sales are usually slow, which means that revenue will be low. The business or entrepreneur will promote the product to increase customer awareness and encourage people to try the product. The people most likely to buy the product are those that like to buy a product as soon as it is available (e.g. people who must have the latest technology). Sales will increase slowly as the product becomes more widely known.

Different businesses will adopt different types of **pricing strategy** (see Section 4.10) when the product is first launched.

- Some businesses may charge a low price to attract customers to try the new product.

- Others may charge a high price to make back the costs of developing the product.

Growth

Sales of the product increase rapidly as the product becomes better known, customers become aware of it and it is sold in an increasing number of places. The revenue from sales will grow rapidy during the growth phase. The product often starts to make a profit, but promotional costs are high. Competitors become aware of the growing demand for the product, and start to bring out similar products. Promotion aims to:

- outline the product's benefits over the competition (i.e. make it stand out)

- develop or strengthen the brand's image (see Unit R069, Section 1.1)

- retain existing customers and attract new ones.

Maturity

Sales and profits reach their peak. The revenue generated will be high. Most customers who are interested in the product will have already bought it. The product is likely to be a mainstream product. Competition is likely to be high, so customers have a lot of choice. Promotion should therefore focus on keeping the product competitive (e.g. by reducing the price to keep customers loyal) and retaining loyal customers.

Decline

Sales of the product and profits start to fall. The revenue generated will also decline. The product is likely to be viewed as 'old' as new technology and/or products may have come to the market.

Due to reduced customer demand, the business may decide to withdraw the product from sale. Sales revenue may not be enough to cover the costs of producing and/or offering the product. If the business decides to withdraw the product, it will often need to develop new ones or find a new target market in order to survive.

In some cases, if there is still some demand for the product, because other businesses have withdrawn from the market for example, the business may continue to offer the product. This will maximise the income generated from it and cover the money invested in the product's development.

The price of the product is likely to fall to maintain desirability against other new, more advanced or more appealing products.

Over to you!   10

1   Carry out some research to identify an example of a good or service in each of the five stages of the product lifecycle.

2   Explain why you chose the specific product lifecycle stage for each good or service you selected.

3   What do the manufacturers of the products that you have identified do to try to encourage sales? How do they adapt the elements of the marketing mix?

Test your knowledge   7

1   Name the stages of the product lifecycle.

2   How can an entrepreneur use the product lifecycle when making marketing decisions?

3   Many businesses offer a range of products that are spread across the product lifecycle. Analyse the benefits of this approach.

4.8 Extension strategies for products in the product lifecycle

Let's get started   8

What happens to a product when it reaches the decline stage of the product lifecycle?

Think of a specific product, such as a type of car or snack bar, and discuss some ways of extending the life of the product to create new interest.

Tip: Think about price, promotion, place and the product itself.

If a product, i.e. the good or service offered, is entering the decline stage of the product lifecycle (Figure 1.44) and the business has not developed a new product, it may decide to extend the lifecycle of the product. An **extension strategy** is a way of extending the product lifecycle before it goes into the decline stage.

If successful, extension strategies can enable products that were considered out of date to benefit from increased levels of sales. Vinyl records are a good example of this. They went out of fashion, but then benefited from increased sales due to the growing popularity of vinyl amongst millennials (people aged between 25 and 40). However, sometimes extension strategies just delay the end of the lifecycle.

Over to you! 11

In the Lucozade case study in Section 4.2, you learnt about how Lucozade changed its marketing mix to prevent a decline in the sales of its product. The strategies that Lucozade used helped to 'extend' the life of the Lucozade drinks brand.

Re-read the case study and explain how each of the four marketing mix elements was changed to extend the life of the drinks brand.

Table 1.31 covers the different extension strategies that a business may use.

Table 1.31: Extension strategies

Extension strategy	Description	Advantages	Disadvantages
Advertising	The business undertakes a new advertising campaign for the product	• Reminds existing customers of product's features or benefits • Can target a specific type of customer depending on the medium used	• Advertising is expensive and it may not increase sales of the product • May only lead to a short-term increase in sales. Sales may return to previous levels when the advertising stops
Price changes	The business increases or reduces the price of the product	• Increasing the price of the product generates more revenue and profit • Reducing the price encourages current customers to continue buying it • Customers may be encouraged to switch to it from other brands/products if the price is reduced	• Customers may not be willing to pay a higher price, and will switch to a cheaper brand/product • Customers will expect a higher-quality product if they are paying a higher price • Reducing the sales price decreases revenue and profit • Reducing the price means that more products have to be sold to break even • The price reduction may harm the product's image • Price reduction may not lead to an increase in sales

Table 1.31: Continued

Extension strategy	Description	Advantages	Disadvantages
Adding value	The business improves the product by adding new features or functions (e.g. adding a better camera to a mobile phone or improving the taste of a food product)	• Makes it more desirable to customers, resulting in increased sales • Can charge more for an improved product • Can help make the product stand out from the competition	• Developing a product further can be costly as the new features and functions need to be researched, tested and promoted • Customers may not be interested in the new features or functions
Exploring new markets	The business revives the existing product so that it appeals to a new: • geographic area such as a new town, region or country • target market, such as males as well as females	• Sales and profits increase if the product is successful in the new market • Spreads the risk because if one market is in decline, the other might be growing	• Some products may only be popular in a certain geographic location, e.g. Barbie dolls were not successful in the Chinese market due to cultural differences • May need to employ new staff in new regions/countries, which increases costs • Existing customers may be put off by the expansion to a new market. E.g. if a product targeted at higher-income customers is made available to lower-income groups, it may lose its prestige with the higher-income groups
New packaging	The business refreshes old packaging with new-look packaging (e.g. Lucozade case study in Section 4.2)	• May increase sales as customers think that the product has been improved • May be more eye-catching and attract customers' attention • Customers may be willing to pay a higher price if they think the product has improved • May help the product appeal to a new market, e.g. Lucozade's new packaging appealed to those looking for a sports energy drink rather than appealing to families	• Costly to change packaging • Loyal customers may not recognise the product • Increase in sales from new packaging may be negated (undone) by loss of loyal customers • Customers who think that the product has changed may be disappointed when they find the product itself has not changed

Stretch   1

Explain how the organisers of sporting events, such as the Olympics and the football World Cup tournament, can use the product lifecycle model to plan the marketing of their sporting events.

Test your knowledge   8

1   Identify some ways that a soft-drink manufacturer can extend the life of a brand of one of its drinks.

2   For each of the soft-drink extension strategies that you have identified, explain the disadvantages.

3   Recommend which method the soft-drink manufacturer should adopt. Justify your decision.

4.9 Factors to consider when pricing a product to attract and retain customers

Pricing is a key factor when purchasing a product. Customers often have limited budgets. They need to ensure that the product they are buying is value for money and they can afford it. There are a number of factors that an entrepreneur/start-up business needs to consider when setting a price for a product.

Income levels of target customers

A customer's income will determine how much they can afford to spend on a product. Generally, a customer with a higher income is able to pay a higher price than someone with a lower income. To determine an appropriate price, businesses need to carry out market research to find out the income levels of their target customers.

The income levels of target customers are an important factor to consider when setting the price of a product. However, the degree to which this affects customers may vary according to the value that the customer places on the product. For example, a customer with a low income may purchase premium-priced baby food as they feel it is essential for their baby to have the best nutrients. However, they may choose basic low-price brands of food for themselves due to affordability.

> **Stretch   2**
>
> Other than the example of baby food outlined in the text, can you think of any other premium-priced products which customers with low incomes may buy?

Price of competitor products

A start-up business/entrepreneur needs to consider the prices that its competitors charge, especially if their products are very similar. Customers are unlikely to pay a high price for a product if they are able to buy a similar item from a competitor for a lot less.

Many companies offer price matching. Tesco offers price matching to Aldi so that a number of essential products cost the same as those from Aldi. An 'Aldi Price Match' bubble, both online and in store, shows which products have been price matched.

Figure 1.45: Why does Tesco price match Aldi?

A start-up business/entrepreneur also needs to consider how their product compares with competitors' products. For example, is the product better quality than the competitors' product? Do customers see the brand as being superior? If so, how much extra are customers prepared to pay for it?

Cost of production

The selling price of a product must cover all of the production costs in order to make a profit. If the price does not cover all of the costs of production, the business will make a loss and will be unable to survive for long. If a product costs £10 to produce, the price must be more than £10 to make a profit. If the entrepreneur aims to make £8 profit on each product, the selling price needs to be £18.

Stage of the product lifecycle

The stage of the product lifecycle (see Section 4.7) will determine the type of pricing strategy that a business/entrepreneur uses. For example:

- **Introduction stage:** A brand-new product may be introduced at a lower price for a short period of time so that customers try it, or with a higher price to create a premium-brand image.

- **Growth stage:** Due to increased competition, the price may be reduced to stimulate sales and increase market share. Alternatively, a high introductory price may be retained to emphasise the appeal of the product as a luxury brand and/or because of advanced technology.

- **Maturity stage:** The business may keep prices in line with those of their competitors so long as they are able to make a profit. This will prevent competitors taking market share as overall market demand will be fairly constant.

- **Decline stage:** The product may be given a lower price to stimulate and prolong customer demand for as long as possible.

Test your knowledge   9

1. Name some examples of costs of production that a business may need to consider when setting a price for a new laptop computer.

2. Explain why the income levels of target customers may influence the price of products within a new greeting card shop.

3. Using an example of a product of your choice, outline how the price of a product may change as it progresses through the stages of the product lifecycle.

4.10 Types of pricing strategies

Let's get started   9

Why might the products in the photos (Figure 1.46) be priced at £4.95 and £1.99 rather than £5 and £2? How does this benefit a business?

Figure 1.46: Why might these businesses use these prices?

There are four main pricing strategies that a business can choose when deciding on a suitable price for a product (Table 1.32). The most appropriate pricing strategy will depend on the type of product, its stage in the product lifecycle (see Section 4.7) and the competition.

Table 1.32: Pricing strategies

Pricing strategy	Description	Advantages	Disadvantages
Competitive pricing	The business sets a price in line with that of competitors Not suitable if there are no competing products	• As the price is in line with that of competitors, customers will be willing to pay it • Prevents competitors from having a price advantage	• Can lead to low prices and low profits • Low prices may not cover the costs of production and may result in the business making a loss • May be difficult for a small business to set prices at the same level as large competitors who can often buy supplies more cheaply as they buy larger quantities • Regular market research is required to keep up to date with the prices charged by competitors • If the business sells online to customers across the world, it will be hard to price match every business across the world • Could lead to a price war if the competitor is keen to maintain a price advantage in the market (i.e. offer the lowest-price product within the market)
Psychological pricing	Setting a price that makes customers think the product is cheaper (e.g. £4.99 rather than £5) The use of persuasive language (e.g. 'only' £2)	• The selling price is only reduced slightly, which will not have a significant effect on revenue • As customers may have a limited budget, they may view the product as being better value/more affordable • Attracts customer attention as £1.99 has more of an impact than £2	• As this is a common pricing strategy, the product will not stand out if all of the competitors are also doing it • Customers may feel like it is taking advantage of them • Customers might see the product as being low quality • There is no guarantee that it will increase sales (i.e. if more customers do not purchase the product, revenue will be reduced)

Table 1.32: Continued

Pricing strategy	Description	Advantages	Disadvantages
Price skimming	Selling the product at a higher price for a short period of time when it is first launched onto the market as customers want to own the latest product (e.g. Apple iPhone) Price is reduced over time as new products/competitor products are launched	• Need to sell fewer products at the higher price to break even • Increased revenue and profit help to recover the high development costs of the new product • The high price may create an image of a high-quality product/brand	• Some customers may not be prepared to pay the high price • Revenue and profit may be low if customers are put off by the high price • Competitors may quickly introduce new products at a lower price and take market share • Customers may feel it is taking advantage of them if the product does not live up to their expectations or if the price drops considerably

Price penetration	Starts with a low price to get customers interested and gain market share
	
	As product awareness grows and the number of customers increases so does the price
	
	Often used by start-up enterprises if their product is not well known
		• The low price will
		  • encourage customers to try the new product and build interest in the product
		  • help it become established and increase market share
		  • create customer loyalty as customers switch from competing brands, as long as the product is better
		• The low price is only for a short period, so revenue and profits should recover over time
			• A low price:
			  • means lower revenue and profits in the short term
			  • may not persuade customers to switch from another product that they trust and are loyal to
			  • may create an image of a poor-quality product
			  • may not cover the costs of production and may result in the business making a loss
			• Some customers may only buy when the price is low, and return to competitor products when the price increases to 'normal'
			• Customers may be unhappy when the price increases

Over to you!   12

1   Which of the four pricing strategies would be most appropriate for each of the following situations? Explain the reasons for your choice.

   a   A shampoo manufacturer wishes to launch its product in the UK. The brand is successful in Germany, but it is unknown in the UK.

   b   A market-leading computer manufacturer is planning to launch a new laptop. The product includes all of the latest features.

   c   A car manufacturer is planning on launching a new model and its finance manager has calculated that the price should be £20 000 to achieve the target revenue.

Review your learning

Test your knowledge   10

1   Which pricing strategy is a business using if it is launching a product with a high price?

2   Explain some advantages of using a competitive pricing strategy for a new dog food product.

3   Analyse the advantages and the disadvantages of a price penetration strategy for a new hairdressing salon.

What have you learnt?

	See section
• The marketing mix elements for a good/service.	4.1
• How the elements of the marketing mix work together.	4.2
• Types of advertising medium used to attract and retain customers.	4.3
• Sales promotion techniques used to attract and retain customers.	4.4
• What public relations is.	4.5
• How to sell the good or service to the consumer.	4.6
• What the product lifecycle model is.	4.7
• Extension strategies for products in the product lifecycle.	4.8
• Factors to consider when pricing a product to attract and retain customers.	4.9
• Types of pricing strategies.	4.10

Factors to consider when starting up and running an enterprise

Let's get started   1

Think of a project or activity when you have worked with one or more partners. It could be a project or activity you've done in school or in your free time. How well did you work with your partner(s)? What were the advantages and disadvantages of working with a partner? What advice would you offer to someone looking to work on a similar project or activity in future?

What will you learn?

- Forms of ownership for business start-ups.
- **Limited** and **unlimited liability**.
- Sources of **capital** for business start-ups and expansion.
- The different sources of support for enterprise.

5.1 Forms of ownership for business start-ups

One of the first decisions an entrepreneur has to make for a new business is choosing the form of ownership (Figure 1.47). It is very important to choose the correct form of ownership as it influences:

- how profits are shared
- business decision making
- **liability** for business debts.

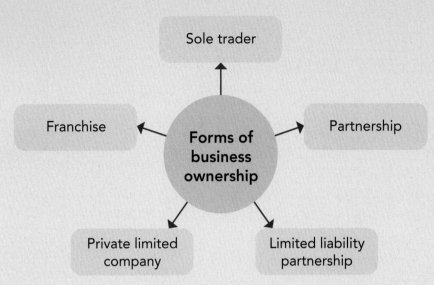

Figure 1.47: There are different forms of business ownership for a start-up business

Liability

In order to understand the features of the different types of business ownership, it is important to understand about the two types of liability and the advantages and disadvantages of each type (Table 1.33).

Table 1.33: The two types of liability

Type of liability	Definition	Advantages	Disadvantages
Limited liability	If the business fails or gets into debt, the owner can only lose the amount of money that they originally invested in the business, i.e. the amount of their personal liability for the debts is limited They cannot be forced to sell their personal possessions, e.g. their house	• The amount that the owner can potentially lose is limited, so they cannot lose any more money than they originally invested. This can give the owner peace of mind and help the business attract people to invest money • The owner cannot be forced to sell any of their personal possessions, such as their house or car, to repay business debts	• Some people and organisations that the business owes money to may never recover the full value of the debt

Table 1.33: Continued

Type of liability	Definition	Advantages	Disadvantages
Unlimited liability	The owner of the business is personally responsible for the total debts of the business. There is no limit to the amount that the owner could lose, which may mean that someone that the business owes money to, such as a supplier or lender, could force the owner to sell their personal items to repay the business's debts. The implications can be very serious as the owner may lose everything!	• There is generally less paperwork/fewer formalities to set up the business	• The amount that the owner can potentially lose is unlimited, so they could lose more money than they originally invested • As the amount they can lose is unlimited, they may be forced into bankruptcy • The owner can be forced to sell their personal possessions, such as their house or car, to repay business debts, which could leave their family homeless

Sole trader

A **sole trader** is a business owned and run by one person (the sole trader). Sole traders are often known as 'self-employed'. It is one of the most common forms of ownership for business start-ups. Many local businesses, such as plumbers, electricians and gardeners, are sole traders.

Sole traders have to complete all of the tasks related to their business even if they are not experienced in those tasks. For example, a gardener may be very knowledgeable about plants but may have less experience of marketing their business or managing the financial aspects, such as doing the accounts. This could affect the quality of the decisions they make.

A sole trader can keep all of the profits that they make, but they have to make all of the business decisions on their own.

Sole traders have unlimited liability, so they are fully responsible for all business debts. If the business gets into debt, they may have to sell some of their personal possessions, such as their car or home, to repay the debts.

Partnership

A **partnership** is a business owned and run by two or more people who are known as partners. The partners usually draw up a legal contract, a **partnership agreement**, which states each partner's role and share of the profits.

The partners jointly share responsibility for decision making, which can lead to disagreements if the partners want different things or feel the business should develop in different ways.

The profits are shared equally by the partners (unless the partnership agreement states otherwise).

Each partner invests capital into the business and may also bring different skills and experience to the partnership. This allows each partner to specialise in specific tasks or areas of the business. For example, one partner may be responsible for marketing the business whereas another may do the financial tasks.

Most partnerships have unlimited liability. So, like with sole traders, the partners are responsible for the business's debts and may have to sell some of their personal possessions to repay them.

An entrepreneur needs to choose their partners carefully as they are liable for decisions made by all of the other partners. For example, if one partner makes a bad decision which loses a lot of money, all of the partners are jointly liable, even if they were not consulted about the decision.

Over to you!   1

You and three of your friends have decided to set up a café business as a partnership.

1   Identify three decisions that you need to agree on before you start the café.

2   Explain two advantages of setting up the café as a partnership.

3   Analyse two disadvantages of running the café as a partnership.

Limited liability partnerships

A **limited liability partnership** is similar to a traditional partnership except that the partners (i.e. owners) benefit from limited liability. This means that each partner (i.e. owner) is not personally responsible for the full debts of the business. They only risk losing the amount of money that they invested into the business. Limited liability partnerships can be identified by the letters 'LLP' after the business name. Many **solicitors** and **accountants** operate as limited liability partnerships.

Private limited company (Ltd)

A **private limited company** is usually a small or medium-sized business that is owned by **shareholders**. However, some larger well-known businesses, such as Dyson and Specsavers, are private limited companies. They can be identified by the abbreviation 'Ltd' after the company name.

Each shareholder invests capital into the business by purchasing shares in the company. In return for their investment, the shareholder may receive a share of the profits made each year. This is called a **dividend**. The shareholder may also benefit financially if their shares increase in value.

A board of directors is employed by the shareholders to run the company and make decisions on their behalf.

Shareholders benefit from limited liability so they are not responsible for the full debts of the business. They only risk losing the amount of money that they invested in the shares.

Many private limited companies are small, family-run businesses. Shares in a private limited company can only be bought and sold with the permission of the other shareholders. This ensures that the shareholders control who becomes an owner. For this reason, the shareholders of many private limited companies are friends and family members of the individual who set up the business initially.

A private limited company has to make some of its financial information publicly available for everyone to view. This includes information on profit and loss, and the business's assets (the things it owns) and liabilities (its debts). This can cause issues, especially if competitors access the information.

Over to you!   **2**

Research examples of private limited companies in your local area.

Tip: Remember that you can identify them by the abbreviation 'Ltd' after the business name.

1 Identify three examples of businesses that operate as a private limited company.

2 For a business example of your choice, analyse two benefits of operating as a private limited company rather than as a partnership. Within your answer, think about the type of business and its activities.

Franchise

Many entrepreneurs choose to run a **franchise**, which involves running a business using an existing idea and brand name. A **franchisor** (the owner of the brand/business idea) sells the right to operate the business/ business idea under their brand to the **franchisee** (entrepreneur/ another business).

Figure 1.48: Did you know that these businesses are operated as franchises in the UK?

The franchisee typically pays the franchisor a fee to set up the franchise and has to follow the rules set by the franchisor. These rules often cover many aspects of running the business, such as the decor of the premises, staff uniforms, prices and menu. This ensures a 'standardised' experience for customers.

Many well-known fast-food restaurants, such as Subway, Domino's and Burger King, are franchises in the UK. Although fast-food franchises are very common, franchises also operate in a range of other industries, such as hairdressing (Toni & Guy), convenience stores (Spar), pet food (Trophy Pet Foods), CeX (digital entertainment product and device retailer) and gardening services (GreenThumb Lawn Treatment Service). While some franchises, such as the fast-food examples above, are large **global businesses**, others are very small and might only operate in a specific town or area. For example, Sparkle Cleaning offers commercial cleaning services in Bristol, Bath, Weston-super-Mare, Birmingham and Newport.

The franchisor is responsible for making all of the key business decisions. This means that the franchisee may have no influence over how the business operates. Every year the franchisee has to pay a percentage of their profits, known as a **royalty fee**, to the franchisor.

Remember: A franchise is not a true form of business ownership as it can be owned and run as a sole trader, partnership or private limited company.

Case study

Fast-food business success

Tawanda worked for a well-known fast-food restaurant for over ten years. He enjoyed his job role and after several promotions he became the assistant manager of a restaurant in Manchester two years ago. However, Tawanda was keen to use his experience to run his own restaurant. He decided to leave his job and set up his own business as a franchise of Brilliant Burgers, a leading burger chain looking to expand within the UK.

Figure 1.49: Many entrepreneurs choose to run a franchise

Tawanda had to pay a fee of £175 000 to become a franchisee. He signed a franchise agreement that covered all aspects of operations, including which suppliers to purchase food from, staff uniforms, restaurant opening hours, rules about the local advertising that Tawanda could organise, and the decoration within the restaurant.

Each year, Tawanda has to pay a share of the profits he makes to the franchisor. However, Tawanda's restaurant has been very busy from the start as loyal customers recognise the Brilliant Burgers brand. Tawanda has also benefited from a national TV advertising campaign prepared by Brilliant Burgers' marketing department.

Check your understanding

1   Explain why Tawanda has chosen to run his burger business as a franchise.

2   Explain why Brilliant Burgers might want to control the local advertising that Tawanda may organise.

3   Evaluate Tawanda's decision to become a Brilliant Burgers franchisee rather than set up his own restaurant business from scratch. Do you think it was the best way to set up the business?

Advantages and disadvantages of different forms of business ownership

Table 1.34: Advantages and disadvantages of the different forms of business ownership

Type of business ownership	Advantages	Disadvantages
Sole trader	<ul><li>The sole trader is their own boss and can make all business decisions</li><li>They can keep all of the profit that is made</li><li>Relatively cheap and easy to set up (i.e. no complex paperwork)</li><li>May provide more flexibility as the sole trader can usually choose their own working hours and holidays etc.</li></ul>	<ul><li>Unlimited liability – the sole trader is responsible for all business debts and may have to sell their personal possessions (e.g. their home or car) to pay those debts</li><li>They may lack experience in some areas of business</li><li>The sole trader may have to work long hours as they are working alone</li><li>They are not paid when they are unwell or take time off for a holiday</li><li>Limited capital – to set up the business, the sole trader can only use their own money or money that they personally borrow</li><li>It may be challenging to secure external finance to start the business and/or expand because, for example, a bank may reject a loan application due to the high risk of failure</li><li>Business decisions cannot be shared</li></ul>
Partnership	<ul><li>Relatively cheap and easy to set up (i.e. no complex paperwork)</li><li>Greater investment of capital into the business as more than one person is investing</li><li>Partners can bring different skills and experience to the business so that decision-making and work can be shared according to experience and strengths</li><li>Shared workload and responsibility for the business risk</li></ul>	<ul><li>Unlimited liability – the partners are jointly responsible for all business debts and may have to sell their personal possessions (e.g. their home and car) to pay business debts</li><li>There may be disagreement and conflict amongst partners regarding business decisions and workload</li><li>It may take longer to reach business decisions as all the partners need to be involved</li><li>Profits must be shared amongst the partners</li></ul>

Table 1.34: Continued

Type of business ownership	Advantages	Disadvantages
Limited liability partnership	• Limited liability – the owners (the partners) will not have to sell personal possessions to repay the business's debts • Greater investment of capital into the business as more than one person is investing • Partners can bring different skills and experience to the business so that decision-making and work can be shared according to experience and strengths • Shared workload and responsibility for the business risk	• More paperwork to set up compared with a partnership • There may be disagreement and conflict amongst partners regarding business decisions and workload • It may take longer to reach business decisions as all the partners need to be involved • Profits must be shared amongst the partners
Private limited company	• Additional capital can be raised easily by selling shares • Limited liability – the owners (the shareholders) will not have to sell personal possessions to repay the business debts • Shares can only be bought and sold with the permission of the other owners	• More complex and costly to set up. There are legal requirements in relation to setting up the business and accounting • Certain financial information needs to be made publicly available, so competitors can see it • Slower decision-making as all shareholders have to agree decisions
Franchise	• Greater chance of success as the business brand/name is already known • The franchisee is supported by the franchisor (e.g. given advice and training) • The franchisee requires limited industry knowledge as they follow the franchisor's business model • After paying the royalty fee the franchisee can keep the remaining profit	• Many important decisions are made by the franchisor • The franchisee has to follow the rules of the franchisor (e.g. use specific suppliers) • Can be expensive to set up • A proportion of the profits made each year must be paid to the franchisor (royalty fee) so the franchisee needs to make enough profit

Features of each form of business ownership

Table 1.35: Features of each form of business ownership

	Who owns the business?	Type of liability	Who is responsible for decision making?	Who receives the profits made by the business?
Sole trader	One owner (the sole trader)	Unlimited	The sole trader	The sole trader keeps all profits
Partnership	Two or more owners (partners)	Unlimited	Each partner will have equal responsibility for decisions unless agreed differently in the partnership agreement	Generally, each partner receives an equal share of profits unless agreed differently in the partnership agreement
Limited liability partnership	Two or more owners (partners)	Limited	Each partner will have equal responsibility for decisions unless agreed differently in the partnership agreement	Generally, each partner receives an equal share of profits unless agreed differently in the partnership agreement
Private limited company (Ltd)	Shareholders	Limited	The board of directors, who are appointed by the shareholders	Shareholders receive a share of the profits (i.e. a dividend) proportional to the value of shares owned, e.g. if a shareholder owns 10 percent of the shares issued by a company they will receive 10 percent of the value of the profit shared amongst the shareholders
Franchise	Franchisor	Depends on form of ownership of business	Franchisor is responsible for high-level decisions, such as using specific suppliers Franchisee responsible for day-to-day decisions, such as working hours	The franchisee has to pay the franchisor an agreed percentage share of the profits (i.e. a royalty fee) The franchisee keeps the remaining profits

Over to you! 3

Toby runs a childminding business from his home.
He works alone and owns the business.

1   What type of business ownership is Toby likely to have?

2   Describe two advantages and two disadvantages of this type of business ownership.

3   What type of liability is Toby likely to have?
    Explain the implications for Toby of this type of liability.

4   Explain how the business's profits are distributed.

Test your knowledge 1

1   What are some types of business ownership with limited liability?

2   State the name of the contract that can be drawn up to outline how profit is shared amongst partners.

3   State the type of fee that a franchisee pays each year to give the franchisor a share of the profits that they make.

4   What are some disadvantages of running a business as a limited liability partnership?

5   Explain two advantages of limited liability to someone looking to invest in a business.

5.2 Sources of capital for business start-ups and expansion

Let's get started 2

An entrepreneur needs money (capital) to start up or expand a small business. Make a list of some of the things that an entrepreneur might need to purchase when starting up a small business. How can the entrepreneur get the capital that they need to start the small business?

To finance the start-up of their business and to support ongoing expansion of the business, entrepreneurs need to raise sufficient capital. Figure 1.50 shows the sources of capital that they can use. Before choosing which source of finance to use, they need to consider the advantages and disadvantages of the different sources. Often entrepreneurs use a combination of different sources of finance.

Own savings

Many entrepreneurs use their own savings to start up or expand their business. This money may have come from:

- **personal savings** – money that they have saved up

- a **redundancy payment** after being made redundant from a previous job

- an **inheritance** from a relative.

Table 1.36 shows some of the advantages and disadvantages of own savings as a source of capital.

Table 1.36: Advantages and disadvantages of own savings as a source of capital

Advantages	Disadvantages
• Do not have to repay interest on the capital • No bank or lending fees • Do not have to submit an application to borrow the money • Do not have to repay the money	• Not all entrepreneurs have savings • The amount of capital that is available may be limited to how much the entrepreneur has in their savings, and they may also need to use other sources of capital • The entrepreneur's savings are tied up in the business so they cannot use them in an emergency or for a personal purchase

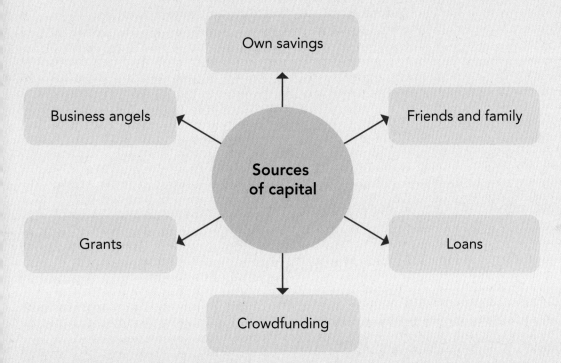

Figure 1.50: Sources of capital that can be used to finance a business start-up or expansion

Friends and family

Many entrepreneurs receive financial support from friends and family in the form of:

- a **gift**, which does not have to be returned

- a **loan**, that is repaid over time.

Such an arrangement is often informal, with no contract. Friends or relatives may fall out with the entrepreneur if they do not agree with their decisions for the business, and they may ask for their money to be repaid.

Table 1.37 shows some advantages and disadvantages of using friends and family as a source of capital.

Table 1.37: Advantages and disadvantages of friends and family as a source of capital

Advantages	Disadvantages
• Do not have to pay interest, or pay less interest on the capital • No bank or lending fees • An informal agreement so there is no formal contract • Do not have to submit an application to borrow the money	• As the arrangement is informal, it may lead to disagreements with family or friends • The friend or family member may interfere with decision making and/or the operations of the business • Funds may have to be repaid at short notice if the friend or family member needs their money back • The entrepreneur may not be able to repay the money at short notice, which may lead to closure of the business • The amount of capital that is available may be limited, so the entrepreneur may need to use other sources of capital as well

Case study

Mia's driving school

Mia decided to set up her own business as a driving instructor. Her aunt gifted her £20 000 to help with her set-up costs. Mia advertised her business on social media offering lessons at £28 per hour but struggled to attract customers.

Mia's aunt is not on social media and does not understand how it works. She felt that Mia would be better off advertising her business in the local newspaper and that she should reduce the price to boost demand.

Figure 1.51: Friends and family can be a source of capital for entrepreneurs when setting up a business

Mia refused to advertise in the local newspaper, so her aunt went ahead and placed a series of adverts offering one free lesson to customers who booked a block of ten.

Mia was furious. The situation resulted in Mia and her aunt having a disagreement and Mia's aunt asking for her money back. Mia did not have £20 000 available to repay the money.

Check your understanding

1 State two advantages to Mia of being gifted the money by her aunt.

2 Explain the difference between capital offered as a gift and capital offered as a loan.

3 Assess two disadvantages to Mia of using capital gifted by her aunt to set up the business.

Loans

Loans are capital that is borrowed from a bank or other lender. The entrepreneur repays the loan and interest in fixed instalments over a period of time. The amount that they repay depends on the amount they borrowed, the length of the repayment period and the rate of interest. The bank or lender makes money by charging interest. Table 1.38 shows some advantages and disadvantages of loans as a source of capital.

Table 1.38: Advantages and disadvantages of loans as a source of capital

Advantages	Disadvantages
• The entrepreneur repays a fixed sum each month, which helps with financial planning • The lender will not ask for the funds to be repaid at short notice (unless the entrepreneur defaults) • The bank often asks for a detailed business plan; this can also help the entrepreneur to run their business effectively and support planning	• Interest is paid on a loan – over time the entrepreneur will repay more than they borrowed • Fees may be charged by the bank or lender when the loan is applied for • The lender may ask for security (i.e. assets owned by the business or entrepreneur) in case the loan is not repaid • The entrepreneur may need to complete a lengthy application (including a business plan) to help the lender assess the risk • More 'risky' business ideas are less likely to be accepted for a loan

Over to you!   4

Most high street banks offer business loans. Visit the websites of four banks and research the business loans they offer.

1   State which bank asks for the highest rate of interest.

2   Identify whether any of the banks offer specialist loans for specific types of business, e.g. business start-up loans or business expansion loans.

3   Explain what an entrepreneur would need to do to apply for each of the business loans.

Crowdfunding

Crowdfunding is where a business raises small amounts of capital from a number of different investors or 'sponsors'. Crowdfunding can be used by new and expanding businesses. The money is raised by advertising the business idea on a crowdfunding website, such as GoFundMe and Indiegogo, to attract different investors or 'sponsors'. Crowdfunding is a popular option for innovative and risky business ideas that banks or traditional lenders may not accept.

Sponsors can:

- **lend money**, which has to be repaid over time (usually with interest)

- **donate money**, which does not have to be repaid

- **invest money** and become a part-owner of the business.

Table 1.39 shows some advantages and disadvantages of crowdfunding as a source of capital.

Table 1.39: Advantages and disadvantages of crowdfunding as a source of capital

Advantages	Disadvantages
• The entrepreneur may raise a large amount of capital • The entrepreneur does not need to provide security • It is a good way to test the public's reaction to a new or innovative idea • More suitable for more risky business ideas	• May not generate the required amount of capital • Sponsors may want to become a part-owner, which reduces the entrepreneur's level of control in the business • By putting details about the business/product online, competitors may get access to valuable information

Grants

A **grant** is a sum of money given to a business to help it with start-up costs or to expand. Grants are offered by many organisations including the government, local councils and charities. Grants are popular as the money usually does not have to be repaid and there is no interest or fees. Grants may be specific to a certain type of business or project or have certain conditions attached to them. So the entrepreneur needs to research the different grants available to find suitable ones that they can apply for. Table 1.40 shows some advantages and disadvantages of grants as a source of capital.

Table 1.40: Advantages and disadvantages of grants as a source of capital

Advantages	Disadvantages
• The business does not have to pay interest on the grant • There are many different grants that a business can apply for • Applying for grants can promote a business and its products	• The process of researching and applying for grants may be time-consuming • The entrepreneur may need to complete a business plan and a lot of paperwork to meet the grant's requirements • May not be eligible as the grant may be specific to certain businesses or projects and have conditions attached • The grant provider may be very specific about how the funds can be used within the business • The amount of capital may be limited so the entrepreneur may have to find other sources

Business angels

A **business angel** is a successful and wealthy entrepreneur who offers capital to help new and expanding businesses.

The business angel may provide the entrepreneur with advice/guidance to increase the chances of their business being successful. They may also have contacts who can support the entrepreneur, such as a website developer who could develop a new website for the business. In return for investing the capital, the business angel may wish to be actively involved in decision-making and/or receive a share of the business's profits. Table 1.41 shows some advantages and disadvantages of business angels as a source of capital.

Table 1.41: Advantages and disadvantages of business angels as a source of capital

Advantages	Disadvantages
• Entrepreneurs can benefit from the business angel's experience and contacts • A large amount of capital may be available • Suitable for more risky business ideas	• They may interfere with business decisions and/or the operations of the business • They may require a share of the business's profits

Over to you!   5

Jessica completed an engineering degree last year and has designed an innovative robot that will help people living with disabilities to carry out household chores. She needs to raise capital to design a prototype product and carry out some market research as she plans to set up a business selling this new product. Jessica's friends feel that the idea is very innovative but risky, but Jessica is determined to prove that it will be successful.

1   Identify two sources of capital that may be appropriate for Jessica's innovative business **proposal**.

Tip: Would you consider Jessica's business to be risky?

2   Explain two advantages of each of the sources of capital that you have identified for Jessica's business.

3   Justify which source of capital is most suitable for Jessica.

Test your knowledge   2

1   Identify the different sources of capital that an entrepreneur could use to start a business.

2   What are the advantages of raising capital via crowdfunding?

3   What are the disadvantages of obtaining funds by way of a grant?

5.3 Support for enterprise

Let's get started   3

Why might an entrepreneur need to talk over their business ideas or get further support? What might they need advice on? For each type of advice, who might they go to?

Starting and running a small business can be very complex and few entrepreneurs are knowledgeable about all aspects, especially at the start. Fortunately, there are many organisations and individuals that entrepreneurs can seek specialist support from (Figure 1.52).

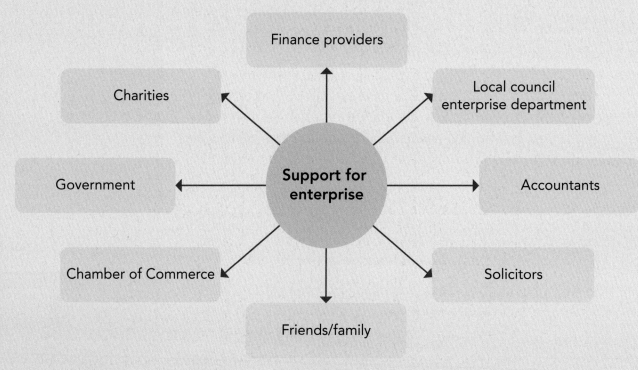

Figure 1.52: What sources of support for enterprise are available?

Finance providers

When financial providers, such as banks and business angels, offer capital to an entrepreneur they also often offer free business advice. The financial provider wants the business to use the capital wisely to ensure that it is successful. If the business fails, the capital is not likely to be repaid to the financial provider.

- Banks employ specialist business banking managers who can offer expert guidance to help the entrepreneur plan the future of the business and manage its financial affairs effectively. However, the advice may be linked to the bank's products (e.g. loans, insurance, etc.) or investments so the advice may not be unbiased.

Figure 1.53: Other than banks, what sources of financial support can entrepreneurs access?

- Business angels are typically successful business owners who have a lot of influential contacts. They can share their experiences and contacts with the entrepreneur.

- When a local council or charity offers a grant, they may offer advice to the entrepreneur to help them use the funds in a specific way.

Over to you!   6

For the four banks that you identified in Over to you! 4, research what help and services they provide to their business customers.

Local council enterprise department

Most local councils have an enterprise department which is responsible for encouraging new businesses to set up in the area and the expansion of existing businesses within the area. The department offers a wide range of support. For example, it:

- employs officers who are knowledgeable about the local area and who can offer free, or low-cost, advice and information to entrepreneurs

- offers financial support such as grants and loans to small businesses/ entrepreneurs

- may deliver training sessions to provide local people with the skills needed to run a small business

- publishes data, such as statistics about households in the area or types of business, which is valuable secondary market research for new businesses

- may run competitions to recognise business success in the area, with successful businesses/entrepreneurs winning prizes and awards such as 'Small Business of the Year'. The winning businesses benefit from a lot of publicity which can help the business to grow further.

However, due to reductions in public spending, many councils have needed to cut back on the services that they provide, so there may be less support available. Also, the quality and range of services may vary according to the local council area.

The local council will often work with other organisations such as the local **Chamber of Commerce** and major businesses to target the support.

Over to you!   7

Visit your local council's website and find the pages about business and enterprise support in the area.

1   Identify the support offered by the local council to encourage new businesses to set up and/or the expansion of existing businesses.

2   Explain how each type of support could help an entrepreneur to run a business more successfully.

3   Explain two advantages of the support offered by your local council.

Accountants

An accountant prepares and analyses financial records and accounts. Many entrepreneurs and small businesses employ an accountant to prepare the business's financial accounts and **tax return**. Accountants are highly qualified professionals so they can provide an entrepreneur with expert advice that they can trust. Accountants can:

- advise an entrepreneur about the most effective way of running their business in terms of tax and other financial decisions
- help the entrepreneur to make financial decisions.

Entrepreneurs have to pay for the services of an accountant, which can be expensive. However, an accountant may be able to save the business more money than the cost of their fees by reducing its outgoings (e.g. the amount of tax that the business has to pay), so the business is better off in the long run.

Solicitors

A solicitor offers advice about legal matters. Entrepreneurs may need to seek legal support from a solicitor specialising in business matters to ensure that they operate in line with the law. Solicitors specialise in different areas of the law as outlined in Table 1.42.

Table 1.42: Different types of solicitors available to businesses

Type of solicitor	Type of advice they provide
Commercial solicitor	Contract law (e.g. writing contracts)
	Other business-related legal issues (e.g. handling business disputes, drafting a partnership agreement)
	Guidance on the most appropriate form of ownership for the business (e.g. sole trader or partnership, etc.)
Tax solicitor	Tax-related legal matters (e.g. issues related to the tax system)
Employment solicitor	Disputes related to employment matters regarding employees (e.g. unfair dismissal, discrimination, or health and safety at work)
Consumer protection solicitor	Consumer rights (e.g. if a product is faulty or causes an injury to a customer)
Conveyancing solicitor	Buying and selling property (e.g. if a business is buying or selling premises)

A solicitor may provide a free consultation to give the entrepreneur some initial advice before they decide whether to go ahead and pay for the solicitor's services.

Like accountants, solicitors:

- are highly qualified professionals, so they can provide expert advice that can be relied upon

- charge a fee for their services, which can be expensive.

Friends and family

Many entrepreneurs know friends or other family members who run small businesses. These friends and family members can offer free practical advice and guidance based on their own experiences.

This support is more informal than that provided by professional organisations. But it can be valuable as the entrepreneur may feel more comfortable asking friends and family questions, particularly about smaller day-to-day matters.

However, it may be some time since friends or family set up their business and they may not have kept up to date with changes or current requirements. The information that they provide might be out of date or incorrect. They may also run a different type of business, so while a lot of the information and advice could be useful, it might not all be relevant.

Chamber of Commerce

A Chamber of Commerce is a network of local business owners and entrepreneurs that promotes the interests of local business within a particular area or town/city. Local business owners and entrepreneurs can become members of the Chamber of Commerce and attend regular meetings and training sessions.

Belonging to a Chamber of Commerce gives the entrepreneur an opportunity to meet and network with other small business owners who offer services that might be beneficial to them. For example, through the Chamber of Commerce, an entrepreneur may get to know a local builder who they can employ to renovate their shop premises.

The type and level of support that is offered to businesses can vary from one Chamber of Commerce to another.

Government

The government is keen to support enterprise as successful small businesses contribute positively to the economy. Figure 1.54 shows how the government helps small businesses in a number of ways:

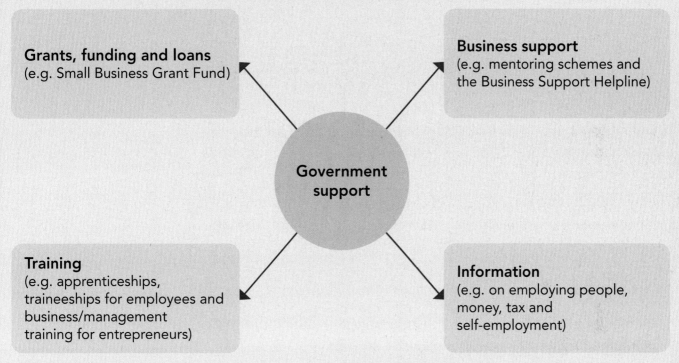

Grants, funding and loans (e.g. Small Business Grant Fund)

Business support (e.g. mentoring schemes and the Business Support Helpline)

Government support

Training (e.g. apprenticeships, traineeships for employees and business/management training for entrepreneurs)

Information (e.g. on employing people, money, tax and self-employment)

Figure 1.54: What kinds of support does the government provide for small businesses?

The government is seen as a trusted source of support, which may be offered free of charge.

However, it can be quite time-consuming finding specific information. The government provides lots of information in different places, so the entrepreneur may not know which government department is responsible or where to start looking.

Charities

Many charities, such as The Prince's Trust and UnLtd, offer support free of charge to assist entrepreneurs in setting up and expanding a business.

The type of support that charities offer varies according to the charity, but may include:

- financial support and investment in the form of grants or loans

- training to develop business skills

- access to a business adviser or mentor to help with business planning and skills that the entrepreneur may lack

- information and advice.

Some charities have a specific aim and will only support enterprises who have the same aims. For example, UnLtd focuses on supporting **social entrepreneurs**, whose business aims to solve social, cultural or environmental issues.

Charities have limited funds, which may restrict the support available to entrepreneurs.

Stretch

Find out about two charities that support entrepreneurs, such as UnLtd or the Centre for Entrepreneurs, and answer the following questions.

a   How do they work?

b   What support do they offer to entrepreneurs?

Over to you!   8

Copy and complete Table 1.43 comparing the different sources of support for entrepreneurs. Add a row for each of the different sources of support.

Table 1.43: Sources of support for entrepreneurs

Source of support	What support does it offer?	Advantages	Limitations
Finance providers			

Case study

Kye's jewellery business – Support and success

Kye was made redundant from his previous job. Despite applying for lots of jobs, the 21 year old was unable to find work. So he spent his time making jewellery for friends and family.

After positive feedback about the jewellery he had made, Kye decided to apply for a bank loan to set up his own business. However, the bank refused his application.

Figure 1.55: There are charities that support entrepreneurs to set up new businesses

His parents suggested that he should contact The Prince's Trust for support to set up his own jewellery business. The Prince's Trust is a charity set up by the Prince of Wales to help 18–30 year olds to start their own businesses.

Kye did some research online and found out about the Enterprise programme that the Trust offers. After attending a free information session, he enrolled on a four-day interactive workshop. There he met other young people who wanted to start their own business. He also worked with expert business advisers to plan the marketing and financial aspects of his jewellery business.

The Prince's Trust provided Kye with a dedicated mentor who helped him to organise market research and **refine** his product ideas. The Trust also provided financial support of £2000. After producing a detailed business plan, he was ready to launch his business.

Three months on from launching his business, Kye is very busy with orders and is enjoying running his own business.

Check your understanding

1   Identify three types of support that The Prince's Trust offered Kye.

2   Explain two advantages of the support offered by The Prince's Trust.

3   Analyse two reasons why Kye's application for a bank loan may have been refused.

Review your learning

Test your knowledge   3

1   Name some examples of the support that the following professionals can offer an entrepreneur:

   a   an accountant

   b   a solicitor.

2   What are the disadvantages of using a solicitor for business support?

3   What are the advantages to a business of using an accountant?

What have you learnt?

	See section
• Forms of ownership for business start-ups.	5.1
• Limited and unlimited liability.	5.1
• Sources of capital for business start-ups and expansion.	5.2
• The different sources of support for enterprise.	5.3

Design a business proposal

Let's get started

What is this product? How might the designers behind this product have come up with the idea for it? How did they know that people would buy it?

What will you learn in this unit?

Developing new products is essential for businesses. It helps them to stay ahead of the competition. New products not only need to make a profit, they must also meet the needs of the customer and stand out from the competition. Whether you want to own a business in the future, work for a small business or work in a creative job role, you need to know about the process of designing a product and creating a business proposal. You also need to be able to review whether your ideas are likely to be successful.

In this unit, you will be developing a new product. To develop your product, you will carry out effective market research. Then you will use your research findings to identify your customers and create an initial product design. You will gain feedback on your initial design ideas and use this to create your final design. Finally, you will assess whether your product and business proposal are financially viable and likely to be a success.

When making decisions, you will be developing skills that will be useful to your future career, whatever that may be. In addition to learning more about being an entrepreneur, you will also develop your creative thinking, planning, research, self-management and verbal communication skills.

In this unit you will learn how to:

- carry out market research to help make decisions relating to a business proposal **TA1**

- identify a customer profile **TA2**

- develop a product proposal **TA3**

- review whether a business proposal is financially viable **TA4**

- review the likely success of the business proposal **TA5**.

How you will be assessed

This unit will be assessed through a series of coursework tasks that show your understanding of each topic area. You will complete the assignment independently in class with teacher supervision. The assignment will be marked by your teacher. The assignment contains six tasks. For example:

- identifying the aims of market research, carrying out the market research and reviewing the results

- using your market research findings to describe your customer profile

- creating a product for the selected customer profile.

TA1
Market research

Let's get started 1

Describe what is happening in the photo. Why is it important to complete this task before designing a new product?

Figure 2.1: What is happening in this photo?

The first step in designing your product and business **proposal** is to carry out **market research** using suitable methods. Once you have completed your research, you will need to **review** the results to make sure that the research has met its **aims**.

What will you learn?

- How to carry out market research to help make decisions relating to a business proposal.

- How to review the results of market research.

1.1 Carry out market research

Select appropriate market research methods and data types

Identifying the overall aims of market research

Before carrying out any market research, **entrepreneurs** must decide what the aims of their research are – in other words what they need to find out.

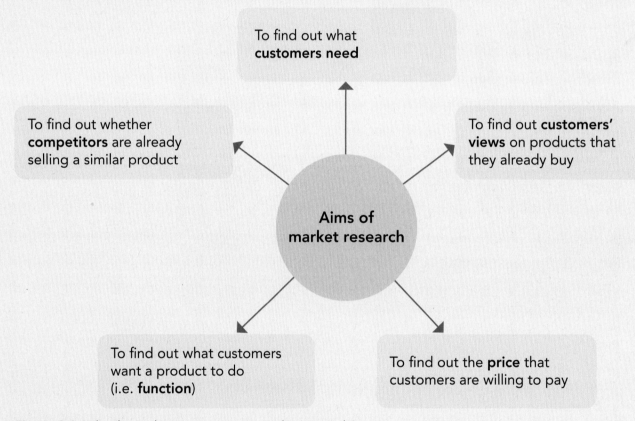

Figure 2.2: Why does a business carry out market research?

Over to you!   1

You have an idea for a new chocolate biscuit. You know that you need to carry out some market research. List three aims of your research.

Market research methods and data types

Tables 2.1 and 2.2 provide a recap of the primary and secondary research methods and **quantitative** and **qualitative data** types that you have already learnt about in Unit R067, Sections 2.2 and 2.3.

Table 2.1: Market research methods

Method	Definition	Advantages/disadvantages
Primary research	Research that you carry out to collect **data** for the first time (e.g. directly with potential customers)	Advantages • Provides detailed information which is specific to your needs (e.g. customer opinions) • Allows you to ask the questions that you want answers to Disadvantages • Time-consuming to collect • May be costly (e.g. if you have to visit different locations)
Secondary research	Research using existing data and information (e.g. from newspapers, Mintel, gov.uk) The internet contains a wide variety of secondary research sources	Advantages • Can be accessed quickly • Low cost/free to access • Often quicker to analyse than primary research as it does not need collating (e.g. producing tally charts (Section 2.2)) Disadvantages • May be out of date • Might not be relevant to your new product

Table 2.2: Market research data types

Type of data	Definition	Examples
Quantitative data	Data relating to facts and figures	Data that shows: • the number of people who are willing to pay £1.00 for a tin of baked beans • the number of customers who find the label on the baked bean tin attractive
Qualitative data	Data relating to people's opinions or reasons for doing something	Responses to the following questions: • What would persuade a customer to try a new **brand** of baked beans? • What do you like about the baked beans that you buy?

Over to you!   2

You have been asked by a small chain of supermarkets to find out how many tins of baked beans are sold in the UK every year.

1   Where will you look for this information?

2   How quickly can you find it?

Stretch

3   Is the information exactly what you need? If not, how else could you find this information?

Factors that businesses need to consider when completing market research

Businesses may choose to carry out primary research, secondary research or a combination of the two. The type of research will depend on a number of factors, such as those in Figure 2.3.

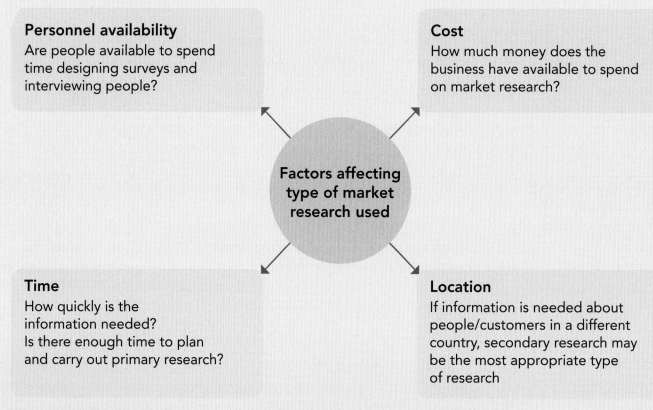

Personnel availability
Are people available to spend time designing surveys and interviewing people?

Cost
How much money does the business have available to spend on market research?

Factors affecting type of market research used

Time
How quickly is the information needed?
Is there enough time to plan and carry out primary research?

Location
If information is needed about people/customers in a different country, secondary research may be the most appropriate type of research

Figure 2.3: What should a business consider when choosing which type of market research to use?

- **Primary research:** In an ideal world, many entrepreneurs and businesses would complete as much primary research as possible before making any decisions about designing and selling new products. This is because primary research data will be specific to their needs. However, this is not always possible as they need to consider the factors shown in Figure 2.3.

- **Secondary research:** Do not assume that primary research is always the best method of market research to use. There are times when a business might also need to carry out secondary research. For example, they might need statistics (figures) about the number of people who are:

  - employed in the retail sector (shops) in the UK

  - using a particular type of product

  - aged 60 or over.

For your design proposal, you need to carry out both primary and secondary research. You will also need to collect both quantitative and qualitative data.

Case study

Greggs PLC

The first Greggs bakery store was opened in Newcastle upon Tyne in 1951. Greggs now has over 1950 bakery stores in the UK.

When Greggs is looking to introduce a new product or modify (change) an existing product, it carries out market research. The main forms of market research that Greggs uses are **surveys** and **interviews**. It also uses taste tests as part of these surveys and interviews, to gain opinions about how the product tastes.

Figure 2.4: Greggs carries out market research using surveys and interviews

Check your understanding

1 Identify two reasons why Greggs uses **primary market research**.

2 Describe how Greggs could use a survey.

3 Explain one benefit and one drawback to Greggs of using taste tests as part of their research.

Sampling methods

Let's get started   2

You work for a biscuit company that is planning to launch a new biscuit. They have asked you to survey potential customers. What do you need to find out? How will you decide who to survey?

When a business plans any market research, it needs to make a decision about who to survey or interview. It would be too time-consuming and too costly to question the whole population, so the business usually surveys a subset (**sample**) of the whole population. The data that it collects from this subset is representative of the whole population.

There are four main **sampling** methods that a business can use when choosing who will take part in primary research:

- cluster sampling
- convenience sampling
- random sampling
- quota sampling.

Cluster sampling

A business might divide the population into groups (clusters) and choose people from each cluster at random. Each cluster might be a geographical area. For example, the population of a city can be divided into clusters by area, and within each cluster a sample of people is randomly surveyed or interviewed. This should give an overview of the opinions and attitudes of the population of the whole city.

Convenience sampling

People are chosen to take part in the research because they are available, so it is 'convenient'. For example, a researcher might stop people in the street or outside a shop and ask if they are willing to take part in the survey.

Random sampling

People are chosen by chance, so every person in the population has the same probability (chance) of being asked to take part in the research. The people in the sample may be any age, any gender, etc.

Quota sampling

The researcher divides the population into groups sharing the same **characteristics**, e.g. age groups or **income** levels. They will then survey or interview a set number of people from each group.

Advantages and disadvantages of sampling methods

Table 2.3: Advantages and disadvantages of sampling methods

Sampling method	Advantages	Disadvantages
Cluster sampling	• More cost-effective than questioning the whole population • Less time-consuming than questioning the whole population	• Difficult to make sure that each cluster accurately represents the whole population • If some clusters are large and some are small, the results may be inaccurate. The clusters must be the same size in order to achieve accurate results • Expensive if large clusters are sampled
Convenience sampling	• Information can be gathered quickly because the people questioned do not have to meet any specific criteria (other than being available) • Reduces possible **bias** in the research **findings** because no specific groups are targeted	• The people questioned may not be representative of the whole population • The location of the research may impact the accuracy of the results (e.g. stopping people outside a college might increase the number of people in the 16–24 age group being questioned)
Random sampling	• More cost-effective than questioning the whole population • Reduced chance of bias because people are chosen at random	• May be time-consuming (e.g. if people from many locations around the UK need to be questioned) • A complete and up-to-date list of the population is required to ensure that a random sample can be chosen
Quota sampling	• Groups can be targeted to make sure that the sample is representative of the population	• **Risk** of bias because people are not chosen at random • It must be possible to divide the population into relevant groups

Choosing an appropriate sampling method

When you carry out the research for your design proposal, you will need to think about which is the best method to use to gather relevant and accurate information for your product (see Table 2.3). You will also need to think about your sample size. The more people that are in your **sample**, the more accurate your research findings are likely to be.

Over to you!   3

A bicycle manufacturer wants to design a new bicycle aimed at people who cycle to school or work in the UK.

1   Which sampling method would you suggest they use for the primary research? Explain your answer.

2   Why will the sample size affect the accuracy of the research?

Use appropriate market research tools for a business proposal

Let's get started   3

What is a **questionnaire**? What is a survey? What is the difference between a questionnaire and a survey? When might you use a survey rather than a questionnaire?

Choosing appropriate market research tools

Look back to Unit R067, Sections 2.2 and 2.3 to remind yourself about the different primary and **secondary market research** tools that a business can use when it carries out market research.

Primary market research tools

Before you can design your new product, you need to choose and create your own primary market research tools to collect the information you will need (Table 2.4).

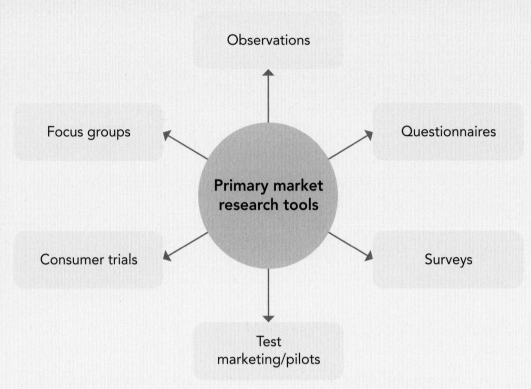

Figure 2.5: What tools could a business use to carry out primary research?

Table 2.4: Market research tools

Market research tool	Key features	Advantages	Disadvantages
Observations	• A research technique where people are observed carrying out their usual actions/tasks • Useful to observe customer shopping habits, e.g. whether a new sales display is attracting attention	• People are behaving naturally rather than saying what they think a researcher wants to hear or what they think might impress the researcher • Collecting qualitative and/or quantitative data gives a detailed insight into customer behaviour	• If people see the researcher, they may not behave naturally • It may not be seen as ethical to observe customers without their permission
Questionnaires	• A list of questions to collect the required information from a target audience • Can include a range of question styles (e.g. multiple choice, ranking, open and/or **closed questions**)	• Using a range of question types means that both quantitative and qualitative information can be collected • Carefully planned questions mean that relevant and up-to-date information is collected	• If the questionnaire is too long, **respondents** might get bored when answering it. This may affect the accuracy of the answers • If respondents do not understand the questions it may affect the accuracy of their answers
Surveys	• Can be digital or paper-based • A survey is the process of collecting, collating and analysing all of the data from questionnaire responses and other market research methods, i.e. a questionnaire can be used as part of a survey to collect data • Platforms such as surveymonkey.com provide a quick and easy way of designing and circulating a digital survey	• Digital surveys can be cost-effective as researchers do not need to be paid to ask the questions face-to-face • Can ask specific questions according to what the business needs to find out	• Some people do not like providing data online and will not take part in digital surveys. This is a significant issue if it applies to the target audience for a product • Paper-based surveys are time-consuming because only one person can be surveyed at a time (by each researcher)

Table 2.4: Continued

Market research tool	Key features	Advantages	Disadvantages
Focus groups	• A selected group of people who meet and discuss their opinions and views • Used to collect qualitative data	• Information is gathered immediately as the group meets face-to-face • Researchers can ask additional questions and collect very detailed information	• Need to be planned in advance (e.g. a venue that will accommodate the selected number of people has to be chosen and booked) • The people who are selected may not be representative of the **target market** or whole population
Consumer trials	• Allowing consumers to try a product for a period of time, free of charge, in return for their **feedback**	• Feedback is received from people who have actually used the product • People who have tried the product for free may continue to buy the product if they like it	• It may be costly providing consumers with free products to try as part of the trial • It may be time-consuming to choose people to take part in the trial, provide them with the product and then collect their feedback • **Competitors** may get to see the product before its full launch onto the market
Test marketing/pilots	• A product is launched to a small part of the target market (e.g. one region) • Research results are used to decide whether to launch the product nationwide or whether changes need to be made first (e.g. to the product itself, **advertising**, price, etc.)	• Research and information are based on a 'real' product rather than questions and answers about a product that has not yet been created • It reduces the financial risk to the business as launching a product nationwide is costly	• Competitors will see the product and may design a similar product before the nationwide launch • Results and feedback are based on a small group of customers who may not be representative of the whole population

Your product proposal 1

Designing a questionnaire

If you choose to use a questionnaire as one of your market research tools, you will need to plan the questionnaire carefully.

What information do I need to collect?

When designing a questionnaire, it is important to think about what information you need to collect. You could write a list of the information you need and then make sure that you write questions which will allow you to collect this information.

What style of questions will I use?

You need to include a range of question styles (Figure 2.6) because you need to collect both quantitative and qualitative data.

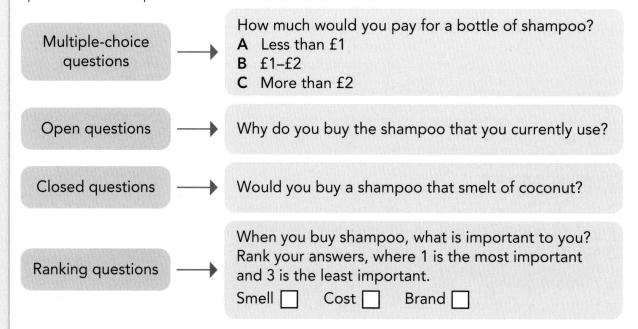

Figure 2.6: What question styles will your questionnaire contain?

How long will it take to complete the questionnaire?

Although you must make sure that you gather all the information you need, you do not want respondents to get bored filling in your questionnaire. If they do, they might rush their answers and they might not be accurate.

Is the language in the questionnaire clear?

Finally, you should make sure that the language you use is clear. Remember that respondents are not likely to be studying enterprise and marketing, so you need to explain any terms or jargon clearly.

Let's get practical!   1

Think back to the business that wants to design a new bicycle (see Over to you! 3). It will be aimed at people who cycle to school or work in the UK.

You have been asked to carry out some research to find out:

- what potential customers need and want from a new bicycle

- any other information that you think the market research needs to answer (e.g. price).

1 Identify three aims for your research.

2 Design a questionnaire to collect information that you need. Your questionnaire should:

    a   include at least five questions

    b   allow you to collect quantitative and qualitative data.

3 Decide whether you will use a digital or paper-based questionnaire. Explain your decision.

4 Ask another student to answer your questionnaire.

5 Review the student's answers. How successful was your questionnaire at collecting the information you needed? How would you improve it?

Secondary market research tools

When using secondary research sources, you need to record any information that you find out from the sources. The two main tools that you should understand and be able to create and use are:

- data collection sheets

- spreadsheets.

Data collection sheets are tools for recording and organising data and information so that businesses can make sense of it. Data collection sheets should have a simple design that makes them easy to fill in and so that the results are clear. For example, if a toy shop wants to know the location and opening hours of local competitors, the researcher could use the data collection sheet in Figure 2.7.

SHOP NAME	LOCATION	OPENING HOURS
Jones Toy Superstore	Clough Road	10 AM–5 PM
Toy Town	Princes Quay	9 AM–5:30 PM
Play Time Toy Shop	Beverley	9 AM–5:30 PM
Toy Shelf	North Point	9 AM–4 PM

Figure 2.7: Data collection sheets should be easy to fill in and show the results clearly

Let's get practical!   2

You have been asked by the bicycle manufacturer to research online bicycle retailers (shops). The manufacturer needs to know:

- the name of the retailer

- the website address

- whether they charge for delivery. If so, what the delivery charge is.

1 Design a data collection sheet that you can use to record your findings.

2 Carry out your research and record your findings on your data collection sheet.

3 Was your data collection sheet useful? Did it enable you to record all of the information that you needed? If not, how would you improve it?

A **spreadsheet** is an electronic document made up of rows and columns. It can help with arranging and sorting data and can also be used to perform calculations.

Like data collection sheets, spreadsheets enable you to organise and analyse market research data. Examples of spreadsheets that you can use are Microsoft Excel and Google Sheets. For example, if a stationery business wants to record the price that its competitors charge for a pad of A4 paper, the researcher could use the data collection sheet in Figure 2.8.

	A	B	C	D	E
1	Competitor	Price	Additional information	Source	Date
2	WH Smith	£3.99	400 pages	whsmith.co.uk	18/02/2022
3	Tesco	£1.50	300 pages	tesco.com	18/02/2022
4	The Range	£2.49	400 pages	therange.co.uk	18/02/2022
5	Amazon	£1.39	80 pages	amazon.co.uk	18/02/2022

Figure 2.8: A spreadsheet can be used to record research into competitors' pricing, e.g. for an A4 pad

Over to you! 4

Look at each column in the spreadsheet shown in Figure 2.8. Why is each piece of information important? Why do you need to know the date?

Your product proposal 2

Which secondary market research tool should I use?

When you are designing your product proposal you must carry out secondary research. You will need to choose and design a secondary research tool to record your findings.

The main difference between a data collection sheet and a spreadsheet is that a data collection sheet is completed by hand and a spreadsheet is completed using a computer.

Your choice of tool may depend on the type of information you are researching. For example, if you are carrying out secondary research using online sources to find telephone numbers, it might be easier and more accurate to handwrite your findings in a data collection sheet rather than having to switch between computer screens. However, if you are researching figures that you will then use in calculations, such as the price of a product or service, it might be easier to use a spreadsheet.

Use appropriate skills when carrying out market research

Let's get started **4**

What skills do each of the pictures show? Why are these skills important when carrying out market research?

Figure 2.9: Why are these skills important when carrying out market research?

In addition to designing and using appropriate market research tools (Table 2.5), you also need to develop and use a range of transferable skills. These are skills that do not just relate to carrying out market research. They are skills that you can use and develop in other subjects that you are studying as well as in your future career.

Table 2.5: What skills do you need to carry out successful market research?

Skill	Explanation
Information and communications technology (ICT)	You will use ICT throughout your research for TA1. This could include: • designing a questionnaire • carrying out online research • producing graphs to present your research findings. Being able to use word-processing and spreadsheet software will help you to produce professional-looking documents. Tools, such as spellcheck and being able to perform calculations, should also improve the accuracy of your documents.
Verbal communication	When you are carrying out your primary market research you will need to talk to people. This could be asking them questions in a survey or a focus group that you are leading. Good verbal communication includes: • speaking clearly • speaking with confidence • being an active listener (i.e. listening carefully to what people say to you, repeating what they have told you and/or asking questions to show that you have heard what they have said) • varying your tone of voice (e.g. do not just read out your questions or presentation in a monotone voice because that will not engage respondents).

Table 2.5: Continued

Skill	Explanation
Non-verbal communication	Communication with another person is not just about talking to them or writing to them. If you can see the other person then you can also see how they are feeling by their facial expressions (e.g. smiling or frowning) and their body language (e.g. folding their arms or shaking their head). This is important when you are carrying out market research because you can see: • how interested a respondent is in the questions you are asking. This might affect the honesty and accuracy of their answers • if they look confused and therefore whether they understand the questions that you are asking.
Written communication	This is an important skill when you are writing questionnaires, collating and analysing your findings and presenting your results. Good written communication skills include: • writing short sentences that make your point clearly • carefully checking your spelling, punctuation and grammar • using professional language rather than slang, jargon or inappropriate language • reading your work through to check that it makes sense.

Over to you!   5

Can you interpret a person's facial expressions and body language?
Look at the images below.

1   How do you think the people in the images are feeling?
2   Who do you think would be most willing to take part in your market research? Why?

Figure 2.10: How are the people in the images feeling?

Checking the accuracy of secondary research

Checking the reliability of sources

Secondary research has been collected by someone else, so you need to check the **reliability** of the information to make sure that it is accurate, up to date and **unbiased**.

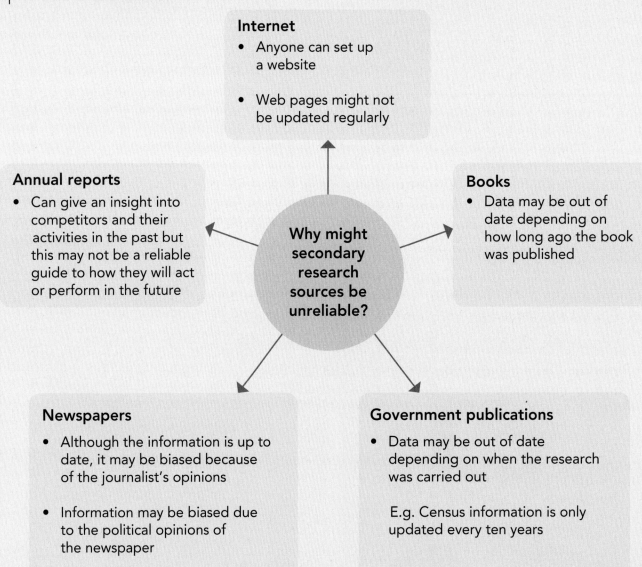

Internet
- Anyone can set up a website
- Web pages might not be updated regularly

Annual reports
- Can give an insight into competitors and their activities in the past but this may not be a reliable guide to how they will act or perform in the future

Why might secondary research sources be unreliable?

Books
- Data may be out of date depending on how long ago the book was published

Newspapers
- Although the information is up to date, it may be biased because of the journalist's opinions
- Information may be biased due to the political opinions of the newspaper

Government publications
- Data may be out of date depending on when the research was carried out

  E.g. Census information is only updated every ten years

Figure 2.11: Why might secondary research sources be unreliable?

The various sources include:

- books/newspapers/trade magazines
- competitors' data
- government publications and statistics
- market research reports such as Mintel.

It is important to check the reliability for every source because you could be using inaccurate or out-of-date information. That might lead to you make badly informed (wrong) decisions in your design proposal, which could lead to your product not being **financially viable** or successful.

Checking the accuracy of information against a second source

Checking information that you have researched against a second source is good business practice, even if you think that the original source is reliable. Even official sources, such as government publications, may contain minor errors in them or the information may not have been updated recently.

Over to you!   6

An office supplies business has carried out secondary research and found the information shown in Table 2.6.

Table 2.6: Secondary research findings

Population of the UK in 2020*	UK government spending in 2020**
67 886 011	Around £928 billion

* Source: United Nations, Department of Economic & Social Affairs

** Source: Statista.com

1   Find two more sources of secondary information to check the accuracy of both pieces of information.

2   Is the data above accurate? Explain your answer.

1.2 Review the results of market research

Once a business has carried out market research, it needs to collate and review the findings. This is the information that the business will use to make decisions. You will need to collate and review your market research findings in order to make decisions for your design proposal.

> **Let's get started   5**
>
> How could you present the results of your primary market research findings? How could you present the results of your secondary research findings? Would you use different methods? Why/why not?

Methods of collating data

Businesses need to collate market research findings so that they can analyse the information more easily. You will also need to collate the findings of your primary and secondary research for your product proposal.

There are three methods for collating data:

- tally charts
- frequency tables
- tables.

Collating your findings will also give you an opportunity to check:

- the answers on your questionnaire to see if anyone has missed out a question or written an inappropriate answer

- that you have recorded/written down any verbal answers accurately.

Tally chart

A tally chart is a simple way of recording and counting the number of times something occurs. It can be used to record answers or observations.

Each time an answer is given (as in Table 2.7) or you observe an action (e.g. every time a customer buys a can of fizzy drink) you draw a vertical line (or tally mark). The fifth line is a diagonal line drawn across them (so that it looks like a gate). These groups of five tally marks make it easier to count your results.

For example, a chocolate manufacturer asked potential customers to complete a questionnaire about a new chocolate bar. One question asked how many times a week each person eats chocolate. The tally chart in Table 2.7 was used to collate the number of people who gave each answer.

Table 2.7: A tally chart is a simple way to record the number of people giving each response

People who eat chocolate every day	People who eat chocolate twice a week	People who eat chocolate three times a week	People who eat chocolate four times a week	People who eat chocolate more than four times a week
ⅢⅢ ⅢⅢ	ⅢⅢ ‖	ⅢⅢ ⅢⅢ ∣	ⅢⅢ ∣	ⅢⅢ

Frequency table

Frequency is the number of times that something happens or occurs. A frequency table allows you to record and see very easily the most frequently occurring data.

A tally chart is also used when calculating frequency. For example, in the questionnaire about a new chocolate bar, another question asks how much customers would be willing to pay for the chocolate bar. Table 2.8 shows the responses; this is the raw, unsorted data from the research.

Table 2.8: Responses to survey showing how much customers would be willing to pay for a chocolate bar

26p	46p	49p	69p	65p	40p	31p	62p
51p	55p	40p	55p	62p	33p	49p	58p
26p	58p	26p	33p	31p	51p	51p	63p

The manufacturer arranged the data in ascending order and then used a tally to collate the number of people who gave each response. The number of 'lines' in each tally was then counted to give the frequency of each response. This is shown in Table 2.9.

Table 2.9: Frequency table stating the number of people willing to pay each price

Price	Number of potential customers willing to pay that price	Frequency
26p	III	3
31p	II	2
33p	II	2
40p	II	2
46p	I	1

Table 2.9: Continued

Price	Number of potential customers willing to pay that price	Frequency
49p	II	2
51p	III	3
55p	II	2
58p	II	2
62p	II	2
63p	I	1
65p	I	1
69p	I	1

Frequency tables are useful when you have collected a lot of data from many respondents. It helps a researcher to collate the data into a format that is easier to understand and interpret. This can be done by sorting the data into groups or ranges when it has been tallied. For example, a table in the format of Table 2.10 below could also be used to sort the data from Table 2.8 to show the range of prices people are willing to pay.

Table 2.10: Frequency table showing the number of people willing to pay each price range

Price	Number of potential customers willing to pay that price	Frequency
20p–29p	III	3
30p–39p	IIII	4
40p–49p	NN	5
50p–59p	NN II	7
60p–69p	NN	5

Over to you!　　7

In the survey, the chocolate manufacturer also asked a question about which type of chocolate people prefer. Using the raw data shown in Table 2.11, produce a frequency table to collate the responses.

Table 2.11: Responses to survey showing which type of chocolate customers prefer

White	Milk	Caramel	Dark	Milk	Dark	Milk	Orange
Milk	Milk	Nutty	White	Dark	Caramel	Nutty	White
Orange	Orange	Dark	Milk	Mint	White	Dark	Caramel

Table

A table is a simple and effective way of collating your research findings. A table could take the format of a spreadsheet or a handwritten table. Tables are useful for presenting both quantitative and qualitative information. For example, a business that is looking to create a new cat grooming product has carried out some research into the size of the pet market in the UK. Table 2.12 shows the collated quantitative findings of research into the number of households in the UK that own a pet.

Table 2.12: Table collating data from research into pet ownership in the UK in 2019–20

Type of pet owned	Percentage of UK adults owning each type of pet*
Cat	16
Bird	1.4
Dog	23
Horse	0.2
Rabbit	1
Snake/lizard	0.7
Other	2.56

*Note that not every adult in the UK owns a pet so the table does not add up to 100 percent

If you choose to present your findings in a table, you must make sure the headings in the table are clear and contain any units of measure (e.g. 'percentage' or '%').

Methods of presenting data

Once you have collated and reviewed your research findings you will then need to present this information. This will allow you, and anyone else viewing the information, to easily see and understand your results.

Let's get started   6

Think about the other subjects you are studying. What ways of presenting data do you already know about?

You can present your market research data as charts, diagrams or tables. These can be produced using software or you can hand draw them. You must include the appropriate labels on each of these (e.g. axis labels, measurements, a title, column headings), so that the audience (anyone looking at these results) can understand what they show.

Charts

There are four main types of chart that you can use to present data.

Bar chart

A bar chart uses bars to display data. The height of each bar represents a value. It can be used to compare data. For example, the business that is looking to create a new cat grooming product can easily see from Figure 2.12 that more people own dogs than cats or horses.

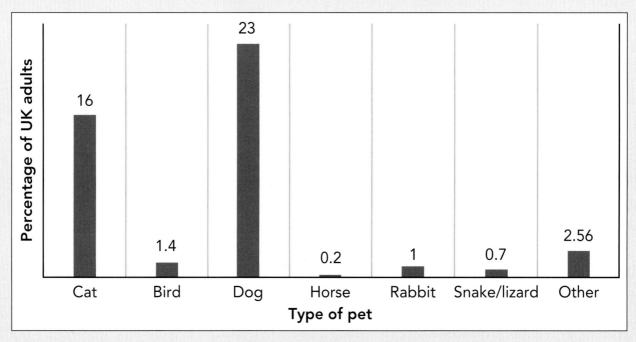

Figure 2.12: This bar chart uses bars to show the percentage of UK adults owning each type of pet

Pie chart

A pie chart displays data in a circle. It is a good way of showing relative sizes. For example, Figure 2.13 shows which is the most common birthday month in a Year 10 form and which is the least common. The chart is divided into 'slices' that represent values of different sizes. In Figure 2.13, the whole circle represents the 32 students in a Year 10 form. Each 'slice' of the circle represents the percentage of the whole form who have their birthday in a specific month. The bigger the 'slice', the higher the value (and percentage). So in Figure 2.13, May is the most common month for students to have their birthday. A pie chart can be used to easily compare data visually.

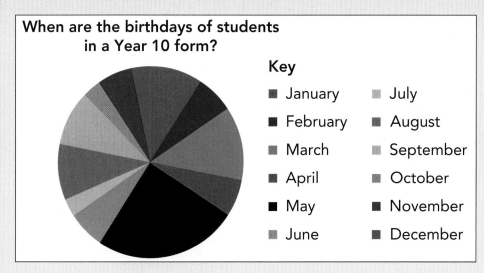

Figure 2.13: A pie chart is a good way of showing relative sizes

Stretch

Why is a pie chart **not** an appropriate method of presenting the data in Table 2.12?

Line chart

A line chart or graph is used to show data over time. Figure 2.14 shows the number of coats sold in a clothes shop over a six-month period. A point is drawn on the chart to represent each value (the number of coats sold each month) and the points are joined by straight lines to show a pattern in the data over time.

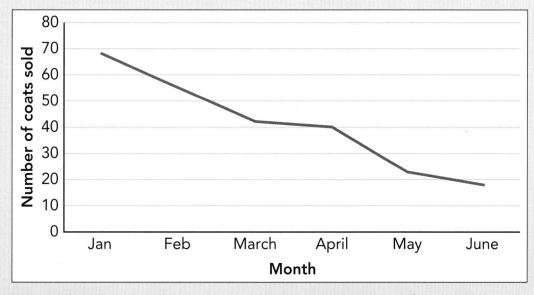

Figure 2.14: A line chart shows data over time, such as the number of coats sold in a clothes shop

Over to you!   8

Why is a line chart **not** an appropriate method of presenting the data in Table 2.12?

Tip: What does the line on a line chart show?

Scatter graph

A scatter graph is used to show whether there is a relationship between two sets of data (variables). The closer the relationship (correlation) between the two sets of data, the closer the dots on the scatter graph will be to the diagonal straight line. Each dot on the scatter graph in Figure 2.15 represents the sales of coats versus the outside temperature. In this instance, the trendline shows that there is a good relationship between the two sets of data because the dots are quite close to the trendline (i.e. the colder it is, the more coats that the clothes shop sells).

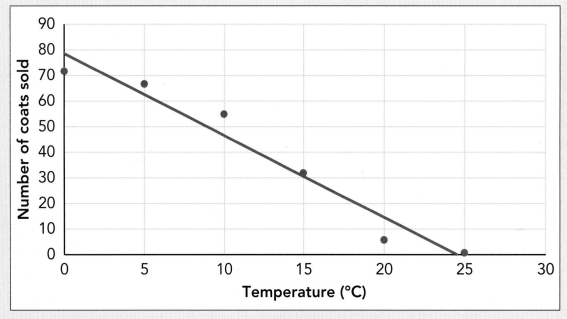

Figure 2.15: A scatter graph can show a relationship between data, such as the number of coats sold in a clothes shop at different outside temperatures (°C)

Diagrams

You could present your data using a diagram. A diagram is a visual way of presenting information. It could be a graph, a chart, a drawing or a plan that explains your results and makes them easy to interpret.

Diagrams can include Venn diagrams, Carroll diagrams, pictograms and flow charts.

Tables

You have already learnt in Section 1.2 that a table is a simple and effective way of collating your research findings. A table can also be used as a method of presenting your results. Tables can be used to present complex (detailed) information clearly by using appropriate column and/or row headings.

Review your learning

Test your knowledge

1   What is the difference between primary and secondary market research?

2   How would you describe some of the primary market research tools to a friend?

3   Explain one method of collating market research data.

4   Explain two methods of presenting market research data.

What have you learnt?

	See section
• How to carry out out market research to help make decisions relating to a business proposal.	1.1
• How to review the results of market research.	1.2

TA2

How to identify a customer profile

Let's get started

What kind of customers are likely to buy these products?
What characteristics are they likely to have?

Figure 2.16: Think about why a customer is buying the product

What will you learn?

- How to identify potential customers and build a **customer profile** based on market research findings.

2.1 Identify potential customers and build a customer profile based on market research findings

When entrepreneurs and businesses come up with an idea for a new product, they carry out market research to help them decide who their potential customers are likely to be (i.e. who will buy it). They do this by trying to identify the likely characteristics of these customers.

Case study

Ford Motor Company

Ford customers in the UK can choose from a range of 13 different models of car and 18 different vans and pick-up trucks. Many of these have the option of petrol, diesel, hybrid or electric engines. Each of these vehicles is aimed at a different market **segment**. For example:

Figure 2.17: Customers can choose from a range of Ford vehicles aimed at different market segments

- the Fiesta is the smallest and lowest-cost car in the range, aimed at single people, couples and small families

- the option of a hybrid engine appeals to people concerned about the environmental impact of petrol and diesel cars

- the Galaxy is a seven-seater people carrier aimed at larger families

- the two-seater Ford GT is a high-performance supercar aimed at high-income drivers with an interest in fast cars.

The cost of these cars varies, with starting prices from £16 645 for the Fiesta up to approximately £450 000 for the Ford GT.

Check your understanding

1   Other than the Ford cars mentioned in the case study, use your own knowledge of the car market to identify:

   a   one car aimed at families

   b   one car aimed at people wanting a sports car

   c   one car aimed at people who are concerned about the environment.

2   Explain two benefits to car manufacturers of selling a range of cars that are aimed at different customers.

3   Do you think Ford will sell the same cars to the US market? Explain your answer.

Market segmentation

Market segmentation is where a business divides its potential customers into groups based on similar characteristics. By segmenting the market for a specific product, the business can learn more about the needs and wants of customers within that segment. The design of the product, the price and any advertising can then be targeted at these customers (Table 2.13). If the product meets the needs of these customers, the business is likely to have higher sales and therefore earn higher **profits**. Figure 2.18 recaps the characteristics that can be used to segment a market (see Unit R067, Section 2.4).

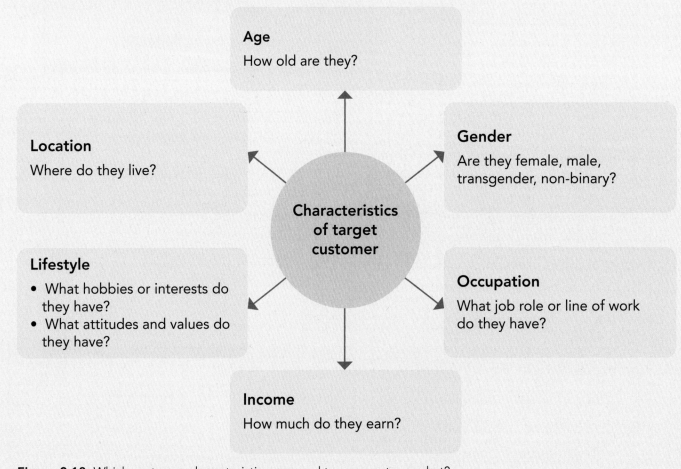

Figure 2.18: Which customer characteristics are used to segment a market?

Table 2.13: Products aimed at specific customers

Customer characteristic	Examples of products targeted at customers with each characteristic
Age	• Toys aimed at babies • Toys aimed at young children • Holidays aimed at the over 50s • Mobility scooters, walking sticks and walk-in baths aimed at older customers
Gender	• Floral-smelling perfumes and deodorants aimed at women • Unisex perfume, e.g. CK Everyone • Male grooming products for facial hair, e.g. a beard trimmer
Occupation	• Stethoscopes aimed at doctors • Electric power tools aimed at people in construction jobs
Income	• Range Rover cars aimed at higher income levels • Primark clothing aimed at people with more limited income • Supermarket finest and premium food ranges aimed at medium to high income levels
Lifestyle	• Fitness trackers aimed at people wanting a healthier lifestyle • Electric cars aimed at people who are environmentally aware • Vegan products being sold in supermarkets as more people become vegan or want to eat meat-free on some days
Location	• A car sold in the UK needs to be right-hand drive, but a car sold in France needs to be left-hand drive (the French drive on the right-hand side of the road) • UK supermarkets sell different products in different stores based on the preferences and ethnic and cultural background of the people in the local area

Over to you!

Give two examples of products that are aimed at each of the customer groups below:

a   people aged 60 years and over

b   females aged 20–30 years

c   people earning £100 000 per year or more

d   people earning £15 000 per year or less

e   people living in a rural area.

Once a business has carried out market research, based on its findings it needs to decide who is most likely to buy the new product and which market segment it will target the product at. Once it has identified the characteristics of its target customer, it can design the product to meet the needs and wants of those customers.

How to apply market segmentation to build a customer profile

By detecting any trends in the collated market research findings, a business is able to identify the likely profile of customers who will buy its product. The customer profile summarises the key characteristics of the target customers for the new product, such as age, income level, occupation, location, gender and lifestyle (Table 2.13). For example, are most of the people interested in buying the product students who are under 18 with low incomes?

When you carry out your research for your own product proposal, you need to not only identify the customer profile but also justify (give reasons) why you have identified a particular customer profile. For example, a company looking to introduce a new healthy fruit drink carried out some market research. Figures 2.19 and 2.20 show their findings for age and lifestyle interests. Each piece of information helps to identify a characteristic of their potential customer.

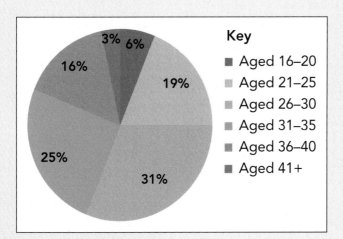

Figure 2.19: Key characteristics, such as ages of potential customers who would buy a new healthy fruit drink, can be shown in a pie chart

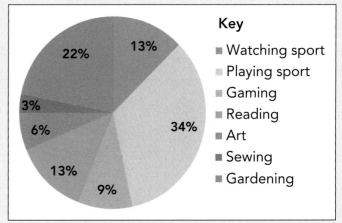

Figure 2.20: Lifestyle interests of potential customers who would buy a new healthy fruit drink can also be shown in a pie chart

The business can then put these characteristics together to start building a customer profile (Figure 2.21).

1. Identify customer characteristics

- People aged 26–35 (Figure 2.19)
- People interested in playing sport and gardening (Figure 2.20)

2. Justify customer characteristics

- 31% are aged 26–30; 25% are aged 31–35 (Figure 2.19)
- 34% play sport; 22% enjoy gardening (Figure 2.20)

Figure 2.21: Stages to identify and begin to justify customer characteristics to build a customer profile. Further research may be needed to identify additional characteristics

Using the customer characteristics identified by market segmentation, the drinks business can start to build a customer profile. Based on the research that they have conducted, the main customer profile for the new drink is people aged 26 to 35 who are interested in playing sport and gardening. These are the people that the business needs to target and whose needs it must meet in order for the drink to be successful.

However, by conducting further research the drinks business could identify additional characteristics that customers may have. For example, what income level are they likely to have, where are they likely to live? This would help them to create a more detailed customer profile and better meet the needs of potential customers.

When you create the customer profile for your new product you will need to consider a range of features that your target customers will have.

Let's get practical!

The bicycle manufacturer from Let's get practical! 2 in TA1 has carried out market research to identify who might be interested in buying a new lightweight folding bicycle. The charts below present the findings of the research.

Based on the findings, identify the profile (characteristics) of the people most likely to buy this new bicycle. Justify your decisions.

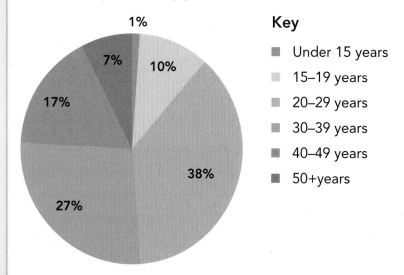

Key
- ■ Under 15 years
- ■ 15–19 years
- ■ 20–29 years
- ■ 30–39 years
- ■ 40–49 years
- ■ 50+years

Figure 2.22: What age range do most of the people interested in buying a new folding bicycle fall into?

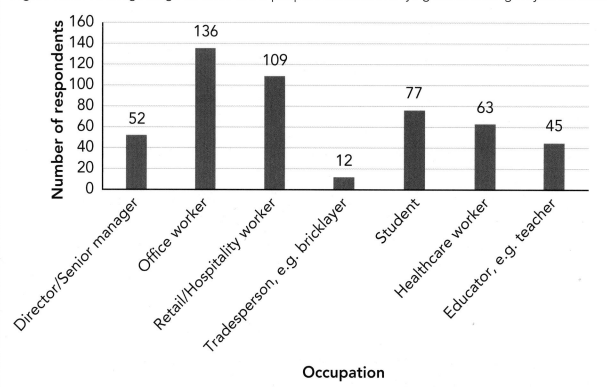

Figure 2.23: What is the occupation of most of the people interested in buying a new folding bicycle?

Continued

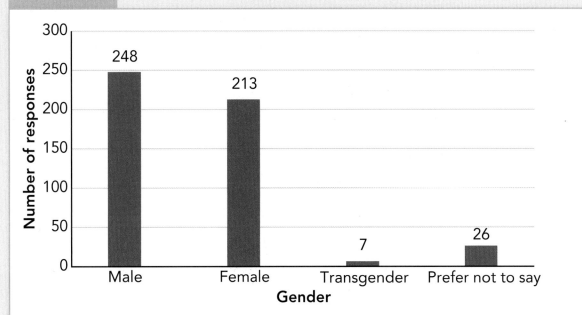

Figure 2.24: What does the bar chart tell you about the gender of the people interested in buying a new folding bicycle?

Tip: You could justify your decisions by giving the percentage of people or, for example, by stating '10 out of 20 people surveyed said …'

Review your learning

Test your knowledge

1   Identify three characteristics that a business can use to segment a market.

2   For each characteristic, give an example of a product aimed at customers with that characteristic.

3   For each product, explain why you think the business aims the product at customers with that characteristic.

What have you learnt?

	See section
• Identify potential customers and build a customer profile based on market research findings.	2.1

Develop a product proposal

Let's get started   1

What are these products? What three words would you use to describe each of these products? Who are the target customers for each product?

Figure 2.25: Think about what each product does and who would want or need it

What will you learn?

- How to create a **design mix** for a new product.
- How to produce designs for a new product.
- How to review designs for a product proposal.

3.1 Create a design mix for a new product

Good product design is essential if a new product is to be successful. A well-designed product will attract customers and make them want to buy it. A product must be suitable for its intended purpose. Businesses often create many **prototypes** before they decide on a final design.

Case study

Fitbit Force

In October 2013, Fitbit launched the 'Force' fitness tracker. It enabled users to track daily activity, sleep patterns and the number of stairs that they had climbed. However, in February 2014, Fitbit removed it from the market after almost 10 000 reports that the wrist strap caused skin rashes.

Check your understanding

1   State why the Fitbit Force was not suitable for its intended purpose.

2   Explain the impact that the problem with the Fitbit Force could have had on Fitbit's **brand image**.

3   Explain the impact that the problem with the Fitbit Force could have had on Fitbit's profits.

When creating and developing a product, a business needs to consider three key elements of design, known as the design mix. Figure 2.26 shows the three elements that make up the design mix.

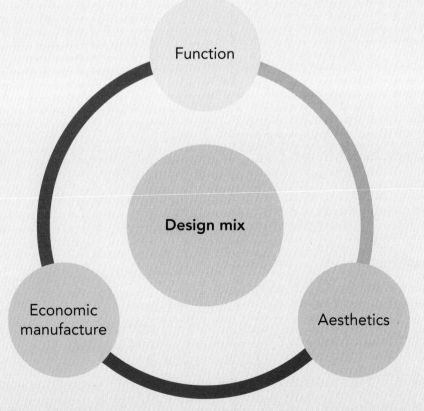

Figure 2.26: The three elements of the design mix

Function

Function is what the product can 'do' and what it needs to do, how it works and whether it is reliable. The product needs to be able to do the job it is being sold to do and must work every time it is used. Customers will always consider a product's function when buying it.

For example, the function of a car is to transport people from one place to another. It has an engine which runs on fuel or a motor that is powered by electricity, and that turns the wheels. The car also needs to be reliable because you do not want it breaking down all the time.

Similarly, if you buy a new coat you might want it to be waterproof or you might want it to be warm. These are the functions of the coat. Knowing what you want it to 'do' will help you to choose the right coat.

Aesthetics

Aesthetics relates to how the product appeals to customers' senses and includes how it:

- looks
- smells
- feels (e.g. shape, size and material)
- tastes (if the product is edible).

Aesthetics are a key way of differentiating a product (making it stand out) from a competitor's product.

Features that make a product attractive

A business needs to think about what product design features will make a product attractive to potential customers. For example:

- colours (e.g. the iPhone comes in a range of colours)
- style/shape (e.g. the Fiat 500 is based on the iconic, retro shape and style of the original car from the 1950s)
- materials used (e.g. luxury cars may use leather on the seats as some people think it makes the car smell nice and creates a luxurious appearance)
- aromas (e.g. perfumes have a range of scents to appeal to different people).

Features that create a USP

A business also needs to make sure that a product has a **unique selling point (USP)**. The USP should encourage a customer to buy this business's product rather than a competitor's product. USPs such as **logos** and brand names can be built into the product's design (e.g. BMW cars, Mulberry handbags and Gucci clothing). USPs can also be created by the shape of a product, for example the shape and design of a vintage Coca-Cola bottle or a Harley Davidson motorbike.

The influence of market segments on aesthetics

Lastly, the business needs to think about how the customers in the target market segment want the product to look. For example, a product aimed at men may be a different colour to a product aimed at women. Similarly, products aimed at children might need to be more brightly coloured and patterned or have a cartoon character on them.

Another consideration is whether or not aesthetics is important to some target market segments. For example, the target customer for a power drill or a mattress is less likely to be influenced by aesthetics as they are buying the product mainly for its function.

Function vs aesthetics

Although some products are designed with a focus on either function *or* aesthetics, many products are designed with a focus on both of these elements. For example, a sofa needs to be functional (e.g. comfortable to sit on) but it also needs to look attractive (e.g. a modern style or an on-trend colour).

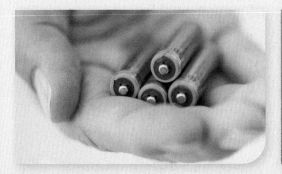 

Figure 2.27: Which are the most important elements of the design mix for these products?

Over to you! 1

1   A battery is an example of a product where function rather than aesthetics is the key element of the design mix. Identify two other products where function is the most important element of the design mix.

2   A pair of designer trainers is an example of a product where aesthetics is the key element of the design mix. Identify two other products where aesthetics is the most important element of the design mix.

3   A sofa is an example of a product where both aesthetics and function are key elements of the design mix. Identify two other products where aesthetics and function are **both** important elements of the design mix.

Economic manufacture

A new product needs to at least **break even** or hopefully make a profit. A business therefore needs to consider whether the design is feasible enough that it allows the product to be made in a cost-effective way to make a profit. To do this, the selling price needs to at least cover the **costs** of making (i.e. producing) the product.

The selling price of a product is affected by the:

*   **the price that customers are willing to pay**. If the price that they are willing to pay is low, then the design may need to use less costly materials to keep the production costs low. If they are willing to pay more, it might be possible to use more expensive materials

*   **target market segment** that the product is aimed at. A customer purchasing a luxury product will be willing to pay a higher price as the quality should be better than a standard product. So a business might be able to afford slightly higher production costs, i.e. it could make the product from higher-quality materials or use a more complex design. For example, a coat aimed at a lower income group may be priced at £15, whereas a coat aimed at a higher-income group may be priced at £300

*   **added value**. The production process adds value to the product. **Added value** is the difference between the cost of the materials used to produce the product and the selling price. That means that

the finished product has a higher value (price) than the sum of all the parts that make up the product. Adding value is very important if a product is to be successful and profitable. For example, if the cost of the materials (fabric, buttons, thread, etc.) to make the coat is £6, the production costs are £3 and the coat is sold for £15, then the business has added value of £6 per coat

- **the cost of producing the product**. A business needs to make sure that the production costs are lower than the selling price in order to break even and hopefully make a profit. It may have to consider using cheaper materials if it cannot afford to use the materials in the original design. For example, the coat priced at £15 is likely to be made with thinner and cheaper material than the one priced at £300.

Case study

Product design mix for a new coat

Two years ago, Jamie set up his own business making and selling clothing. This season, Jamie is looking to expand his product range and introduce a new coat to the current range that he offers. He has carried out market research and identified his customer profile. The target market segment for the coat will be young children. To decide on his design mix, he will need to answer the following questions.

Function

- Does it need to be waterproof?
- Does it need to be warm?

Aesthetics

- What colour(s) will the coat be?
- What style will the coat be?
- What material will it be made of?
- Will it have a hood?
- What will the buttons be like? Or will it have a zip?
- Will it have a brand logo to differentiate it and create a USP?
- How can it be designed to appeal to the target market? Does it need a cartoon animal on it? Does the fabric need to be a bright colour?

Continued

Economic manufacture

- What is a customer in the target market segment (the child's parent) likely to pay? Are they willing to pay, say, £25 or are they willing to pay much more, say £300?

- How much will it cost to produce the coat? What do the materials cost? What are the labour costs?

- Based on the price that parents are willing to pay, what materials can Jamie use to make the coat? Will the materials need to be cheaper and thinner for the £25 coat?

- How much value can be added to the coat? How much will the coat be sold for? What will be the difference between the selling price and the cost to produce the coat?

Check your understanding

1 State the key function of a coat that is aimed at young children. Explain why you have chosen this function.

2 Outline what you think the coat should look like to appeal to the target market. Explain your ideas.

3 Explain why it is important to add value during the production process.

3.2 Produce designs for a new product

Use market research to inform product designs

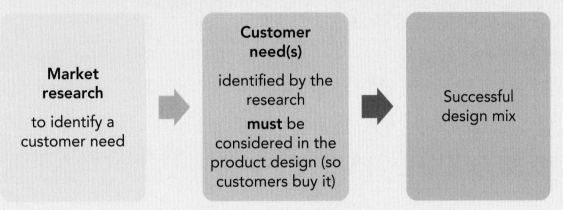

Figure 2.28: The three steps to creating a successful design mix

When a business is considering the steps of creating a design mix (Figure 2.28) it needs to make sure that customers are at the heart of its decisions. If the business does not take into account customer needs, wants and opinions, the customers are unlikely to want to buy the product.

Let's get practical! 1

Jamie's clothing business (see the case study, Product design mix for a new coat in Section 3.1) is also considering launching a new range of bags. Based on the market research, they have asked you to produce a design mix for one of these new bags. It can be a handbag or a backpack.

The market research found that:

- the people most likely to buy a large bag were between 10 and 39 years old

- the people least likely to buy a large bag were over 40 years old

- both men and women were equally likely to buy a bag

- 61 percent of the people who were interviewed earned between £15 000 and £35 000, and 22 percent earned less than £15 000

- the most popular hobbies amongst those interviewed were watching TV, shopping and playing sport.

Continued

1   Create a design mix for the bag. In your design mix, you need to identify:

    a   the characteristics of the target customer

    b   the function of the bag

    c   how the aesthetics of the bag will meet the needs of the target customer

    d   the selling price of the bag.

2   Do you think your bag will make a profit? Give a reason for your answer.

Your product proposal   1

Market research and the design mix

The market research that you have carried out will help you decide on the design mix for your own product proposal. It should have:

- its function – what customers want the new product to do

- the aesthetics – what customers want the new product to look like, feel like, smell like, taste like

- selling price – what customers are willing to pay for the product.

When producing design ideas for your product, be sure to think about the research findings so that you design a product that:

- does what customers want and meets their needs (rather than designing a product to meet your own tastes, needs and wants)

- is appealing to your target customers

- is affordable, i.e. the price matches what your customers are willing to pay

- can be produced at the right cost (e.g. by using cheaper material for a lower-price product, or more expensive material for a higher-price product).

Using current creative techniques

Creative techniques allow product designers to think about and view their ideas and findings in a new way and to find innovative ideas and solutions.

Your product proposal   2

Creative techniques

You will need to use creative techniques to come up with your initial design ideas for your assessment. You should show evidence of these in your assessment task. Some of the techniques that you could use are explained below.

Brain shifter

The brain shifter technique requires you to 'put yourself in the shoes' of the target customer. By doing this you may come up with ideas that you might not have thought of if you were focusing on your own needs and wants. To use this technique:

- identify the target customer and their key characteristics

- imagine that you are this target customer and answer these questions:

  - What are your likes and dislikes likely to be?

  - What needs and wants might you have?

  - What needs might you want a new product to meet?

You can then use these ideas to inform (come up with) designs that will meet the needs and wants of the target customer.

Mind map

A mind map is an effective and visual way of structuring information about a product design idea. To create a mind map:

- start by writing the name of the product in the middle of a sheet of paper (you can also use word-processing or mind mapping software)

- as you come up with ideas, words, phrases and images relating to your product idea, add them around the product name using radiating lines.

This will build up a visual map of your ideas. Your mind map should include:

- information about your target customer (e.g. your customer profile)

- price (e.g. what price do competitors charge? What price do you think your target customer will pay?)

- product design ideas (e.g. clippings/photos from magazines or pictures found online)

- product features (e.g. a list of features for your product or a list of features that competitor products have. What will be your USP?).

Try to link similar ideas/topics together (e.g. those relating to your target customer or product features). Use different colours, shapes, images and different-sized writing to make the mind map as visual as possible.

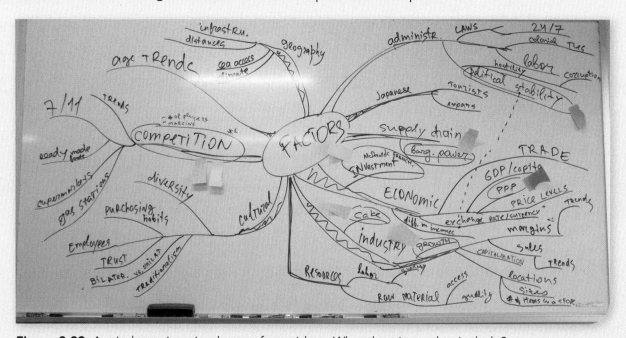

Figure 2.29: A mind map is a visual map of your ideas. What does it need to include?

Mood boards

A mood board is a type of collage that consists of images, text, drawings and material samples. These can all be pinned onto a board or glued to a large sheet of paper. Mood boards communicate a designer's vision for their product and allow the audience to see what the designer is thinking.

A mood board should be full of ideas, textures and images, but it also needs to be organised and based around a theme so that it is not just a messy collage. To create a mood board:

- decide whether you are going to create a digital mood board or a hard copy one

- choose the materials that you will need in order to create it

- decide how you will organise your ideas – for example, it is a good idea to choose one central image with smaller images and text around it

- decide on a theme

- choose what you will use to illustrate your ideas:

  - text: pick out some key words and make them stand out

  - photos: think about using photos from a variety of sources, online images, images cut out from magazines; use your phone to take photos of things in the real world that inspire you

  - samples of materials: these add a tactile element to your mood board, so think about what materials you might include and where you might get them.

Figure 2.30: How does a mood board help to communicate the vision for a product?

Sketches and drawings

Do you ever 'doodle'? Do you find that it helps you to think? A sketch is similar to a doodle because it may stimulate your thoughts and ideas and help you to put them on paper. You could sketch a few different design ideas very quickly and roughly to see what they look like before you start to focus on your final designs. You could:

- sketch an outline of your product

- add any design features that your target customers are interested in

- think about what the product looks like and where you could add any decoration or patterns

- add any other design features that you would like to try out.

You could then use these sketches as a basis for your product designs.

Let's get practical!   2

Using one of the creative techniques described here, produce a design idea for the bag that you suggested for Jamie's new range (Let's get practical! 1). You need to:

a   identify which of the creative techniques you will use to collate your ideas and then use it to come up with one design idea

b   generate your design idea. The design must include:

  i   at least two accessories (e.g. a detachable strap, a decoration (e.g. metal studs) or a key ring)

  ii   a logo or brand

c   write a short explanation of how you used your chosen creative technique to come up with a design idea for your bag.

3.3 Review designs for a product proposal

Let's get started   2

How might an entrepreneur find out whether target customers will like a new product design? Why do they need to know this?

When an entrepreneur designs a new product, they will think that it is a great idea and a great product. However, as part of the design process it is important to find out what customers think of the design and whether it meets their needs. Otherwise, the entrepreneur may spend money **manufacturing** the product, packaging it and advertising it only to find that no one buys it. Reviewing the product design is therefore an essential part of the product's development.

How to review designs for a product proposal

Self-assessment

Self-assessment involves the entrepreneur looking at their designs and deciding what they personally think are the strengths and weaknesses. The entrepreneur needs to ask themselves:

- What are the design's strengths – what is good about it?

- What are its weaknesses – what can I improve?

- Does it meet the needs of my target customers?

- Have I based my design on my market research findings?

Methods of gaining feedback

Feedback from others is also an important part of the review process. Balanced feedback not only tells the entrepreneur what people like about the product, but also what people dislike about the product or what does not work, so that they can make improvements. For example, you could gain feedback from friends, family or peers.

Table 2.14 outlines the three different methods of obtaining feedback and the advantages and disadvantages of each method.

Planning methods of gaining feedback on your design proposal

In the same way that you planned the market research which you carried out for Topic Area 1, Let's get practical! 1, you now need to plan how you are going to gather feedback on your designs. The more detailed your planning is, the more likely you are to gain useful feedback. This will help you to **finalise** which design you will take on to the next stage of the design process.

Table 2.14: Methods of feedback

Market research tool	How to gain feedback	Advantages	Disadvantages
Verbal feedback	• Discuss your designs individually with peers (e.g. friends and other students in your class) • Telephone surveys. You would need to send people your designs (e.g. by email) and ask them verbal questions to find out what they think • Focus groups (e.g. arranging for a group of people, who would be in your target group, to meet together and discuss your designs)	• You can gain detailed information and opinions by asking additional questions • Individuals can ask if they do not understand a question • Individual discussions or focus groups allow you to see people's reactions to your designs (e.g. non-verbal communication) • If face-to-face, you can show people the design and see their reaction	• It is very time-consuming to speak to lots of people • Telephone surveys mean that you have to find a way to send your designs to the people you are surveying, e.g. by email or via social media • It can be harder to convey opinions face-to-face as people may be embarrassed to express their true feelings • You might forget what was said if responses were not written down accurately
Written feedback	• Design a questionnaire that you print out and then ask people to fill in • Email your questionnaire to potential customers and ask them to fill it in and return it	• You will have written evidence of the responses that people give • You can ask lots of people to give feedback, particularly if you email the questionnaire to participants	• Creating and printing a questionnaire is time-consuming • It may be quite costly if you need to print out lots of questionnaires • Feedback might not be as detailed as it would be with verbal responses
Online feedback	• Post your designs on social media and ask for **constructive feedback** • Post your designs on an online community (e.g. TikTok) to receive feedback • Design a questionnaire on a platform such as SurveyMonkey for people to complete	• You will have written evidence of the responses that people give • It is a fast way of showing your design to lots of people • You may receive feedback from a wide range of people in different locations	• It may be harder to target the relevant audience as not everyone will have access to the online platforms • Feedback posted online may not be constructive or fair, and anyone viewing the post can see unrepresentative/unfair feedback. • You will have less control over who the feedback is from than with verbal and written feedback • Competitors may see your design and copy it before it is launched onto the market

Over to you! 2

Have you ever been asked to provide feedback for anyone? This could include commenting on another student's work or presentation, an online survey or someone asking your opinions in the street.

1 What was the feedback about? Who was it for?

2 Which method of feedback was used?

3 Do you think that the method used was appropriate? Why/Why not?

Your product proposal 3

Gaining feedback

The areas that you need to think about in your planning include:

- What methods will I use? Remember that you have to gain verbal **and** written feedback.
- How many people do I need to interview or survey? How many people do I need to talk to?
- If I am going to use a questionnaire, what questions do I need to ask?
- If I am going to arrange a focus group, what will we discuss and how quickly can I arrange a venue etc.?
- If I am going to use online feedback, which platform is the best to make sure that my target customers see the designs?

Your product proposal   4

Identifying your designs' strengths and weaknesses

Once you have your plan, you need to follow it and collect the feedback. You will then be ready to identify the strengths and weaknesses of the designs you have created for your assessment (Figure 2.31).

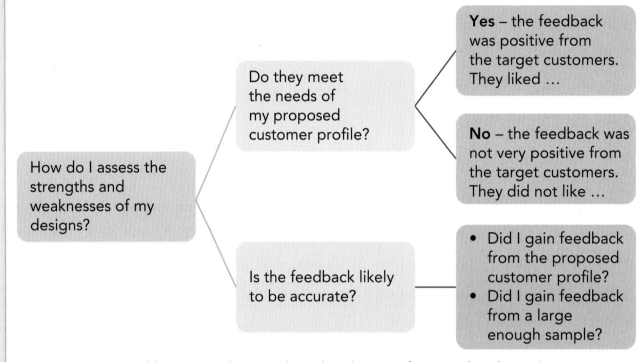

Figure 2.31: How would you assess the strengths and weaknesses of your product designs?

Let's get practical!   3

You have designed a new bag for Jamie's range. Now you need to get feedback about your design to find out whether it meets the needs of the target customers.

1   Write three questions that you could ask to gain verbal or written feedback about the bag you have designed.

2   Based on your own self-assessment of the design:

    a   identify **two strengths** and **two weaknesses** of the design

    b   explain how it will meet the needs of the customer profile that you identified (Let's get practical! 1).

How to finalise a design after feedback

Once the entrepreneur has gathered feedback on their designs, and they have identified the strengths and weaknesses, they need to decide which of the designs is likely to best meet customer needs. For your assessment, you will need to decide which of your designs best meets customer needs.

Depending on customer feedback, the entrepreneur is likely to need to make **modifications** (changes) to their chosen design to make sure that it successfully and fully meets customer needs. For example, customers might think that the product is too big, so the entrepreneur will need to see if they can make it smaller. Customers might have thought it was likely to be too expensive based on the materials used. So the entrepreneur will need to consider whether they can use cheaper materials to make the product less expensive, without affecting the quality. Negative feedback does not mean that the product is a failure or that the design is poor. Rather, negative feedback gives the entrepreneur an opportunity to identify weaknesses and make improvements so that the product is even more suitable.

Your product proposal   5

Finalising your design

For the designs you have created for your assessment, you need to think about your initial market research findings:

- What did potential customers actually want?

- What was your self-assessment of the designs?

- What was the feedback from others on your designs?

- What were the strengths and weaknesses that you identified?

Once you have all of this information you need to:

a decide which of the designs meets customer needs the most closely

b decide which of the designs has the most strengths and fewest weaknesses

c choose which of the designs you are going to finalise (i.e. make modifications to) so that it meets the customers' needs and overcome any weaknesses

d make the relevant modifications and explain why you have made these.

Let's get practical! 4

Think back to the weaknesses that you identified for the bag which you designed (Let's get practical! 3). What changes would you make so that it better meets the needs of the target customers?

Review your learning

Test your knowledge

1. What are the three elements of the design mix?
2. Explain how the requirement to break even might impact the design mix.
3. Identify one advantage and one disadvantage of using verbal feedback to review product designs.
4. Identify one advantage and one disadvantage of using written feedback to review product designs.
5. Explain one reason why an entrepreneur might need to make changes to a design.

What have you learnt?

	See section
• Create a design mix for a new product.	3.1
• Produce designs for a new product.	3.2
• Review designs for a product proposal.	3.3

Review whether a business proposal is financially viable

Let's get started   1

Think back to Unit R067, Topic Area 3. What does the term 'financial viability' mean? What makes a product financially viable? Why must a new product be financially viable?

What will you learn?

- How to calculate costs, **revenues**, break-even and profit relating to a business proposal.

- How to apply an appropriate **pricing strategy**.

- How to review the likely **financial viability** of a business proposal.

4.1 Calculate costs, revenues, break-even and profit relating to a business proposal

Once an entrepreneur has finalised their design, they need to calculate the:

- costs of making the product

- revenue that they are likely to receive from selling it

- likely **break-even point**

- likely profit.

These calculations allow them to assess the financial viability of the product. If a product is not financially viable, it is unlikely that the entrepreneur will be able to continue with the plan to produce and sell the product.

Costs

When producing a product, a business/entrepreneur needs to consider the different types of costs that they will incur. Managing costs is therefore essential for all entrepreneurs and businesses.

- If a business's costs are higher than its revenue, the business will not make a profit. If this continues in the longer term, then the business is likely to fail.

- If a business's costs are too high and it is only just making enough revenue to cover them, the business will see low profits.

Table 2.15 provides a recap of the types of costs.

Table 2.15: Different types of costs

Type of cost	Definition
Fixed costs	<ul><li>Costs that do not vary with output (i.e. they are the same whatever the quantity that the business produces)</li><li>Examples: factory rent, advertising, **salaries** paid to employees and **insurance**</li></ul>
Variable costs	<ul><li>Costs that vary with output (i.e. they change if the business produces more or fewer units/products)</li><li>Examples: **raw materials** (e.g. the wool to make a jumper), packaging, **wages** (paid by the hour or per unit produced)</li></ul>
Total costs	<ul><li>Fixed costs + variable costs</li></ul>

For more information on costs, see Unit R067, Section 3.

Knowing the costs of producing a product will also help a business to determine the proposed selling price for the product.

Proposed selling price per unit

An entrepreneur needs to think carefully about what the selling price for a new product should be. There are a number of factors that they should consider, including:

- **the costs of producing the product** – setting a selling price that is lower than the costs of producing the product would result in a **loss**

- **the price that competitors are charging for similar products** – this is found by researching competitors' products and pricing. The entrepreneur should charge a similar price to those of similar competing products, otherwise customers are likely to buy the competitor's product because it is cheaper

- **the price that customers are willing to pay** – market research will have identified the price that target customers are willing to pay. This should be the maximum price that the entrepreneur charges, otherwise the product will be seen as too expensive.

In the real world, the entrepreneur would decide on their pricing strategy (see Section 4.2) before deciding on the actual price.

Revenue

Revenue is the income that a business earns from selling a product or service. A business needs revenue to pay the costs that it incurs and to **break even** or make a profit. The formula for total revenue is:

> **total revenue = selling price × number of products sold**

For more information on revenue, see Unit R067, Section 3.2.

Over to you!　1

How do each of the businesses listed below earn revenue? How many ways can you think of for each business?

a　A large supermarket (e.g. Tesco)

b　Amazon

c　A petrol station.

Break-even

For a business to survive, it needs to at least break even (see Unit R067, Section 3.4). To break even, the business has to receive enough revenue to cover all of its costs.

A business can use the **break-even level of sales** calculation to:

- estimate the level of sales required to cover all costs – so the business knows the number of products they need to sell in order to not make a loss

- **estimate profitability** – if the predicted level of sales is greater than the break-even level of sales, the product will make a profit

- **make future business decisions** – if the calculation shows that the product will not break even or is only just breaking even, the business/entrepreneur can take action to improve profitability. This could include increasing or reducing costs or increasing revenue by raising the price.

The formula for break-even is:

$$\text{break-even level of sales} = \frac{\text{fixed costs}}{(\text{selling price} - \text{variable costs per unit})}$$

Impact on break-even of changing the price

- **Increase in price** – if a business increases the price of a product, it needs to sell fewer products to break even. However, if it increases the selling price, some customers will probably think that the product is too expensive. They may choose not to buy it at all or buy a competitor's product that is cheaper. As a result, the number of sales may fall. If they fall significantly, the business may not break even.

- **Decrease in price** – if a business reduces the price of a product, it needs to sell more of the product to break even. However, the lower selling price might encourage more customers to buy the product. If sales increase significantly, the business should break even and hopefully make higher profits.

For more information on break-even, see Unit R067, Section 3.4. For more information on the impact of changing price on break-even, see Section 4.3 in this unit.

Profit

Most entrepreneurs set up a business and design and produce a new product with the aim of making a profit. If the entrepreneur's product does not make a profit, or at least break even, the product and the business are likely to fail.

The formulae for calculating profit per unit and total profit are:

> **profit per unit = selling price (for one item) − total cost (for producing one item)**

> **total profit = total revenue − total costs**

For more information on profit, see Unit R067, Section 3.3.

Let's get practical!   1

1 Challenge Sports is a sports shop that sells a wide variety of sports equipment and clothing.

For each of the items sold by Challenge Sports last year, use the information in Table 2.16 to calculate:

a   total cost per unit

b   total costs

c   total revenue

d   the break-even level of sales and explain what your answer shows

e   profit/loss per unit

f   total profit/loss.

Table 2.16: Financial information relating to items sold by Challenge Sports last year

Product	Variable cost per item (£)	Fixed costs (£)	Selling price per item (£)	Number sold in the last year
Football	2.00	14 000	9.00	5 000
Hockey stick	6.00	27 000	24.00	850
Sports socks	0.50	15 000	4.00	16 000

Stretch

2 Is the proposed selling price for each item appropriate? Explain your answers.

3 The sports socks are selling very well, so Challenge Sports is thinking about increasing the selling price to £5.00.

a   How many will they need to sell at the new price to break even?

b   Do you think that they will sell as many pairs of sports socks if they increase the price? Explain your answer.

4.2 Apply an appropriate pricing strategy

Let's get started 2

The following are two terms that entrepreneurs might need to use when thinking about pricing strategies.

P_IC_ P_N_TRA_ION

_R_CE _K_MM_NG

Can you work out what the terms are by putting the missing letters in the gaps? What do you think the terms mean?

Tip: Look back to Unit R067, Section 4.10 to refresh your memory.

There are a number of pricing strategies that a business can use, as shown in Table 2.17.

Table 2.17: Pricing strategies

Pricing strategy	Definition and purpose	Advantages	Disadvantages
Competitive pricing	• The price is set at the same or a similar level to competitors' prices • Supermarkets price match one another on essential products (e.g. milk) • If a new version of a product (e.g. a technology product) has been launched, the price of older versions may be reduced to match prices charged by competitors for similar products	• Competitors do not have a price advantage • Customers are willing to pay that price	• If all competitors charge the same price, the market will be very competitive (e.g. businesses will need to provide the best customer service to stand out) • Can lead to low prices and low profits
Price penetration	• Setting a low price (at least to begin with) to attract people to try/buy the product, build brand loyalty and gain **market share** • Once the product is established and customers have become loyal, the price can be increased • A new cereal might be introduced in a supermarket at half price and then eventually go up to full price	• Customers might be attracted to try the product • May create customer loyalty as customers switch from competing brands	• Likely to mean lower profits while the price is low • The business must be able to survive while selling at the lower price, i.e. the price must cover the production costs so that the business is not making a loss

Table 2.17: Continued

Pricing strategy	Definition and purpose	Advantages	Disadvantages
Price skimming	• Initially setting the price at the highest price that customers are prepared to pay and reducing it as competitors enter the market or the product is updated (e.g. to the latest technology). Apple launches products, such as the iPhone and iPad, at premium prices making higher profits. Within a few months they usually drop the price	• Need to sell fewer products at the higher price to break even • The high price may create an image of a high-quality product/ brand	• Price skimming can only be used while the product has a USP (i.e. no direct competitors) • Some customers may not be prepared to pay the high price • Revenue and profit may be low if customers are put off by the high price • Competitors may quickly introduce new products at a lower price and take market share
Psychological pricing	• Setting a price that makes customers think the product is cheaper • Selling a laptop for £479 rather than £480	• Customers may see the product as being better value/ more affordable • As the price is only reduced slightly (e.g. by £1) it will not have a significant effect on revenue	• Customers might feel that the business is taking advantage of them • There is no guarantee that the number of sales will increase

A business may have designed an attractive product that is fit for purpose, but if it is priced incorrectly it will not be a success.

• If the price is too high then, unless it is a premium product, customers may not be willing to pay the price and the business will not sell many products.

• If the price is too low, the business may not be able to break even or make a profit. Also, if the price is too low, demand might be so high that the business cannot make enough of the product to keep all customers happy.

Select an appropriate pricing strategy

Although a business needs to make a profit, this is not the only thing that it should consider when it is deciding on a price to charge and a pricing strategy. It also needs to think about:

- the type of product (e.g. if it incorporates new technology then people may be willing to pay a higher price so that they can be the first to own it)

- how competitors price their products (e.g. if competitors use psychological pricing, then the business may need to use the same pricing strategy, otherwise they might appear to be more expensive)

- how unique the product is (e.g. is it a well-known brand name that people are willing to pay a higher price for?)

- the amount of competition (e.g. a new product entering a competitive market might need to use price penetration to get customers to try the product rather than continuing to buy their current brand)

- the price that the target customers are willing to pay based on market research findings.

Case study

Tea 'n' Cake

Last year Naomi, the owner of Tea 'n' Cake, decided to add a new cherry and almond cake to the range of products she was selling. The normal selling price is £10. To attract customers to try the new flavour, she placed an introductory offer on Tea 'n' Cake's website where the cake cost £5. The offer was very successful and she received hundreds of orders. She had to employ six extra staff to meet the additional demand, which meant that she made a loss of £1.50 on every cake she sold.

Check your understanding

1   Which pricing strategy is this an example of?

2   What does the success of this discount deal suggest about the price that Naomi usually sells her cakes for? Explain your answer.

3   Explain two drawbacks to Tea 'n' Cake of making a loss of £1.50 per cake.

Over to you! 2

1 Which pricing strategies do you think are used for the products in the images in Figure 2.32?

2 For each product, explain why you think the chosen pricing strategy is appropriate.

Figure 2.32: Which pricing strategies are used for these products?

Your product proposal 1

Selecting an appropriate pricing strategy and selling price

- You will need to select an appropriate pricing strategy and selling price for your design proposal for your assessment, and give reasons for your decisions.

- This pricing strategy and selling price need to fit with your market research and customer profile (i.e. to show that people are willing to pay the price you have chosen).

- Your selling price ideally needs to cover your costs to help you to break even and make a profit.

- However, the price must also fit with your chosen pricing strategy (e.g. if you choose price penetration then it may be that your product will not break even during the introductory period).

- Over to you! 3 will help you identify how to make pricing decisions based on the target customers' profiles.

- Remember that choosing the right selling price and pricing strategy is important because the price must be one that target customers are willing to pay. Just because it is a price that will allow you to break even or make a profit does not mean customers are willing to buy the product at that price.

Over to you!   3

Using Table 2.18, identify the likely customer profile for the following scenarios. For each one, explain your decision.

a   Nike launch a new range of white fashion trainers.

b   Sony launches a new 16K resolution Smart TV.

c   Primark launches a new range of sportswear.

d   A new hotel opens in London that is aimed at couples who are holidaying without children.

Table 2.18: Different customer profiles can impact pricing strategies

Customer profile A	Customer profile B	Customer profile C
• Aged 14 to 18 • Student • Interested in music • Receives pocket money of £8 per week	• Aged 25 to 35 • Earns £35 000 to £50 000 per year • Likes playing sport and socialising • Lives in a town or city	• Aged 65+ • Receives a pension of £16 000 to £25 000 per year • Interested in gardening and watching TV

Customer profiles can impact pricing strategy decisions. See Table 2.18 for examples of three different customer profiles.

Apple is most likely to target a new product at customer profile B, because this group has a relatively high income.

Price skimming would be an appropriate pricing strategy for Apple to use when launching the product to take advantage of people who are willing to pay a high price for the latest technology and for an Apple-branded product.

A year later, when Apple has launched a newer version of the product, the price of the older version may become more competitive and more targeted at customer profile C. People in profile C are likely to be less willing to pay a high price for the latest technology but may still be interested in owning an Apple product.

A new range of Primark sportswear is most likely to be aimed at customer profile A. As the income level for customer profile A is low and there are likely to be many other businesses selling similar sportswear, Primark is most likely to use a competitive pricing strategy.

Over to you! **4**

Research three completely different types of products that have been launched in the last year.

Which pricing strategy has each business used for the products? Why?

For more information on pricing strategies, see Unit R067, Section 4.10.

4.3 Review the likely financial viability of a business proposal

Let's get started **3**

What might happen if a new product does not break even? Might it depend on the size of the business? Why/why not?

Once a new product has been designed, a business will need to work out whether the idea is financially viable (Figure 2.33).

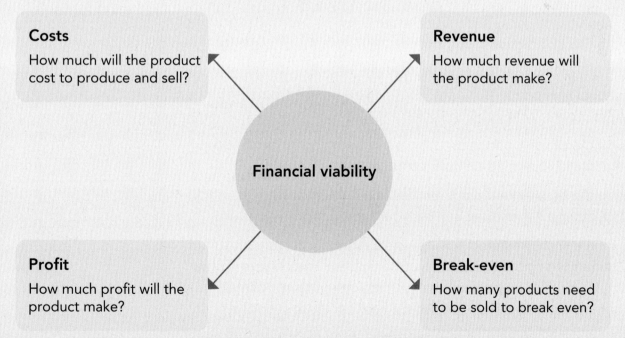

Costs
How much will the product cost to produce and sell?

Revenue
How much revenue will the product make?

Financial viability

Profit
How much profit will the product make?

Break-even
How many products need to be sold to break even?

Figure 2.33: What needs to be calculated to decide whether a new product is financially viable?

Likelihood of breaking even

In order to survive, a business needs to at least break even (i.e. receive enough revenue to cover their costs). Most large businesses produce more than one product. So if one product does not break even, they can hopefully survive by breaking even and earning profit on other products. For an entrepreneur who may only produce and sell one or two products it is important that all of their products at least break even.

Your product proposal   2

Calculating the likelihood that your product will break even

1   Identify and calculate the total fixed costs and total variable costs for the product you have designed in your assessment.

2   By referring to your primary and secondary market research, predict the number of sales you are likely to achieve. For example:

   a   How many people said they would be interested in buying your product?

   b   How many people said they would be interested in buying your product at the price you intend to sell it for?

   c   Did you have any secondary information about how many of a similar product your competitors sell?

Tip: You need to make sure that your predicted sales are realistic for a new product and a small business. You are very unlikely to sell millions in your first year!

3   Using the primary and secondary market research information, identify a selling price for your product.

4   Using the break-even formula in Section 4.1, calculate how many products you will need to sell for your product to break even.

5   Compare your predicted number of sales to the actual number of sales needed to break even. Is your predicted sales figure higher than, lower than or the same as the break-even level of sales? What impact is this likely to have on your business proposal?

Let's get practical!   **2**

Challenge Sports is launching a new range of tennis rackets. Table 2.19 shows the variable costs, fixed costs and predicted level of sales for the new range.

Using the information in the table and the formula in Section 4.1, calculate whether each product is likely to break even. Show your workings.

Table 2.19: Predicted financial information for a new range of tennis rackets

Product	Selling price (per item) £	Variable cost (per item) £	Fixed costs allocated to that item (per month) £	Predicted sales (per month) £
Shot X racket	12.00	4.20	56 000	50 000
Storm racket	22.00	8.80	56 000	32 000
Majestic racket	35.00	14.50	56 000	28 000

Changing the sales price

Changing the selling price of a product is one way that an entrepreneur can influence the number of sales. The lower the price, the higher the level of sales is likely to be. However, the revenue per item will be lower. This means that reducing the selling price will not always increase the likelihood of breaking even. Sales would need to increase significantly to balance out the reduction in price.

Case study

Amazon Fire phone

In 2014, Amazon tried to break into the mobile phone market in the USA by launching the Amazon Fire phone. However, the product was not popular with customers, and only 15 months after the phone had been launched Amazon decided to withdraw it from sale. Amazon made approximately $170 million in losses mainly due to a lack of customers purchasing the Fire phone product.

Check your understanding

1   Identify two variable costs that Amazon would have had when manufacturing the Amazon Fire mobile phone.

2   What could Amazon have done to encourage more customers to buy the Amazon Fire mobile phone?

3   Explain one reason why Amazon would have wanted the Amazon Fire mobile phone to break even.

Figure 2.34: Amazon launched its Amazon Fire phone in 2014

Stretch

4   Amazon reduced the price of the Amazon Fire mobile phone from $649 when it was launched to $149.

    What impact would this have had on Amazon's break-even level of sales?

Your product proposal   3

Calculating the impact of a change in price on break-even

Once you have calculated your break-even level of sales, you might find that this does not match the price that your market research says customers are willing to pay. As a result, you may need to look at reducing your selling price.

By reducing the price you may increase sales, but the revenue will be lower. To break even, you will need to make enough extra sales to make up for the reduction in price and the fall in revenue.

1   If a lower selling price was suggested by your market research, calculate the new **break-even quantity** and describe what the results show.

2   Describe the impact of the lower price on the level of sales needed to break even and the impact on your business proposal.

Case study

Cana Sauces – A new BBQ sauce

Cana Sauces is a family-owned food manufacturing business that produces tomato sauce using a traditional family recipe. When it started out, it carried out market research and used the information to decide on a selling price and their monthly sales. It also calculated the variable and fixed costs (Table 2.20).

Table 2.20: Predicted financial information for tomato sauce

Product	Selling price £	Variable cost (per bottle) £	Fixed costs allocated to tomato sauce (per month) £	Predicted sales (number of bottles per month)
Tomato sauce	1.45	0.59	£36 000	12 000

Figure 2.35: Cana Sauces is launching its new sauce with an introductory offer price to get customers to try it

Cana Sauces has decided to launch a new BBQ sauce. As the product is new to the market, it has decided to launch it with an introductory offer price to get customers to try it. Table 2.21 shows the variable cost, fixed costs, selling price and predicted sales for both the introductory offer and the normal selling price.

Table 2.21: Predicted financial information for BBQ sauce

Product	Pricing strategy	Selling price (per item) £	Variable cost (per item) £	Fixed costs allocated to BBQ sauce (per month) £	Predicted sales (number of bottles per month)
BBQ sauce	Introductory offer (price penetration)	1.80	0.64	39 000	90 000
BBQ sauce	Normal selling price	2.20	0.64	39 000	65 000

Continued

Check your understanding

1 a Using the break-even formula in Section 4.1, calculate Cana Sauces' break-even level of sales for their tomato sauce.

   b Looking at the predicted sales per month, did the tomato sauce break even? If so, by how many bottles?

2 a Calculate the break-even level of sales for the BBQ sauce at the:

      i introductory price

      ii normal selling price.

   b For each price, explain whether the product will break even.

3 Calculate the predicted profit/loss at the:

   a introductory price

   b normal selling price.

Stretch

4 Should Cana Sauces consider continuing to sell the new BBQ sauce at the introductory price rather than increasing it to the normal selling price? Justify your answer.

Likelihood of making a profit

Let's get started 4

Why does an entrepreneur need to make a profit? How might the business benefit if it makes a profit?

In the short term an entrepreneur can survive by breaking even. In the long term they need to make a profit, otherwise there is no **reward** for their time, effort and ideas. The business is unlikely to survive if it does not make a profit. The entrepreneur therefore needs to work out the likelihood of their product/business making a profit.

Your product proposal 4

Calculating the likelihood of making a profit

For your design proposal in your assessment, you will need to calculate the likelihood of it making a profit for the first month.

Start by calculating the predicted:

a **Total revenue:** total revenue = selling price × predicted sales

b **Total costs:** total costs = variable costs + fixed costs

Then you can use the formula below to calculate total predicted profit:

c **Total profit:** total profit = total revenue − total costs

When a small business launches a new product, it may take time for customers to become aware of the product and buy it. This means that profit figures may be low initially, but the product may be profitable in the long run. The business will need to decide whether it thinks that its new product is likely to make a profit.

Over to you! 5

What impact could it have on a new business if the predicted revenue and profit figures are inaccurate?

Review your learning

Test your knowledge

1   Which of the following is the formula for calculating total costs?

   a   fixed costs – variable costs

   b   fixed costs + variable costs

   c   revenue – fixed costs

2   Explain why it is important for a business to break even.

3   Explain psychological pricing and give an example of a business that uses psychological pricing.

4   A business has total costs of £450 per week and revenue of £460 per week. Is the business making a profit or a loss?

5   A business is not breaking even. Explain what the business can do to try to reach the break-even level of sales.

What have you learnt?

	See section
• How to calculate costs, revenues, break-even and profit relating to a business proposal.	4.1
• How to apply an appropriate pricing strategy.	4.2
• How to review the likely financial viability of a business proposal.	4.3

Review the likely success of the business proposal

Let's get started   1

What is the product shown in the photo? It was first launched in 1974. Do you think this product would be successful today? Why/why not?

Figure 2.36: Do you think this product would be successful today?

What will you learn?

• Risks and challenges when launching a new product.

5.1 Risks and challenges when launching a new product

Having designed the product and made sure that it is financially viable, it is now time to launch the new product. Whilst this is an exciting time, there are many risks and challenges involved with launching a product. Entrepreneurs need to consider these to ensure that their product proposal is successful. Even large, well-known businesses have to **minimise** or overcome risks and challenges when developing and launching a new product.

Figure 2.37 identifies possible risks and challenges that an entrepreneur may face when launching a new product.

Figure 2.37: What are the risks and challenges when launching a new product?

Impact of external factors

External factors are factors outside of the business's control. Some external factors can have negative impacts and some can have positive impacts. If a business/entrepreneur spends time thinking about which factors might impact the launch of the new product, they can put plans in place to try to minimise (reduce) any negative impact.

As businesses operate in an ever-changing world, external factors can have a huge impact on them. Table 2.22 gives some examples of external factors that a business should research, be aware of and plan for.

Table 2.22: Examples of external factors that may impact a business

Political	• **Government policy and incentives:** are **grants** available to help fund new businesses/business ideas? What will Brexit mean for the UK in the long term? • **Taxation:** what is the rate of corporation tax that a business has to pay? What is the rate of VAT? If taxes increase, the business's costs will increase. • **Laws:** the Government can introduce new laws (e.g. minimum wage or health and safety) which may change the way a business works and increase its costs.
Economic	• **Employment/unemployment rates:** if people are unemployed, will they have enough money to buy the new product? • **Rate of economic growth:** in an **economic boom** period people are more likely to spend money than in a **recession**, which may affect the selling price that a business can charge. • **Interest rates:** when interest rates are high, people save their money and spend less. When they are low, people are less likely to save and may be more willing to spend money on new products.
Social	• **Population growth rates:** this relates to whether the population is growing or shrinking. What is the size of the overall market? Is it growing? • **Age distribution of the population:** if a product is aimed at teenagers, is this a growing or shrinking market? • **Consumer buying patterns and trends:** these are continually changing according to what is in fashion. • **Changing lifestyles, attitudes and opinions:** there is a greater focus currently on preventative health, such as healthy eating and exercise, so businesses need to consider this.
Technological	• **Level of innovation:** new technologies are continually emerging (e.g. artificial intelligence, 5G). A product that needs cutting-edge technology may have very high start-up costs and the product might need to be updated regularly. • **Online selling:** selling online reduces costs and increases the number of customers that the business can reach.
Legal	• **Copyright** and/or **patenting** (e.g. if a brand or logo is included on a product): obtaining copyrights and **patents** can be costly and time-consuming for the business. • **Local, national and international laws:** what laws does the business need to follow, e.g. health and safety regulations, employment law, environmental legislation?
Environmental	• **Environmental values:** is the product made using **sustainable** materials? Is the production process environmentally friendly, e.g. does it use renewable energy sources, such as solar or wind energy?
Ethical	• **Producing ethical products:** are the workers who produce the product and any materials in it treated fairly? Ethical practices may increase production costs, but customers are becoming increasingly aware of ethical issues so these practices may lead to increased sales. • **Paying fair wages:** paying workers the minimum wage permitted in a country will result in higher profits, but, even though legal, it might not be viewed as fair to the workers.

Copyright and patents

Copyright: If a design is under copyright, no one else can copy or use it without the owner's permission. Anyone who wants to use the design will have to pay a fee to the copyright owner to do so. This means that if an entrepreneur wants to use a logo that is under copyright, they will have to pay to do so and this will increase their costs.

Patent: A patent gives a product's inventor/creator the legal right to stop other people producing their invention. This gives that product a unique selling point (USP) because a competitor cannot produce and sell an identical product. Applying for a patent is a complex process that can take a few years. It is also quite costly.

Over to you!   1

Imagine that you are currently designing a new version of the following products. For each product listed below identify two external factors that are likely to impact the development of the product.

Tip: Work through the external factors in Table 2.22 to help you think which might be relevant in each case.

a   An instant coffee   c   A washing powder

b   A pair of denim jeans   d   A laptop

Competitors

A competitor is a business that sells the same or similar products. To be successful a business needs to make sure that its product has a USP that will differentiate the product (i.e. make it different) from those sold by competitors. Having a USP minimises the risk that customers will choose to buy the competitor's product instead.

When an entrepreneur is designing a new product there is always the risk that a competitor is designing a similar product. Therefore the entrepreneur's product might not be as unique as they had intended. This is a risk that an entrepreneur must consider as:

- it may have a negative impact on the likely success of the new product

- the entrepreneur is unlikely to be aware of competitors' products until they launch.

Over to you! 2

What might be the impacts on a Tesco store if a Lidl store opened next door to it?

Lack of business experience

When an entrepreneur starts a new business, they may not have much experience of running their own business. Even if the entrepreneur has worked for other businesses, they may not have been in overall charge. They are therefore unlikely to have been responsible for decisions relating to all of the different business functions (e.g. finance, marketing, legal requirements (such as making sure that the appropriate copyrights and patents have been applied for)).

This lack of experience may mean that the entrepreneur overlooks an important task which could impact on the business. For example:

- the entrepreneur might have no experience of working in finance, so they could make a mistake when calculating the break-even level of sales. As a result, they may set the price too low, so the business does not break even or make a profit

- the entrepreneur may forget to carry out a crucial process, such as applying for and registering a patent as they did not know it was needed. Forgetting to register a patent might mean that a competitor copies the entrepreneur's product idea and sells it without their permission.

Making a loss

No matter how much research the entrepreneur has done before launching a new product there is still a possibility that not enough people will buy the product to enable the business to at least break even. When starting a new enterprise, an entrepreneur with only one or two products will struggle if they are making a loss or only breaking even. Unlike bigger businesses, they cannot rely on other successful products that are making a profit to support the new product.

Over- and underestimating consumer demand

Market research findings are the basis for many decisions about new products. There is no guarantee that this research is accurate and it could have:

- **overestimated** consumer demand – fewer people than expected buy the actual product. This could lead to fewer sales and the business not breaking even

- **underestimated** consumer demand – more people than expected buy the product. The business could run out of products, leaving some customers disappointed, which could damage the business's reputation.

Case study

Panic buying in the UK

In March 2020, shops in the UK sold out of basic items such as toilet rolls, rice and flour. The government was about to announce a lockdown due to the COVID-19 pandemic and the public started panic buying. The shops had underestimated consumer demand for these products as they did not anticipate panic buying. As a result, they had not ordered enough stock from their suppliers. The problem was made worse because the suppliers of these products had also underestimated demand and had not produced enough to meet the unexpected increase in sales.

Figure 2.38: Underestimating consumer demand may mean that items sell out

Check your understanding

1. Why does underestimating consumer demand mean that items sell out?

2. Explain one financial impact on the shops that had sold out of the items.

3. Evaluate what the suppliers of these products could do to make sure that they do not underestimate consumer demand in the future.

Overspending on a budget

A **budget** is a prediction of likely income and expenditure over a period of time. For example, a business predicts that it will spend £10 000 in the next six months on all of its costs, e.g. wages, stock, electricity.

If the business spends £15 000 rather than the £10 000 it predicted, it may not break even because its costs are higher than it budgeted for.

The business has therefore overspent on its budget. The business will now need to sell more products to break even. If it does not, it could struggle to pay its day-to-day bills, which could put the business at risk.

How the impact of risks and challenges can be minimised or overcome

Let's get started　　**2**

Imagine that an entrepreneur needs to calculate their break-even level of sales, but they have very little knowledge about finance. How could they overcome this challenge?

If a new product is going to be successful an entrepreneur must think about potential risks and challenges. Once an entrepreneur has identified potential risks and challenges that may impact the launch of a new product, they need to think about different ways of overcoming them (Table 2.23).

Table 2.23: Methods of minimising or overcoming risks and challenges

Method	How does it minimise or overcome risks and challenges?	Example
Use of experienced advisors	An entrepreneur is unlikely to be an expert in every area of a business. Also they may not have much experience of running their own business. To help them overcome risks and challenges, they can use advisors who have experience in different business functions (e.g. financial advisors, legal advisors, sales and marketing consultants)	• A financial advisor could give advice about how to record the money coming into and going out of the business to minimise the risk of inaccurate financial calculations • A business mentor with experience of running a business can give an entrepreneur support and advice about dealing with challenges. They can share their own knowledge and be a role model
Contingency planning	A **contingency plan** is a plan that a business/entrepreneur puts in place in case an unexpected event or situation occurs. It helps to ensure that an entrepreneur is prepared for whatever may happen	• If a bakery's oven breaks down then it will not be able to bake the bread to meet customer demand. If the bakery has planned for this situation, it could have some pre-baked loaves in a large freezer that it can defrost and sell. • The bakery will still be able to sell bread so its customers will not go to a competitor. • Even if it does not have enough bread in the freezer for all of its customers, by having a contingency plan in place it has minimised the risk of losing all revenue until the oven is repaired
Detailed research	Detailed research gives an entrepreneur a thorough knowledge of the **external environment**. Detailed research could be: • market research • competitor research • research into **economic conditions** • research into costs	• **Market research** will help the entrepreneur to find out what products customers might want to buy or what price they are willing to pay. That way, the products meet customers' needs and the business minimises the risk of products not being sold • **Competitor research** will find out whether they are currently selling a product similar to the one the entrepreneur is designing • How might **economic conditions**, such as the long-term effects of Brexit, affect the business? The business will know in advance what paperwork and documentation is needed to sell products to Europe. This will minimise the risk of it not being completed and thereby delaying the supply of raw materials, for example • Researching **costs** will show whether these can be reduced (e.g. can a cheaper supplier be found for materials, but at a similar quality?)
Attending training courses	Entrepreneurs may have gaps in their knowledge or need to extend their knowledge about business functions that they lack experience in. Training courses are a great way of learning and developing knowledge, understanding and skills	Online training courses that teach the basics of setting up a business or book-keeping courses on how to keep business **accounts** will help the entrepreneur to obtain new knowledge and skills that they may lack. This will minimise the risk of making poor decisions and inaccurate financial calculations

Case study

Innocent Drinks – Contingency planning

When Innocent Drinks first launched its smoothies onto the market in 1999, the business used one company to supply all of its plastic bottles. Not long after the launch, the supplier informed Innocent Drinks that it had received a large order for bottles from another customer and could no longer supply any of Innocent's smoothie bottles. The situation taught the owners a lesson – to focus on Plan A, but to have a contingency plan in case something unexpected happens.

Figure 2.39: Innocent Drinks had to rapidly come up with a solution when there was an interruption to the supply of its plastic bottles

Check your understanding

1   What is a contingency plan?

2   Explain the likely impact of the lack of plastic bottles on Innocent Drinks' smoothies.

3   Assess what actions Innocent Drinks could include in a contingency plan to minimise the likelihood of this problem happening again.

Let's get practical!   1

Read the four scenarios below:

- Layla has designed a new fashion range aimed at teenagers. She has qualifications in fashion design but does not know anything about managing business finances.

- Jasmine has designed a new fitness tracker. Unemployment rates in the UK are starting to increase.

- Ahmed started selling a new folding bicycle last year. He realises that if he is to grow his business, he needs to understand more about marketing and **promotion**.

- Natalie is launching a new flavoured tea next month. She does not know whether any competitors are planning to launch a similar product.

1   State the risks and challenges for each entrepreneur.

2   Which method (from Table 2.23) would you use to minimise or overcome each of the risks and challenges faced by the entrepreneurs?

3   Evaluate how each of your suggestions would minimise or overcome the risk or challenge.

Your product proposal

Evaluating the impact of risks and challenges on the success of your business proposal

Once you have identified potential risks and challenges that may impact on the likely success of your business proposal, you will need to evaluate how significant they might be and whether you can minimise or overcome any of them.

You could use the process shown in Figure 2.40 to help you identify:

- what the risks and challenges are

- whether you can minimise or overcome them

- how big an impact the risks and challenges are likely to have on the successful launch of the product.

| Are there any potential risks and challenges for your new product? | What impact might these have on the success of your new product? | How can you minimise or overcome the risks and challenges? | Will these risks and challenges affect the likely success of your new product? |

Figure 2.40: How would you evaluate the likely success of your business proposal?

Case study

Cadbury Dairy Milk

In July 2020, Cadbury launched three new special edition flavours of Dairy Milk:

- Gillian's Cadbury Dairy Milk Coconutty

- Shannon's Cadbury Dairy Milk Crunchy Honeycomb

- Taylor's Cadbury Dairy Milk Out of the Blueberry.

Figure 2.41: Cadbury launched three new special edition flavours of Dairy Milk in 2020

Continued

The public had the opportunity to vote for their favourite, and the winner was added to the Dairy Milk range. Shannon's Cadbury Dairy Milk Crunchy Honeycomb was the winner.

Check your understanding

1   Identify three risks or challenges that Cadbury may face when launching new products.

2   Explain how Cadbury might try to minimise or overcome each of these risks and challenges.

3   The winning product became part of the Cadbury Dairy Milk range and was launched as Cadbury Honeycomb & Nuts. Why might introducing a new product as part of a competition help it to be a success?

Review your learning

Test your knowledge

1   Identify four external factors that can affect whether a new product is successful.

2   Why might a business struggle to survive if a new product makes a loss?

3   Why might a business overestimate or underestimate consumer demand?

4   Explain how contingency planning can help to minimise risks and challenges.

What have you learnt?

	See section
• Risks and challenges when launching a new product.	5.1

R069 | # Market and pitch a business proposal

Let's get started

What questions would you want to ask about this photo of Times Square, New York? How does the photo link to brands and marketing?

What will you learn in this unit?

From the local baker, who is well known for his high-quality products, to the tech giants fighting for market domination, brand is important to a business. You will learn about and understand the role and the power of brands and how they can separate a business from its competition. By understanding brands and branding, you will be able to create an appropriate promotional campaign for a product of your own.

In addition, you will learn and develop the skills necessary to pitch your business product and brand in a professional manner. The pitch will cover all of the key questions someone might have about your product and its unique selling points. The answers to these questions will enable you to market and sell your product effectively.

You will also develop your verbal and non-verbal skills, as well as your ability to review and evaluate your own work.

In this unit you will learn how to:

- develop a brand identity to target a specific customer profile **TA1**

- create a promotional campaign for a brand and product **TA2**

- plan and pitch a proposal **TA3**

- review a brand proposal, promotional campaign and professional pitch **TA4**.

How you will be assessed

This unit will be assessed through a series of coursework tasks that show your understanding of each topic area. You will complete the assignment independently in class with teacher supervision. The assignment will be marked by your teacher. The assignment contains five tasks. For example:

- developing a brand for your product

- creating a promotional campaign for your brand and product

- developing and delivering a pitch for your brand and product

- reviewing your brand, promotional campaign and pitch.

Develop a brand identity to target a specific customer profile

Let's get started 1

How would you **brand** yourself? List the **characteristics** of 'You' as a brand. Think of adjectives to describe yourself. What sets you apart from your friends?

What will you learn?

- What a brand is.
- Why branding is used.
- **Branding methods**.
- How to carry out a **competitor analysis**.

1.1 What is a brand?

A brand is a unique name and image of a company or a product that sets it apart from the competition. It is how the public sees a product or **business**, and it represents what the company stands for. A strong brand:

- helps a company or product to stand out in the market
- encourages customer loyalty
- leads to repeat sales
- allows a company to target a specific **customer profile**.

Over to you! 1

What does the word 'Apple' mean to you? Write down five words that you think describe the Apple brand.

Branding is made up of three distinct components, which a business must be aware of when creating a strong brand:

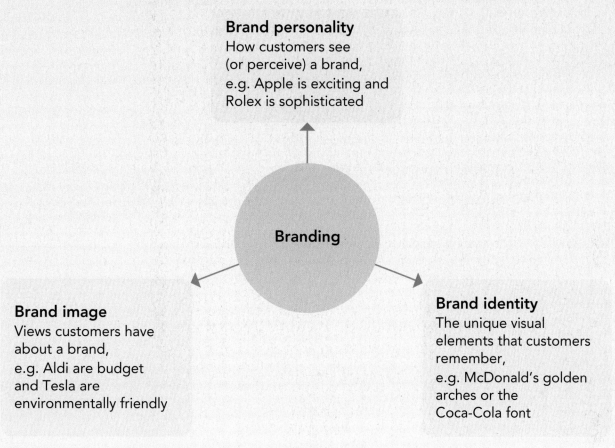

Brand personality
How customers see (or perceive) a brand, e.g. Apple is exciting and Rolex is sophisticated

Branding

Brand image
Views customers have about a brand, e.g. Aldi are budget and Tesla are environmentally friendly

Brand identity
The unique visual elements that customers remember, e.g. McDonald's golden arches or the Coca-Cola font

Figure 3.1: What are the three components of branding?

Brand personality

Think about all of your friends, classmates and family. How many different personality types are there? Brands, like people, develop a personality of their own.

Brand personality is how customers identify with a product or business, how they perceive it, and how they think it will act. For example, Fitbit uses exercise and social events to promote its products so it is seen as an 'exciting' and 'fun' brand. As a result, it attracts a similar kind of customer. Rolex, on the other hand, has a personality of sophistication and luxury, so it attracts a different kind of customer. Brand personality also influences how people feel about a brand.

Figure 3.2 shows different types of brand personality and examples of brands that match these personalities.

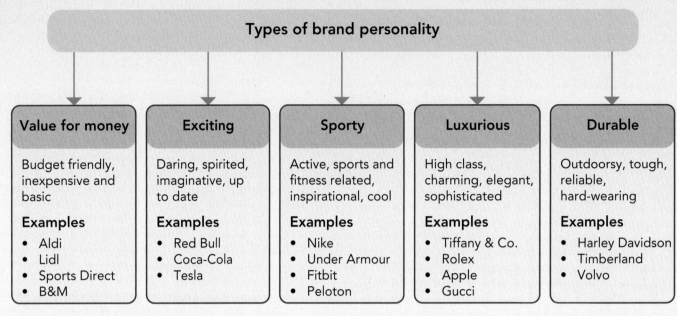

Types of brand personality

Value for money	Exciting	Sporty	Luxurious	Durable
Budget friendly, inexpensive and basic	Daring, spirited, imaginative, up to date	Active, sports and fitness related, inspirational, cool	High class, charming, elegant, sophisticated	Outdoorsy, tough, reliable, hard-wearing
Examples • Aldi • Lidl • Sports Direct • B&M	**Examples** • Red Bull • Coca-Cola • Tesla	**Examples** • Nike • Under Armour • Fitbit • Peloton	**Examples** • Tiffany & Co. • Rolex • Apple • Gucci	**Examples** • Harley Davidson • Timberland • Volvo

Figure 3.2: Different types of brand personality

A strong brand personality can:

- set a business apart from its competition

- help a business last

- emotionally connect a brand and its products with customers.

Case study

The 'Other' games console

In 2021, the global video games console market was worth nearly £99 billion. The market was dominated by three key players:

- Microsoft – Xbox

- Sony – PlayStation

- Nintendo – Switch.

Each brand has its fans and loyal customers, but Nintendo has managed to become the go-to name for family gaming and family friendly entertainment.

Figure 3.3: Each brand of video games console has its own brand personality

Continued

While Sony and Microsoft have spent their time **advertising** the raw power of their consoles and have developed an 'exciting' personality (Figure 3.2), Nintendo has focused on creating a more wholesome and cheerful personality to access the younger and family corners of the market.

So, while Xbox and PlayStation have developed fiercely loyal followers among avid gamers who play regularly, Nintendo, with its Switch console, has developed a strong brand name in family gaming by developing their own 'sincerity' personality. Nintendo is the only games console developer to focus on family gaming.

Even though Nintendo has competition from Microsoft and Sony, the products are viewed differently by many gamers and family entertainment users. Nintendo has successfully used a quirky, cheerful personality to stand out from the rest.

Check your understanding

1   How would you describe Nintendo's brand personality?

2   How has Nintendo achieved this personality? Explain your answer.

3   Explain how important brand personality is in setting Nintendo apart from Sony and Microsoft.

Over to you!   2

1   Think of your favourite brand of mobile phone, games console or clothing. If it was a person, how would you describe it? Which of the five personality types (durable, luxurious, sporty, value for money and exciting) does your favourite brand fit in to?

Stretch

2   Find some advertising for your chosen brand. Do you think its advertising matches the brand personality you have given it? Why/why not?

Brand identity

Just as your identity makes you unique and individual, a business has its own **brand identity** to separate it from its competition. Brand identity is the image that comes to mind when someone says the company's name, and it should reinforce the brand. In other words, it is the face of the brand.

Brand identity includes:

- **Visual look** – This includes all imagery and graphical information. It is what customers see of the brand. Every time you see an Apple advert or poster, the product being advertised is shown in clean, high-gloss surroundings which reflect the high quality of the brand.

- **Colours** – These need to be attractive and suit the personality of the brand, such as vibrant colours for fun and exciting brands or sleek and dark tones for more luxurious brands. McDonald's changed from its signature red backdrop to an earthy green in 2009 so that the colours reflected a more eco-friendly brand identity.

- **Typeface** – This is the font type. The choice of typeface is important as it can represent the tone and values of a brand and support a brand's identity. From the playful and fun typeface of Disney to the luxury style of Ralph Lauren, typeface can support a brand's identity.

- **Logo placement** – A **logo** has to be seen but it should not obscure the packaging, the advert or even the product itself. On the Xbox controller and console, the Xbox logo is front and centre and also functions as the power button.

A business uses brand identity to:

- attract new customers to a brand

- make a brand feel familiar to existing customers

- make a brand stand out from the competition.

Over to you!　3

1　Choose a brand you use or trust. Identify the components of brand identity that it has.

2　As a brand expert, you have been asked to help guide new businesses. Using the components of a brand identity, create five simple rules for designing a strong brand identity.

Having a brand identity makes a brand and product memorable and helps a business to stand out in the market. To be effective, a brand identity needs to be strong, attractive, impactful and consistent.

Businesses need to refresh their brand identity to keep up to date with trends and fashions, which is why their logos go through so many changes.

For example, since 1976 Apple's logo has gone through six changes from the original logo of a man sitting under a tree. A logo or other visual element, such as a font, that customers see as outdated can harm a brand if it is trying to stay on trend or be cutting edge.

Brand image

Brand image is how customers think of a brand (i.e. how they perceive the brand right now). This image develops over time and is informed by customers' personal experiences with the brand. In today's world, many consumers (especially those under 25 – Generation Z) do not buy products simply because they are the best. They buy them because of what they stand for, or because of how they think of the brand (e.g. it is cutting edge or ethical, or environmentally friendly, etc.). There is a lot of competition between products, so a strong brand image is essential in order to stand out from the crowd.

Brand image includes:

- logo design
- **customer perception**
- **brand association**.

Logo design

A business logo should grab customers' attention and make a strong first impression. It is the first point of contact between a brand and its customers or potential customers. A logo can create a strong visual link to a business, so it is important to get the design right. The right design can make a brand immediately recognisable and inspire customer loyalty. It says a lot about a business. When designing a logo, you need to think about logo colours, logo font and logo image.

Customer perception

Customer perception relates to the feelings a customer has about a brand or a business. What a customer hears about a brand, what they see in the media, what they read about it and what they experience themselves, in terms of both product quality and customer service, all contribute to the customer's perception. Positive brand perception will lead customers to choose one business rather than another.

Brand association

Brand association can make or break a brand name. Brand association is anything that creates links in a customer's mind to a particular brand. This could be a phrase, a jingle or even a celebrity that triggers the customer to think of a particular company. Nike, for example, has a strong brand association with athletic excellence. Nike sponsors athletes who have achieved sporting excellence, such as Cristiano Ronaldo. It uses them within their advertising to further strengthen their brand association.

Case study

Coca-Cola's brand image

Logo design: The Coca-Cola logo is one of the most recognisable logos in the world. It is so recognisable, in fact, that even when it is in another language, people recognise it because of the familiar typeface (font and style), and the red and white colour scheme.

Customer perception: Coca-Cola is one of the oldest and most successful brands in the world. It promotes its products by using adverts that show positive lifestyles which are about bringing people together. This paints a very positive picture in the mind of the customer and results in a strong brand image.

Figure 3.4: Coca-Cola has an internationally recognised brand image

Brand association: In 2013, Coca-Cola ran a 'Where will happiness strike next?' campaign. As part of the campaign, the company created a pop-up park. It put down some temporary grass in a location, put up a sign saying 'Take off your shoes to open happiness', and installed a vending machine which dispensed free Coke to people who did take their shoes off to relax. The **promotion** associated Coca-Cola with the outdoors, happiness, relaxation and togetherness.

Check your understanding

1   What makes the Coca-Cola logo so effective?

2   What brand image do you think Coca-Cola is trying to portray?

3   Identify five words or phrases that come to mind when you think of Coca-Cola. Analyse whether this is the brand association Coca-Cola is hoping for.

Over to you!   **4**

In 2016, Samsung had a problem with its Galaxy Note 7 phone. Some of the phones were catching fire while they were charging.

1   What do you think this did for Samsung's brand image?

2   Explain how this would have impacted customer perception and brand association.

Stretch

3   Research Samsung's response to the problem with its Note 7 phones catching fire.

   a   What actions did it take?

   b   Do you think its actions helped the brand? Why/why not?

Let's get practical!   **1**

You work for a new technology company. You have been asked to design a concept phone to help the business enter the mobile phone market.

1   Draw/sketch your ideal mobile phone, highlighting key features you think are unique.

2   Create a brief outline of each of the following for your new mobile phone product:

   a   **Brand personality:** What characteristics do you think would make your product most successful? Why?

   b   **Brand identity:** What are the visual factors of the brand going to be? Why?

   c   **Brand image:** What image are you trying to create for your brand?

1.2 Why branding is used

Let's get started   **2**

Think about a brand you know and like. Why do you like it?
Do you always buy the same brand or do you switch between different brands?

Building a successful brand involves a lot of hard work, time and money. So why do so many businesses take the time to create strong branding? Why do they use branding at all? Figure 3.5 shows some of the reasons why businesses use branding.

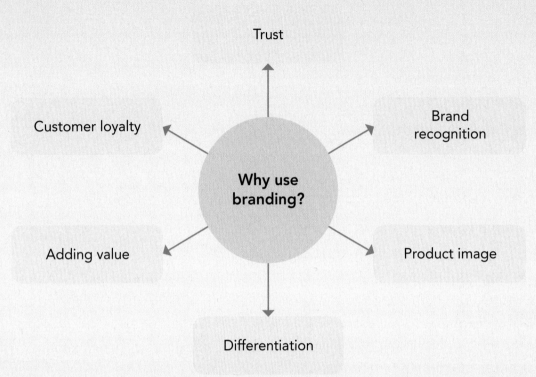

Figure 3.5: Why do businesses use branding?

Trust

Businesses use branding to build trust. Brand trust is when a customer believes that a brand will deliver on its promises and company values. Customers develop trust through their own personal experiences with a brand, and it can take years for a brand to build up trust. Trust is very important to customers. According to the 2018 Global Consumer Insights **survey**, 35 percent of **respondents** said that trust in a brand was in their top three reasons for choosing a company to purchase from.

BMW's slogan 'The ultimate driving machine' is a bold statement. However, BMW has developed enough trust in its brand that this is both believable and expected by the customers. Customers have come to trust the build quality and performance of BMW.

Brand recognition

Brand recognition (or brand awareness) is how familiar a brand is to its customers. Do customers recognise the logo, the slogan and the colours of the brand design? Strong brand recognition can:

- help to increase customer trust
- reduce price sensitivity in relation to some products (meaning customers will not mind paying a little more for the product)
- reduce advertising **costs**.

McDonald's has worked on its brand recognition so that it is now one of the most recognisable brands in the world. A survey conducted by SW Londoner in 2014 found that 88 percent of people surveyed (in six countries) recognised the golden M.

Product image

Brand image is how customers view the brand as a whole. Product image, however, relates to the perceptions and attitudes of customers towards new or existing products. This image can be affected by how well or how poorly the product works or delivers on customer expectations. A strong brand image means that a business does not have to prove this for every new product. For example, the designer brand Louis Vuitton has built a strong reputation for luxury products. A new product from the brand is expected to be of very high quality.

However, a brand's image can potentially be damaged by the performance of just one of its products. When Samsung's Galaxy Note 7s began to catch fire in 2016, the company had a product and brand image problem. Samsung had been recognised by customers all over the world for innovation and high-quality products. It had to regain customer trust and rebuild both the brand and product image.

Samsung recalled all of the affected phones and replaced them quickly, even setting up exchange points at major airports. It introduced new safety tests and changed the phone's design to avoid the problem occurring in future phones. Samsung's brand image with other successful products helped it to overcome this product image problem.

Differentiation

In most markets there are a number of businesses offering a range of products, so a business needs to use its branding to make it stand out from the competition. To differentiate itself, a business or a brand needs to offer something that the competition does not. It needs to give the customer a reason to choose one product or brand over another.

Offering personal experiences is one way that a business can stand out from the competition. Build-A-Bear Workshop sells soft toys, such as bears and other stuffed animals. It sells similar products to many toy stores, but Build-A-Bear stands out due to its unique personalised in-store experiences. Customers can name their bear and create a personalised 'birth certificate'. They can also customise the amount of stuffing to their liking and choose outfits for their new furry friend.

Adding value

A product or a service that is more appealing or desirable to a customer can often be sold for a higher price because customers are willing to pay more for a more attractive product or service. Branding can create this appeal and desire, so a strong or quality brand name can often command higher prices.

The mobile phone industry is very competitive and there are many phones to choose from. The most desirable brands, such as Apple and Samsung, are able to charge much higher prices than competing brands because of the strength of their branding and the position of their brand as market leaders.

Customer loyalty

Customer loyalty is when a customer consistently chooses one business's product over **competitors**' products. Strong branding cultivates customer loyalty as customers often develop a positive association with a brand. They are not easily persuaded to switch to another brand, even if there is a difference in price or there is a special offer on.

Starbucks' strong branding as a provider of quality coffee and its loyalty card scheme, which gives rewards for repeated custom, see people queuing up outside its branches to get coffee. Customers are so loyal to the brand that they will queue up and wait for their coffee rather than go somewhere else less busy, which may also be cheaper.

Over to you!   5

Think of a brand name (one you own or one you would like to own) and explain how using branding benefits that brand.

1.3 Branding methods

Let's get started   3

You now know how important branding is, but how do businesses develop their brands? Pick any brand name you are familiar with. Describe the brand's logo. What else is connected to this brand – a slogan, a song, is there a celebrity that comes to mind when you think of the brand?

Table 3.1: The elements to building a successful brand

Branding method	Description	Benefits	Examples
Brand name	A name given to a business or product that differentiates it from the competition	Brand names can help a business stand out in the market They can make the business easily identifiable	The brand name Hoover became so popular and linked to vacuum cleaners that people refer to different brands of vacuum cleaners as 'hoovers'.
Logo	A logo is a graphic, emblem, symbol or shape that is used by a business to provide a visual representation of its brand name	Logos are linked to a business's identity Logos can often grab attention and make a strong first impression They are easy to place on promotional materials	The Nike tick or 'swoosh' can often be seen on promotional materials without the name 'Nike', but it is easily recognisable as part of that brand
Sound/jingle	A short tune or song that is used in advertising or promotional videos A good jingle is catchy and memorable	A sound or jingle can immediately bring a business to the minds of its customers It helps reinforce the brand's message	McDonald's has one of the most recognisable jingles – the whistle tune along with the line 'I'm lovin' it'
Strapline	A short slogan or simple sentence that sums up the brand's essence or vision	It helps set a brand apart from the competition It can give information about the business and its values The strapline reinforces the brand identity	L'Oréal has one of the most recognisable tag lines: 'Because you're worth it'.
Characters	A character or mascot is the personality of a company This can be a cartoon character or an animal	A brand mascot can add: • a broad appeal to the brand • a familiar, friendly feel to the company Characters can be a softer way to sell a product A character can have its own personality which can be used in advertising	Gio Compario, the Go Compare opera singing mascot is synonymous with the company and stands out as one of the most recognisable mascots in the UK today.

Table 3.1: Continued

Branding method	Description	Benefits	Examples
Animated characters	Animated characters are cartoon or CGI designed characters, such as the Aldi Christmas carrot, Tony the Tiger and many more, that represent the brand values of the company. They are often fun and engaging and are indelibly linked to the brand name.	Characters can add instant recognition to an advertising campaign and give the target audience something to connect with, building an emotional connection with a business's consumer	Mickey Mouse has been the mascot of the Disney corporation since 1928 and is seen as the chirpy, fun face of the Disney corporation. The company has even been nicknamed 'The House of Mouse'.
Celebrity endorsement (can also be used within **public relations** (PR) – see R067, Section 4.5)	Using a celebrity's fame or reputation to sell the brand The celebrity needs to be relevant and familiar to the brand's target customer	Choosing the right celebrity to support or advertise a brand can attract a range of new customers and give the brand credibility Borrowing the popularity of a celebrity can boost sales and link their success with the brand's success Celebrities can inspire customer confidence	Nescafé partnered with the actor George Clooney to help sell their Nespresso coffee pods. George Clooney was well known and popular amongst the potential customers for Nespresso coffee pods

Case study

McDonald's is 'lovin' it'

Brand name: In 1940, Richard and Maurice McDonald opened a burger restaurant in California offering speedy service. When Ray Kroc opened a burger restaurant in 1955, he named it McDonald's after the McDonald brothers' restaurant, which had inspired him.

The McDonald's brand name is instantly recognisable worldwide in the fast-food industry.

Logo: The simple but effective 'golden arches' is one of the most globally recognisable logos.

Figure 3.6: The McDonald's golden arches logo is recognised globally

Sound/jingle: 'Ba da ba ba ba', McDonald's well-known jingle, was launched in 2003 and was originally sung by singer-songwriter, Justin Timberlake. It has become more famous than Justin Timberlake's original hits. The jingle is linked to the strapline 'I'm lovin' it'.

Continued

Strapline: 'I'm lovin' it' is simple and easy to remember. It reflects what McDonald's is about (i.e. people loving their food). It was launched in 2003 at the same time as the jingle, and it is the longest-running McDonald's slogan.

Characters: Ronald McDonald was the clown character used as McDonald's main mascot up to 2016. The character appeared in television advertisements and made appearances at fundraising events. Ronald McDonald was a huge part of McDonald's brand image. However, while Ronald McDonald was a popular character, he was retired by the company following a makeover of the brand as the character didn't fit with the modern-day McDonald's image.

Celebrity endorsement: In 2015, McDonald's used Jessie J and YouTube star Thatcher as part of a competition targeted at younger urban customers. Winners were surprised with an open-top bus performance by Jessie J, Thatcher and other YouTube stars.

Check your understanding

1 Why do you think the McDonald's logo is so recognisable?

2 Explain why McDonald's chose to use a YouTube star for their celebrity endorsement.

3 Explain which branding method used by McDonald's is the most important.

Over to you!   6

For the brand name you looked at earlier (in Over to you! 2), draw a spider diagram showing the methods the company uses to build its brand.

For each method you identify, explain how the company has used it.

Let's get practical!   2

Having worked out its brand personality, the technology company you work for has asked you to suggest what methods of branding it should use for its new mobile phone.

1 Suggest an appropriate mix of branding methods for the mobile phone brand you have been working on. For each method:

   a explain the method you have chosen

   b outline how it would work for your mobile phone brand

   c identify any limitations to using this method.

2 Which methods would you not use? Why not? Explain why you rejected the methods you have not chosen.

1.4 Competitor analysis

You are starting your own restaurant. What would you want to find out about your competitors and why?

What is a competitor analysis?

Businesses do not operate in isolation. They operate in a world with competitors. If a business wants to be successful, it needs to be aware of its competitors and undertake research into competitors' products and **services**.

A business needs to identify and analyse competitors in the market. It should carry out a competitor analysis to look at what each competitor offers, what they do well and whether they have any weaknesses.

By identifying any competitor weaknesses, it can turn these into opportunities to provide customers with a unique product or service not already offered by its competitors.

The business also needs to understand how its own product differs from that of competing brands.

Competitor analysis allows a business to:

*   understand the strengths and weaknesses of its competitors
*   distinguish its product from others on the market
*   understand its competitors' **unique selling point (USP)**
*   identify a **gap in the market**
*   understand how to make its product appeal to customers.

Key factors when researching competing brands

Table 3.2 shows that when carrying out research into competing brands, a business can make use of a range of sources of information.

Table 3.2: Sources of information on competing brands

Source of information	How it is useful
Observed preferences of customers	Market researchers watch how customers behave under normal circumstances to get an idea of their: • preferred products • what they are looking for while shopping • ways of shopping

Table 3.2: Continued

Source of information	How it is useful
Competitor websites	Useful to see: • how the competition approaches customer service • what offers they have on • their range of prices • customer **feedback** • product information
Product information	Usually available on a competitor's website, this information allows a business to see everything about the competitor's product such as: • product options/models • product specifications • prices and added extras
Industry reports and trade journals	These allow businesses to get insight into the industry and its competitors through: • information on trends and best practice in the industry • **interviews** with competitors

Strengths

Strengths are what a business is good at. What it does well or what it is known for can be considered key strengths for a business. For example, Sony's greatest strength is its high-quality electronics.

A business needs to know its competitors' strengths so it can improve on them. Knowing what competitors are good at and being able to offer something extra might gain some more customers. A business may even have a similar strength to its competitors and be able to improve on it to give itself a competitive edge. Questions that a business needs to ask about its competitors' strengths include the following.

- What are they good at?
- Why would customers choose a competitor over our business/product?
- Is their quality better?
- Is their design more appealing?
- Do they have a stronger or more popular brand name?

Weaknesses

Weaknesses (which are the opposite of strengths) are the things that competitors are not so good at. For example, the competition may fail to meet customer needs. This can be considered a weakness. Nokia's slow pace when moving into the smartphone market was a weakness and it lost **market share** to companies such as Samsung and Apple.

By looking at competitors' weaknesses and comparing them to its own strengths and weaknesses, a business can identify opportunities to improve on the weaknesses and 'win'. Maybe one of the weaknesses of a competitor is a strength of your business. The competitor's weaknesses may be down to an industry-wide weakness which a business may be able to turn into a great opportunity. For example, the early smartphones were only aimed at the business market. Apple identified this as an industry-wide weakness, which it turned into a strength by developing the iPhone and apps focusing on the leisure and consumer market. This gave smartphones a much wider appeal.

Questions that a business needs to ask about its competitors' weaknesses include the following.

- What are they not doing so well?
- Where are they failing to meet customers' expectations?
- What weaknesses do they have that are our strengths?
- What characteristics of the business put them at a disadvantage compared to others? (For example, some larger businesses lose that 'personal' touch that smaller or local businesses can offer in terms of customer service.)

Unique selling point (USP)

A unique selling point (USP) is a specific characteristic that makes a business or product stand out from the competition. For example, KFC's unique selling point is its 11 herbs and spices; M&Ms' USP is 'The milk chocolate melts in your mouth, not in your hand'.

Competitor analysis can help a business to identify or build its own USP from its strengths and the competitors' weaknesses. By knowing the competitors' USP, it may give some insight into how to reduce its appeal by offering an improved or different USP. Here are some questions that a business needs to ask about its competitors' USP.

- What is it about the competitors' products that sets them apart?
- What do the competitors offer that no one else does?
- Do the competitors even have a USP?

How a product proposal differs from competing brands

Product proposal **differentiation** is about making sure that the product a business is proposing:

- is not something that is already being offered by the competition, or

- has key differences to something that the competition is offering.

One of the main reasons for conducting competitor research is to ensure that a new product doesn't already exist. If a product already exists, businesses want to avoid following to the market with an identical product. This could damage a brand if the business is seen as copying or falling behind a competitor. For example, Lush, the soap and make-up high street retailer, separate themselves from the competition by highlighting their ethically sourced, all natural, vegetarian and 80 percent vegan ingredients that are never tested on animals.

Questions that a business needs to ask about its **proposal** include the following:

- What products do competitors sell that are similar to ours?

- Do competitors already sell what we are proposing?

- If we are selling a similar product, how can we make our product different (i.e. how can we differentiate ourselves)?

Let's get practical!   3

Developing a brand for your new mobile phone is going to require some consideration of the competitors in the market. Identify who the leading competitor for your new phone would be and conduct a competitor analysis.

1   What are the competitor's strengths?

2   What are their weaknesses?

3   What is their unique selling point?

4   Suggest one way you could differentiate your mobile phone from that of the competitor.

Opportunities and threats in the external environment

The **external environment** is the factors outside of the business that impact on how the business operates and performs. A business has no control over these factors. However, by analysing them, it is possible to gain an insight into the external influences which may impact on the business. An analysis of the external factors can help inform business decisions.

The external environment presents both opportunities and threats for businesses. It is important for a business to look at its external environment so that it is not taken by surprise by changes (threats) and so that it sees and embraces opportunities.

The external factors that can influence a business are:

- economic factors
- social factors

- technological factors
- ethical factors.

Economic factors

Economic factors are those relating to the **economy**. They include tax rates, interest rates, exchange rates, inflation, employment rates and government spending. Table 3.3 explains how these can have a significant impact on the success of a business.

Table 3.3: The impact of economic factors on a business

Factor	Description	Impact on business
Tax rates	<ul><li>A tax is a charge made by the government on businesses, workers or individuals. There are different kinds of tax:<ul><li>Income tax: tax charged on workers, taken from their **wages** or **salaries**</li><li>Corporation tax: a charge on the **profit** made by businesses</li><li>VAT: Value Added Tax is a 20 percent tax added to **goods** and services in the UK</li></ul></li></ul>	<ul><li>An increase in income tax means people pay more tax</li><li>If people are paying more tax, customers' disposable **income** (the money they have to spend after bills) is reduced</li><li>This can result in fewer sales of certain goods or services. For example, sales of luxury and branded goods or services (e.g. restaurants) may fall as tax rates rise and people have to cut their spending</li></ul>
Interest rates	<ul><li>Interest rate is the amount charged for borrowing money and the amount that is rewarded for saving</li><li>People with loans and mortgages pay interest as a charge on the money they borrow</li><li>Higher interest rates mean higher costs for customers</li></ul>	<ul><li>If interest rates are low, the cost of borrowing and mortgages is reduced. This could mean customers with mortgages or loans have more disposable income because their bills are lower. This can then result in increased sales for businesses</li><li>If interest rates rise, customers with mortgages or loans may have reduced disposable income</li><li>If interest rates fall, businesses such as estate agents may see more people able to buy houses as mortgages become cheaper</li></ul>

Table 3.3: Continued

Factor	Description	Impact on business

Exchange rates	• Exchange rates are the value of one currency against another. So, for example £1 = €1.16
	• Currency values change regularly and can impact businesses that trade internationally
		• If the pound falls against the euro, you get fewer euros for every pound. For a UK business, this means that:
		  • it is more expensive to buy goods from Europe and the business will pay more for the same goods and make less money
		  • its products are cheaper to buy in Europe so it may sell more there
		• If the pound strengthens against the euro, you get more euros for every pound. For a UK business, this means that:
		  • the costs for buying goods from Europe will be reduced and the business will pay less for the same goods, spend less money and make more profit
		  • its products are more expensive to buy in Europe so it may sell less there

Inflation	• Inflation is the increase in the price of goods and services over time • For example, in 2020 the inflation rate was 0.62 percent (which is very low). This means that the average price for goods and services in the UK increased by 0.62 percent • If the inflation rate was 1 percent then a product costing £1 would increase to £1.01	• If inflation increases, then it costs customers more to buy the same products, and customers' disposable income may be reduced • This increase in costs to consumers could mean a fall in sales for some businesses as people have less money to spend on luxuries
Unemployment	• The unemployment rate measures the number of people who are able to work, but who are currently without a job	• If people are unemployed and not earning a wage, they will not have as much money to spend. This will mean a reduced demand for more luxury goods and services, such as meals in restaurants and visits to the cinema
Government spending	• The money spent by the government on the public sector such as the NHS, education, defence, etc.	• The more money the government has to spend, the higher the **risk** of tax increases • When the government builds new roads or hospitals, private sector businesses are contracted to carry out the work

The economy

The economy in the UK is measured by tracking **gross domestic product (GDP)**. GDP is the total value of all goods and services produced in a country. The government, economists and businesses track it to see how strong the economy is. A high GDP is related to a strong economy.

Figure 3.7 shows that the economy goes through a cycle of peaks (when the economy grows) and troughs (**recessions**/slumps) which are also linked to employment levels (the number of people in work in the country). This cycle is known as the **business cycle** and can present both opportunities and threats to businesses.

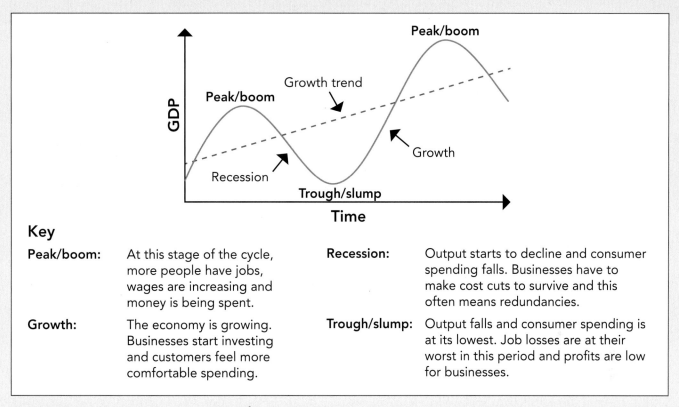

Key

Peak/boom: At this stage of the cycle, more people have jobs, wages are increasing and money is being spent.

Growth: The economy is growing. Businesses start investing and customers feel more comfortable spending.

Recession: Output starts to decline and consumer spending falls. Businesses have to make cost cuts to survive and this often means redundancies.

Trough/slump: Output falls and consumer spending is at its lowest. Job losses are at their worst in this period and profits are low for businesses.

Figure 3.7: The economy goes through a cycle of economic peaks and troughs which can present opportunities and threats for businesses

Over to you!　7

1　What are the impacts of an **economic boom** and a recession on businesses and their customers? Copy and complete Table 3.4 to structure your answers. (An example has been provided for you.)

Table 3.4: Impacts of an economic boom and a recession

	Economic boom		Economic recession	
	Impacts	Response	Impacts	Response
Businesses	Increase in consumer spending leads to higher **revenues** and profits	Due to increase in demand for products, the business expands by opening a new branch		
Customers				

Continued

Stretch

2   Does a recession always mean a loss of sales? Explain your answer.

3   Is an economic boom always a boost for sales? Explain your answer.

Case study

Not all businesses suffer in a recession

Recessions are not good for an economy. There are low profits, fewer employment opportunities and even redundancies – no one welcomes a recession. However, it is not doom and gloom for all businesses.

During the economic downturn in 2011, Aldi saw a 20.7 percent increase in sales. This gave it a record share of the UK grocery market, increasing its market share to 6 percent.

Figure 3.8: Discount retailers often grow in a recession

The economic situation that the UK found itself in during this recession provided many opportunities for discount retailers such as Aldi, Lidl and Primark.

Since 2011, Aldi and other discount retailers have become a mainstay on our high streets and they form part of our regular grocery shopping.

Check your understanding

1   In the lead up to the 2011 increase in sales and revenue for Aldi, the UK was in a period of recession. What does the term 'recession' mean?

2   Explain why Aldi and other discount supermarkets became so popular during a recession.

3   Using two examples, explain how Aldi's competitors might have been affected by the recession.

Social factors

Social factors are the things that affect customers' behaviours, beliefs and spending: Social factors include:

- **demographic** trends and changes
- customer tastes and fashions
- lifestyle changes.

Demographic trends and changes

Is the population increasing or decreasing? What time of year are the birth rates highest? What is the average age of the population of an area?

It is important for a business to understand this information so that it can target its market more specifically and appropriately. It can also use this information to decide who to target its advertising at, and if it is even worth opening the business in a particular area.

The country can be broken into different demographic groups by age, income and ethnicity, for example. By knowing the demographics of the market, a business can design and market its products more effectively. For example, McDonald's aims its marketing at young, urban customers.

Consumer tastes and fashions

Fashions change regularly and it is very important to keep on top of them. If a business does not keep on top of changing fashions it can have a serious impact on the success of the business as it will be out of touch with its customers' needs. For example, since 2015 streaming services such as Netflix and Amazon Prime have grown in popularity as consumer tastes and fashions have changed to a more on-demand and binge-watching culture. As a result of the increased popularity of streaming services, other businesses, such as Disney+ and Apple TV, have also launched streaming services to make the most of changing consumer tastes and trends.

Lifestyle changes

Customers' lifestyles are one of the main factors that dictate their buying habits. If a business does not take into consideration its customers' lifestyles and changes, then it may lose them. Knowing what is important to a customer for their everyday life can help to inform product design.

As people have become more environmentally conscious, supermarkets have started reducing the amount of plastic packaging on their products. In some of its stores, Sainsbury's has removed all plastic bags from its fruit and vegetable aisles. Instead, customers can buy reusable bags or bring in their own containers. Keeping up with these lifestyle changes can give a business a competitive edge.

Case study

Gaming for a lifestyle change

With increased concern over child obesity and children spending too much time in front of a computer screen, games manufacturer Nintendo seized on an opportunity to fill a gap in the gaming market.

It introduced Wii Fit and healthy lifestyle games, such as Zumba and Yoga, on the Wii console to meet the needs of consumers who enjoy a more active lifestyle. These lifestyle games have become a major part of Nintendo's product mix. They were

Figure 3.9: Nintendo seized on an opportunity to fill a gap in the gaming market with its Wii Fit

released not only on the next generation console, the Switch, but have also become a significant part of the console's product design and marketing. Improved motion sensitivity and controls have been included in a wider range of games.

The combination of exercise and fitness games with a console on which other types of game can also be played led to increased sales for Nintendo because of the popularity across whole families.

Check your understanding

1 Identify two ways in which Nintendo was affected by changes in consumer lifestyles.

2 Explain two benefits of Nintendo adapting to consumer lifestyle changes.

3 Explain why Nintendo has concentrated so much on lifestyle games and genres in their consoles.

Technological factors

Technology is a powerful component in business. From faster communication online to more efficient **manufacturing**, developments in technology can change processes, products and markets dramatically.

Technology has made it easier for businesses to:

- produce goods more quickly and with greater precision
- communicate more efficiently within the business and to customers
- create, store and edit data and information
- market and sell products online
- innovate.

Produce goods more quickly and with greater precision

Manufacturing has come a long way in the last hundred years thanks to new and innovative technology. Not only does technology speed up the production process so that products can be mass produced more efficiently and accurately, but it also means fewer staff are required.

For example, car manufacturing used to need a large number of people working on the production line. Each part of the car was fitted by a different worker. Now, car manufacturing is pretty much fully automated, with robots doing much of the heavy lifting and manufacturing, and fewer staff using machines to complete the process.

So as technology improves, businesses often need fewer staff. This can lead to redundancies, poor staff motivation and staff leaving.

Communication

From customer service chat options on websites to selling over the phone, technology has completely changed how businesses communicate and interact with their customers.

Technology has made communication much easier by:

- hosting FAQs, common questions and other information (such as timetables and delivery information) on a company's website
- using chat bots to respond to customer queries
- allowing customers to purchase goods and services online.

These changes mean that businesses need fewer telephone call handlers, and customers can get answers to questions without having to phone the business. However, when customers do want to speak to someone they may struggle to contact a human being.

Create, store and edit data and information

From mobile apps that gather user data to websites that ask customers to complete forms, technology allows businesses to track customer data, such as:

- what a customer purchases

- how a customer interacts with a business's website (e.g. mobile apps, email, social media pages)

- customer feedback and **reviews**

- how frequently a customer purchases a product or visits a website.

All of this information helps a business to create a profile of its customers so that it can target the right ones with marketing.

Improvements in data storage technology mean businesses can record, analyse and retrieve information quickly and efficiently.

For example, Carphone Warehouse has customer information called 'leads' stored on its computer system. A lead is created for every customer who purchases a product from the company. Each lead includes the customer's personal information, purchasing history and financial information. This is kept on Carphone Warehouse's computer network and can be accessed by all of its employees. Therefore, if a customer from Birmingham visits a Carphone Warehouse store in Leeds with a query about their contract, all of the relevant information is there for the member of staff in Leeds to deal with the query.

While customer data stored online is easy to access, it is also at risk from hackers and cyber criminals, who can make use of this data for fraud and other crime. It can be a complicated and expensive process to protect the data. Failure to protect customers' data can have serious consequences for a business's brand image and reputation.

Market and sell products online

The internet has changed how customers interact with businesses. As more and more people are doing things online, customers are turning to online retailers for many things, from groceries to fashion. Businesses are therefore having to adapt how they market and sell their goods to include online marketing and selling.

Online sales were increasing steadily, but as a result of the COVID-19 pandemic, online sales in the UK increased strongly from £77 billion in 2019 to £99 billion by the end of 2020. At the end of 2020, online sales were 27.9 percent of total UK retail sales, compared to just 19.2 percent the year before. Businesses without an online presence have seen a decrease in sales.

Innovation

Technology drives customer choices and innovation. Customers want the most technologically up-to-date products, and the way that customers want to receive or use products has changed as a result of technological innovation.

One example of this is the entertainment industry. Back in the 1980s, if you wanted a band's newest music track or the latest film when it was released, you had to go into a shop and buy the physical product (i.e. a cassette tape, CD, vinyl record or video cassette). Now, as a result of technological developments, you can stream and download them to your phone, laptop, tablet or other digital devices.

While technological innovation has brought benefits for the customer, some businesses, such as HMV, have seen significant drops in sales revenue as consumers no longer visit high street stores to buy their entertainment. Also, while being the first business to adopt new technology can give a business a competitive advantage, new technology may come at a high cost.

Over to you!   8

Identify one technological development that you think has completely changed how things are done in an industry. Discuss the positive and negative consequences of the development.

Ethical factors

When we talk about ethics, we mean the difference between something that is morally right and wrong. For example, if you saw someone drop some money on their way into a shop, would you pick it up and keep it or would you tell them?

Businesses need to act in an ethical way that is fair and right. Ethical awareness also includes acting in an environmentally friendly and **sustainable** way. Customers and governments are putting pressure on businesses to act more responsibly in terms of their use of resources and environmental protection.

A business can be more ethical by:

- reducing exploitation:
  - making sure that it pays workers in poorer countries a fair wage and provides them with good working conditions
  - paying suppliers a fair price for their goods (e.g. see the Fairtrade Foundation case study)
- reducing the amount of packaging on its products and making its packaging more recyclable or biodegradable
- reducing its carbon footprint and cutting down on pollution and carbon emissions
- sourcing its materials sustainably (i.e. using materials that can be replaced easily or come from countries where production is not to the detriment of wildlife and natural habitats).

Customers are increasingly interested in ethics and environmental sustainability. They view companies who act in an ethical and environmentally friendly way more positively. The benefits to the business are customer loyalty and the ability to charge a higher price for more ethical products. Customers may avoid businesses that are seen as unethical.

Sometimes a business may be unclear about how ethical or environmentally friendly it is. For example, a business could make organic products out of sustainable materials but exploit its workers by not paying a fair wage. Likewise, a business may claim to be ethical but may use materials that are not sustainable.

Case study

Ethics and sustainability – The Fairtrade Foundation

Farmers and suppliers in developing countries are often exploited and have to sell their goods for less than it costs to make them, just to survive. While this is not illegal, there are some ethical issues. Fair trade is when the producer, often a farmer in a poorer country, is paid a fair wage for their produce. This ensures better prices, decent working conditions and sustainability for suppliers in developing countries.

Figure 3.10: The Fairtrade Foundation logo can provide a competitive advantage as it shows a business that is ethically minded

The Fairtrade Foundation works with farmers and producers in developing countries to negotiate a fair deal with businesses, so the farmers can make enough money to survive.

Businesses that meet the Fairtrade Foundation's ethical requirements get to put the Fairtrade logo on their products and advertising. In today's ethically minded world, this can be a great competitive advantage.

Many common products such as tea, coffee and chocolate are fair trade products and carry the Fairtrade Foundation logo on their packaging.

Check your understanding

1   Identify three benefits of operating as a Fairtrade partner.

2   Explain the impact on a business of operating as a Fairtrade partner.

3   Explain how operating as a Fairtrade retailer might provide a business with a competitive advantage.

Over to you!   9

Operating ethically can be expensive. If a business's suppliers are paying their staff a fair wage, then they will need to charge more for their goods. Using an example, explain why many businesses operate in an ethical way.

Let's get practical!   4

The technology company you work for likes the idea for the new mobile phone and it wants to make sure it has all the facts before moving on.

Your manager has asked you to outline the key external factors and explain the:

a   **opportunities:** what opportunities exist in the market that the company could take advantage of?

b   **threats:** what threats does the company need to be aware of? What does it need to look out for?

c   **competition:** in Let's get practical! 3 you identified one mobile company as a competitor and explained two of its strengths. Now explain two of its weaknesses.

Tip: As you have already decided on the brand personality, identity and image, are there any opportunities or threats in the external environment specific to your brand idea?

Review your learning

Test your knowledge

1   What is a brand?

2   How does a strong brand help a business to stand out from its competition?

3   The company you work for wants to release a new pair of trainers onto the sports market. Explain the possible impact of one opportunity and one threat from the external environment on the release of the new trainers.

4   Your manager has asked your opinion on whether the company needs to carry out a competitor analysis of other companies selling trainers. Explain two advantages and two disadvantages (limitations) of carrying out competitor research.

What have you learnt?

	See section
• What a brand is.	1.1
• Why branding is used.	1.2
• Branding methods.	1.3
• How to carry out a competitor analysis.	1.4

TA2

Create a promotional campaign for a brand and product

Let's get started 1

Figure 3.11 shows a Cadillac advertising campaign in China. Why do you think they put the car in a fish tank with large goldfish?

Figure 3.11: Why did Cadillac put one of its cars in a fish tank?

What will you learn?

- How to create a **promotional campaign** for a brand or product.

2.1 How to create a promotional campaign for a product or brand

Promotion is the method of informing customers about a product, service or brand and persuading them to purchase or engage with it.

A promotional campaign is a series of activities, such as advertisements and demonstrations, that a business uses to promote and encourage the sale of a product or a service.

Over to you!   1

Think of your favourite device. How were you convinced to buy it?
What made you think 'I prefer this one over that one'?

Explain the objectives of a promotional campaign

The **objectives** of a promotional campaign are the things that a business
or **entrepreneur** wants to achieve from the promotion. Table 3.5 shows
the main objectives of a promotional campaign.

Table 3.5: Promotional objectives

Objective	Description	Examples of promotional materials to achieve the objective

Raise awareness	• Make consumers aware of new products or services and the brand, as customers are not going to buy what they do not know about
	 • Make sure customers understand:
	  ◦ what the product or service is – its features and qualities
	  ◦ how it benefits them as this will encourage them to buy new and existing products/services
	  ◦ how much it costs (price)
	 • To inform customers of changes to existing products or services
		• Billboard adverts in a city centre
		 • Viral social media campaigns
		 • Social media **influencers** raise awareness of products and also inform potential customers about product features and how they work

Differentiate	• Make the product or service stand out from the competitors' products so that customers will buy the business's product instead of the competitors' • To show how a product or service is different from other products/services on the market • To highlight the business's unique selling point (USP) • To target specific market **segments**	• Product innovation, e.g. Tesla, the electric car manufacturer, separates itself from the competition with cars that are not only environmentally friendly, but also very technologically advanced compared to other similar products on the market • Unique marketing campaigns, e.g. Coca-Cola's Christmas advert is one of the most recognisable
Create market presence	• To make customers aware of the availability of a product or service in order to make sales • To create interest around a new product or service • To develop the business's message and brand	• Less is more. A business can generate interest by hinting at the product and enticing customers to find out more. E.g. Hello Games provided a small amount of information about its 'No man's sky' game before release, generating a buzz amongst gamers about its content

Table 3.5: Continued

Objective	Description	Examples of promotional materials to achieve the objective
Increase market share	• To persuade customers to buy the business's product rather than its competitors' • To increase the percentage of total customers in the market that the business sells to	• Reducing prices, offering promotions, and advertising • Loyalty cards and reward schemes to build relationships with customers can increase market share and retain those customers with loyalty points and offers

Case study

'Did somebody say Just Eat?'

In August 2001, Just Eat, a new way to order fast food from local takeaways, was launched in Denmark. The service provides a one-stop shop for takeaways and restaurants in the local area.

The business model is simple. Just Eat provides a platform for local takeaways and restaurants to advertise their menus in one place – on Just Eat's app or website. Customers log onto the Just Eat website or app and order their food through Just Eat, which passes the order on to the local takeaway(s). Customers can either pick up the food or have it delivered.

Figure 3.12: Just Eat's promotional campaign 'Did somebody say Just Eat?' was successful

In May 2020, Just Eat launched and ran a very successful global promotional campaign featuring the catchy slogan 'Did somebody say Just Eat?'. It hired Snoop Dogg to provide the theme tune for the business.

The campaign was extremely successful. In 2020, Just Eat generated a 61 percent increase in revenue on the previous year and 60 million users worldwide. Some of the increase in revenue and the number of users was due to the promotional campaign.

Despite costing Just Eat millions of pounds, the campaign was an astute investment because of the increase in orders and market share.

Just Eat's success depends on customers knowing that it exists and placing their orders through its website or app. So market presence is a vital component of Just Eat's promotional campaign and is one of its key promotional campaign objectives.

Case study

Check your understanding

1 Suggest what Just Eat's main objectives were for this campaign.

2 Rank the order, from most important to least important, of the objectives you have just identified. Justify your ranking.

3 Do you think Just Eat met the campaign objectives? Explain your answer.

Over to you! 2

In 2006, Apple ran a promotional campaign 'Get a Mac'. The campaign saw actors portraying the characteristics of a Mac and a PC, with the Mac seeming newer, faster and more appealing.

1 Suggest two objectives that you think Apple was trying to achieve with this campaign.

2 Why do you think Apple included a PC in the campaign if it wanted people to buy Macs instead?

SMART objectives

Whenever an entrepreneur sets promotional objectives, they should be SMART (Figure 3.13).

S	**M**	**A**	**R**	**T**
Specific	**Measurable**	**Achievable**	**Relevant**	**Time bound**
Are the objectives clear, well defined and specific enough to be achieved?	Will the objectives allow you to measure success and see whether the objective (e.g. increase in market share) has been achieved?	Are the objectives realistic? They should stretch a business's ability but still be possible	Do the objectives help you achieve what you set out to achieve? Do they align with the company values or long-term plans? Are they worthwhile?	Do the objectives have an end date by when they need to be achieved? Set a time limit that is realistic but ambitious

Figure 3.13: Objectives need to be SMART

Over to you!   **3**

The Cherry Tree is a small tea shop in the North of England, offering cream teas, sandwiches and a fine tea-room style experience. Having opened only two years ago, the business now enjoys regular customers and is looking to the future, with plans to expand the business and open further tea shops. Mia, the owner, has set herself the following objective for the business:

'We aim to increase our market share by 5 percent before the end of 2022.'

Why is this a SMART objective? Identify what makes this:

a   Specific

b   Measurable

c   Achievable

d   Relevant

e   Time bound.

Create a plan for a promotional campaign

Let's get started   **2**

Read the quote below from Benjamin Franklin, one of the founding fathers of the USA. What do you think it means? Write down your thoughts on this quote and what it might mean for a promotional campaign.

'If you fail to plan, you are planning to fail.'

Planning is an important part of any business venture. Once an entrepreneur has set the objectives of their promotional campaign, they need to consider and plan how they will achieve each objective. Planning for a promotional campaign includes:

- setting an appropriate timeframe for the whole campaign

- identifying an appropriate timeframe for each activity within the campaign

- scheduling a review phase within a promotional campaign

- setting **key performance indicators** (KPIs).

Appropriate timeframe for the whole campaign

From start to finish, how long will the campaign last? Objectives are likely to be time bound, which means that the entrepreneur needs to complete them within the required timeframe.

Other factors that an entrepreneur needs to consider when setting a timeframe include:

- resources:
  - large companies often have whole departments or teams dedicated to marketing, so an entrepreneur on their own is likely to need more time to complete the different tasks/elements
  - digital versus paper based: for example, collecting people's email addresses on a paper form and inputting that data into a mailing list can take longer than collecting them via a digital method which adds the email address to the mailing list automatically
- experience: less-experienced marketers will need more time to plan and run a campaign than those who have done it before
- the campaign's purpose. For example:
  - when releasing a product or increasing market share the goal is to grab immediate attention and develop initial sales, so the campaign is likely to be shorter
  - a campaign to develop brand image may contain a number of stages, which can take time. E.g. the Specsavers 'Should've gone to Specsavers' campaign was developed over a number of years.

While there is no set timeframe for a promotional campaign, it needs to be long enough that it reaches potential customers, but not so long that customers or the **target market** get bored of it or ignore it. Entrepreneurs may decide to run a short campaign or a longer campaign (Table 3.6).

Table 3.6: The advantages and disadvantages of different lengths of promotional campaign

Type of campaign	Timeframe	Advantages and disadvantages
Short campaign	Less than six weeks	• Need to use promotional materials that target customers quickly, i.e. emails and paid ads on social media • Can be costly paying for adverts • Can be rushed and not carried out well • Limited time to collect data, so the data collected may not meet the objectives
Longer campaign	Over six weeks	• More time to carry out individual elements within the overall campaign • Allows more time to plan the campaign so decisions are not rushed • Allows a business/entrepreneur to collect plenty of data • Can measure results more effectively over a longer period of time • Customers/target market might get bored and lose interest in the product/service if the campaign is very long

Over to you!　4

For each of the promotional campaign types below, suggest the appropriate timeframe (short or long term) and explain why you think this.

a　A local, newly formed rock band has managed to book some local venues over the next six months. It needs to raise awareness of the gigs, with venues, ticket prices and tour dates.

b　After a production error that caused some smart watches to overheat and break down, a technology firm is looking to repair its brand image to regain the trust it once had with its current and former customers.

Your product proposal　1

Campaign considerations

You should identify a timeframe for your promotional campaign. You need to make sure that the timeframe that you have stated allows you enough time to complete all of the individual activities/tasks and that you are able to justify your timeframe. Consider the following.

- What are you trying to achieve with the campaign (are you building a brand or raising awareness of a new product, or are you doing both)?

- What are the available resources (do you have the resources for the size of campaign you are planning)?

- What is your experience (will you need longer as this is new to you)?

- How long is the campaign going to last? What activities will take the longest and what activities can be done simultaneously (at the same time)?

Appropriate timeframe for each activity

As a campaign covers a wide range of techniques and can include a mix of components working together, not all elements will require (or be given) equal time. For example, TV adverts may run for longer than a competition. Radio adverts might run for a shorter time than a magazine or social media advert.

Table 3.7: Promotional activities and timeframe considerations

Campaign activity	Timeframe considerations
Social media The use of social media platforms to engage customers, build a brand, increase sales and drive traffic to the business's website	• They take less time to set up than other promotional materials • It may take time to develop a relationship with customers through social media. Therefore it requires a long-term commitment from the business
Leaflets and 'traditional' media Usually print-based materials that can be used to inform customers of a new product or promote an offer. Often used to get an immediate response from customers	• Planning the content to ensure an appropriate mix of information, images, etc. and printing can take a long time • Once created and printed, it can be distributed fairly quickly
Website Contains information about the business's products and services and may even contain a page from which customers can buy the products/services	• It can be time-consuming for a business to create a page containing suitable, high-quality content, images and information • Takes a while for search engines to find the page so it appears in search results, though this can be sped up if the business pays search engines or through search engine optimisation • Once created, a website can be published immediately and updated quickly

Over to you!   5

Find a real-life promotional campaign for a product or service you have heard of.

1   Identify the promotional materials used during the campaign.

2   For each type of promotional material, assess the likely timeframe for creating and carrying out the promotional activity.

Stretch

3   Research the impact of the campaign and suggest how the campaign may have affected the sales and revenue of the product or service.

Your product proposal   2

Timeframe for the whole campaign

Consider your own promotional campaign for the assessment. By now, you will have an idea of the objectives for your campaign and some ideas about what your campaign will contain. For your assessment, you should consider:

- the timeframe of the whole campaign, from planning to results

- the timeframe for each individual activity (how long each specific element is likely to take)

- the order of activities. Which ones must be done first?

Importance of a review phase within a promotional campaign

Once the campaign has come to the end, there is still a lot of work to be done to determine how effective and successful the campaign has been. Entrepreneurs and businesses need to consider:

- which elements of the campaign worked well and which did not

- whether the objectives have been met

- whether it was worth it

- what recommendations should be made for the next campaign.

You will look at these points in greater depth in TA4.

Importance of key performance indicators (KPIs)

Key performance indicators (KPIs) are measurable values that can be used to track progress and assess whether the promotional campaign has achieved the objectives.

Why are KPIs important?

KPIs are useful not only in assessing whether the objectives have been met at the end of a promotional campaign, but also for indicating progress during the campaign. They can help an entrepreneur to work out whether they need to make any changes to ensure that the promotional campaign is a success.

KPIs can be used to:

- **measure progress** – KPIs can be tracked to measure consumer engagement with the campaign, sales revenue and impact on the brand during the campaign. This can help to identify whether the campaign is having the desired effect

- **help make adjustments** – KPIs can be measured to identify whether the campaign is on track and whether it is going to meet its key milestones (significant stages). If a campaign does not seem to be generating interest in a product and sales are not increasing as expected, for example, the entrepreneur might decide on a change of direction mid-campaign to ensure success

- **evaluate success** – KPIs, such as sales growth, number of new customers, brand awareness and other values, provide a measure of how well a campaign has worked and whether it is worth running a similar campaign again.

Table 3.8: Examples of KPIs used to measure the success of promotional campaigns

Key performance indicator (KPI)	Description
Sales growth	An increase in the number of sales or the amount of sales coming in
Number of new customers	The number of new customers gained during or after the campaign
Search rankings	Where the website comes on search engine results pages, including how often searches are converted to site visits and sales
Website traffic	The number of visits to a website through: • a direct visit (i.e. by typing in the URL) • a link from another website • a link from social media
Number of conversions	When a user takes a particular action, e.g. • opens an email • clicks a link • makes a purchase

Let's get practical!   1

The technology company you work for liked the mobile phone branding ideas so much they are considering releasing the product soon.

Your manager has asked you to provide a short written summary of what the promotional campaign could look like. She wants you to outline:

a   three objectives of the campaign

b   a rough timeframe for the campaign (when it should start and when it should finish), and to explain the timeframe you have suggested

c   what KPIs you would use to judge the success of the campaign for the new mobile phone release and explain their suitability.

Gantt charts

Planning a promotional campaign involves identifying and allocating tasks, setting specific deadlines for when work should be completed, and knowing when tasks should be started and finished by. This can be a complex task.

A **Gantt chart** is a visual planning tool which allows a business to see at a glance:

* the different activities/tasks in the campaign

* the order in which activities/tasks need to be completed

* the start and completion dates for each activity/task

* the duration of each activity/task

* lag time (free time before or after an activity/task takes place) or overlap

* quieter periods in the campaign.

To construct a Gantt chart, an entrepreneur needs to identify the different activities within the promotional campaign and the duration of the activities. Figure 3.14 shows a Gantt chart for a short six-week campaign.

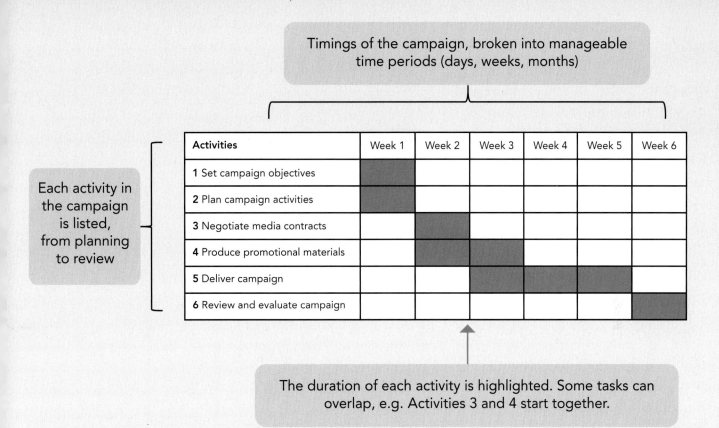

Timings of the campaign, broken into manageable time periods (days, weeks, months)

Each activity in the campaign is listed, from planning to review

Activities	Week 1	Week 2	Week 3	Week 4	Week 5	Week 6
1 Set campaign objectives	■					
2 Plan campaign activities	■					
3 Negotiate media contracts		■				
4 Produce promotional materials		■	■			
5 Deliver campaign			■	■	■	
6 Review and evaluate campaign						■

The duration of each activity is highlighted. Some tasks can overlap, e.g. Activities 3 and 4 start together.

Figure 3.14: Gantt charts help with planning a promotional campaign by showing each activity in the campaign and the time it is likely to take

In Figure 3.14, the duration of each activity is indicated by the shaded boxes so it is easy to see where some tasks overlap.

Over to you!　6

1　In the Gantt chart in Figure 3.14:

　　a　which activity will take two weeks?

　　b　which activities can be completed simultaneously?

2　How would the project be impacted by a one week delay to activity 2, 'Plan campaign activities'?

Setting out the promotional campaign in a Gantt chart allows an entrepreneur to not only see what is happening and when, but also to plan for changes in the campaign itself. For example, if one task is delayed then it is easy to see at a glance the knock-on effects and help the business to decide:

- what other tasks might need to be delayed or rescheduled
- any changes that might need to be made to the end date of the campaign.

Other planning tools

Although a Gantt chart is a useful planning tool, it is not the only one available.

- Simple lists can help to organise a campaign into smaller, manageable tasks by breaking the whole campaign into individual activities. By adding these individual activities to a timeline it is possible to set target deadlines and keep a campaign on track.

- Web-based project management tools, such as Trello, allow users to create activity cards which can be colour-coded and put in columns according to whether the task is 'to do', 'work in progress' or 'completed'.

Over to you!   7

1   Why might using a Gantt chart like this be helpful when planning a promotional campaign?

2   Suggest a limitation of using a Gantt chart in planning and running a promotional campaign.

3   Explain why a Gantt chart might be more use to an entrepreneur than a list.

How to create appropriate promotional materials

Let's get started   3

WhatsApp is trying to increase its user numbers among the elderly and non-traditional digital communication users. How might WhatsApp achieve this goal?

Tip: Think back to R067 and types of advertising mediums.

As discussed previously, a promotional campaign is a series of advertisements and other promotional techniques. A promotional campaign is therefore more than just a single advert.

Strong campaigns use a mix of promotional materials that:

- work well together to achieve the campaign's objectives
- are appropriate for the product that the campaign is promoting
- are appropriate for the customer that the campaign is targeting.

Promotional materials

In Unit R067 you covered types of advertising medium (Section 4.3) and sales promotion techniques (Section 4.4). Tables 3.9 and 3.10 recap these advertising mediums.

Non-digital advertising mediums

Table 3.9: Advantages and disadvantages of non-digital advertising mediums

Medium	Advantages	Disadvantages
Leaflets	• Visually appealing and easy to read • Can target a specific demographic • Can include a lot of information • Quite cheap to make and print	• Often ignored or thrown away • Can use lots of paper, which is wasted if thrown away
Newspapers	• Good at targeting a specific demographic/audience • Can grab the audience's attention with coupons or offers • Can include detailed information in advertisements • National newspapers can have a broad reach	• Images are often poor quality • Newspapers are soon thrown away so advertisements have a short lifespan • People may not read the advertising pages • Lots of competing advertisements • Can be expensive
Magazines	• Can contain colourful, glossy advertisements • Very good at targeting specific readers (e.g. a car product advert in a car magazine) • Can include pull-outs inside (e.g. leaflets inside the magazine)	• Colour advertisements are expensive • Not suitable for reaching a large audience as magazines often appeal to a specific customer group. To reach a wide audience, a business would need to advertise in many publications • Advertising deadlines are months before publication

Table 3.9: Continued

Medium	Advantages	Disadvantages
Radio	• Can target specific demographics (e.g. local area with local radio or specific types of listener) • Fairly cheap, compared to other mass media methods, such as television • Can have an immediate response if promoting offers and events	• Can only use sound to generate impact • Listeners might not be engaged as they may be doing something else while listing to the radio in the background • Advertisements cost more than print or social media advertisements • Need to be run repeatedly to have an impact
Posters/ billboards	• Can be eye catching and engaging in public places, especially as billboard technology is evolving and now includes digital boards • Can be used for regional or local targeting • Builds brand awareness • Less expensive than other mass media • Target a variety of customers	• Provide people with limited information • Exposure time to the message can be brief • As they are everywhere, they are often ignored • Prime locations are expensive
Cinema	• Can have a deep impact because of the use of a large screen • Has a captive audience (you cannot skip ahead during the adverts in a cinema) • Can target the advertisement in line with the type of film and its audience	• Expensive to produce • Low exposure to audiences as cinema screens are only full for a few blockbuster movies

Digital advertising mediums

Table 3.10: Advantages and disadvantages of digital advertising mediums

Medium	Advantages	Disadvantages
Social media platforms (Facebook, Twitter, Instagram, TikTok)	• Can reach a large, global audience • Can be targeted at a specific audience/demographic • Low cost • Easy to update and change • Can drive customers to a website via links	• Not everyone has access to social media • Negative feedback is visible to all customers and potential customers and can impact on the brand • Can be time-consuming as someone needs to regularly update, monitor and respond to social media • Not guaranteed to reach the target market
Websites	• Can reach a wider audience • Thanks to mobile technology, customers can access websites from almost anywhere • Low cost • Easy to update and change	• Difficult to reach potential customers initially if they do not know the website address or that it exists • Need to be updated as out-of-date information may impact the business negatively • Takes time for new websites to appear in internet search rankings • Allow customers to compare products and prices with those of competitors

Table 3.10: Continued

Medium	Advantages	Disadvantages
Banners/pop-ups (Advertisements that pop up on screen when a page is opened or an advert at the top or bottom of a web page (banner))	• Catch attention as they are the first thing that website visitors see • Can generate visitors to a website as they click on the pop-up or banner	• Full-screen pop-ups can be annoying to the customer if they are not shown correctly and block content • Pop-up and advertiser blocker software hides them from customers so the customer does not see the pop-up • Can damage brand reputation if not done correctly
SMS texts (Adverts sent directly to someone's mobile phone via text, often with links to the company's website)	• Cost-effective • Text messages are quick to read • Most people read text messages as soon as they arrive so can respond to offers or deals quickly • Do not get stuck in spam like emails • People take their phones everywhere so they are reachable and can access the internet and websites almost all of the time • Likely to reach target audience as people tend to read all of their text messages	• Messages need to be short, which reduces the information a business can provide • Can be seen as intrusive by some customers, which can affect brand reputation • Need to update content so customers are not sent the same text several times • A customer may change their phone number, so they no longer receive the texts • **SMS text messages** are commonly used by fraudsters, which can make customers wary of clicking on links
Podcasts (A series of spoken audio files on a particular topic)	• Simple and fairly cheap to make with a computer or smartphone and to upload to the internet • Can be fun and engage the customer with the brand as well as introducing the product • Customers can download or stream the file and watch it at a convenient time	• Finding the target audience can be difficult • Not all customers access podcasts

Table 3.10: Continued

Medium	Advantages	Disadvantages
Vlogs/blogs (Videos or written information on different topics that is posted online)	• A more interactive way than websites of creating interest in a product • Can provide detailed information about a product and its benefits • Blogs are relatively cheap to build and run • Can be engaging and build a relationship between customers and a brand • Vlog advertising links the brand with well-known content providers or influencers • Quick and easy to update • Customers can leave comments/feedback • Engaging content creates brand awareness and improves search engine ranking if people share it • Good-quality material will gain repeat visitors and earn customers' trust and respect	• Vlogs can be expensive to produce because of the cost of the equipment and difficult to update • Can be time-consuming to produce regular updates that have good-quality content • Need to be updated regularly to keep up to date with trends • Not all customers engage with companies in this manner • Poorly written or inaccurate content can reflect badly on a brand • If people do not know that the blog/vlog exists they will not read it

Over to you! 8

1 Select three types of promotional material. For each one:

 a describe what the material is and what it does, and find real-world examples of it apart from those mentioned in the text

 b explain one benefit and one drawback of the material to a business.

Figure 3.15: Is a newspaper advert an appropriate method for WhatsApp to advertise to older people?

2 Think back to Let's get started 3 which described how WhatsApp is trying to increase its user numbers among older people. Assess the appropriateness of the newspaper advert as a means of promotion.

Tip: Consider the target audience and the benefits and drawbacks of the advertising medium.

Let's get practical!   2

Your manager at the technology company wants to make sure information about the new mobile phone reaches the customers to maximise sales. She has asked you to:

a   recommend four promotional methods (both digital and non-digital) that would not only differentiate the phone from the competition, but also create market presence

b   justify your recommendations by explaining how the materials you have chosen will meet her requirements.

Appropriate promotional materials for a given business proposal

Not all advertising mediums or promotions are suitable for every promotional campaign. Entrepreneurs and businesses therefore need to consider not only what promotional materials and techniques are available, but also which ones are appropriate to the product it is promoting and the customer it is promoting the product to. They also need to consider whether the various materials and techniques produce a campaign that fits together well. When creating a business proposal, an entrepreneur should consider whether the advertising mediums and the promotional materials they are going to use are a good fit for the product and the business proposal itself. Table 3.11 shows some examples of things to consider.

Table 3.11: Assessing whether the advertising mediums and promotional materials are a good fit for the business proposal

Questions to ask	Why this is important
Is the product a new product?	If a business is releasing a new product, then it is vital to promote the key features and product information. Is this achievable with a billboard poster or would it be better in a full-page newspaper advertisement or through a social media campaign or blog?
What are the product's/business's objectives?	What is the business/entrepreneur trying to do? Building a relationship with customers to strengthen a brand is better done with a social media campaign than cinema advertising, for example
What is the **budget**?	Cost will also be a key consideration. Some mediums, such as TV advertising, will obviously reach a wider audience, but the entrepreneur may not be able to afford a TV spot

Appropriate promotional materials for the customer profile

Another thing for an entrepreneur to consider is whether the promotional materials are suitable for the proposed target customer (Table 3.12).

Table 3.12: Assessing whether the advertising mediums and promotional materials are a good fit for the customer profile

Questions to ask	Why this is important
Who is the audience?	Different audiences will consume different mediums. If a business is aiming to target young, trendy teenagers, then would newspapers and certain TV channels be the right medium to advertise on, or would the business be better off using social media or vlogs, for example?
Who are the customers?	Identifying the target customer allows a business not only to understand customers' interests and what would get their attention in the campaign, but also what medium is appropriate for reaching them

Case study

Sky AdSmart – Appropriateness to customer profile

Sky AdSmart is a modern approach to TV advertising, which allows businesses to use information on customers' viewing habits and entertainment preferences to ensure their advertising is appropriate to the customer profile.

Sky AdSmart uses data it has collected through surveys and viewing habits to identify the viewing preferences of a business's target audience. It then downloads the business's advert directly to those customers' Sky+ HD boxes. The advert will play during a commercial break when the usual adverts are on. For example, a mobile phone company may use Sky AdSmart to target a commercial break during a reality TV show which is popular amongst younger viewers, whereas a company promoting holidays for the over 50s might use it to target a commercial break in a daytime quiz programme.

While Sky AdSmart is used widely by many big brands for national campaigns, it could also be beneficial to smaller businesses that want to reach the right audience at a lower cost than typical TV advertising.

Check your understanding

1 Explain one benefit of this method of advertising.

2 For a product/business of your choice, explain one limitation of this type of advertising.

3 For the business you have chosen, evaluate the overall value of using this method to target appropriate customers.

Complementary to each other and to the promotional materials

As well as being appropriate to the product proposal and to the customer profile, the mix of promotional materials and advertising needs to work together so that:

- they use a blend of both non-digital and digital methods that target a wider range of customers or provide more detailed information to the customer

- the brand and its message are consistent.

Using a blend of non-digital and digital methods

Older people are more likely to read a newspaper while younger people are more likely to get their news from websites on their smartphones, laptops and tablets. Therefore, an entrepreneur or business might place an advertisement in a newspaper *and* online to target both of these groups.

They might also include a link or QR code leading to their website from a printed advertisement or a social media page to provide the customer with additional information. For example, when KFC had some distribution issues that meant its restaurants ran out of chicken, it launched a blended digital and non-digital promotional campaign apologising to customers. KFC printed a link and QR code in a newspaper leading to a website where customers could see when their local KFC was going to be restocked.

Figure 3.16: How is this a blend of print and digital mediums?

Consistency

A business needs to ensure that its promotional materials are consistent so that the audience recognises the brand and the message is consistent. This means making sure that the core information, visual look, and feel, tone and branding are consistent so that the target audience is given a consistent message by the company.

For example, Reebok adapts its marketing message to target different audiences on different social media platforms, from really visual images on Instagram to a more information-based approach on Pinterest. However, the messages have the same feel and tone.

Over to you!   9

1   Consider each of the scenarios below. Write a brief statement that explains why the promotional methods used might not be appropriate.

   a   Advertising in-game currency for a video game through a newspaper advert.

   b   Trying to get more customers in store by sending an email leaflet to customers with an online account.

   c   Using a discount code on a billboard for customers to get 5 percent off their next online grocery shop.

2   For each of these scenarios, recommend one alternative method that would be more appropriate for the business.

Let's get practical!   3

Your manager at the technology company liked the suggestions you made for the promotional materials for the campaign to promote the new mobile phone. But she is worried about whether the materials are appropriate for the campaign.

1   Your manager is concerned about the project budget. She has asked you to choose two of the promotional materials that best suit the project needs. Explain why you have discarded the ones you have chosen to drop.

2   For the materials you have chosen, identify a complementary method that could be used to add to the effectiveness of the campaign. Explain why you think the two methods complement each other.

Review your learning

Test your knowledge

1 State the main objectives for a promotional campaign.

2 Explain why SMART objectives are a useful tool for businesses.

3 What is a KPI?

4 Explain why KPIs are important within a promotional campaign.

5 For two types of promotional materials, outline one benefit and one drawback of each type of material.

6 A business is launching a new laptop. Suggest and explain a promotional material that is complementary to a TV advert for the new laptop.

What have you learnt?

	See section
• How to create a promotional campaign for a brand or product.	2.1

TA3

Plan and pitch a proposal

Let's get started   1

Think back to a presentation you have given in class or one that you have attended. Was it a good experience? What was good about it? What was not so good about it? What could have been improved?

What will you learn?

- Considerations when planning a professional **pitch**.
- How to use and development of personal and presentation skills.
- Benefits of using a practice pitch.
- How to deliver a professional pitch.

3.1 Considerations when planning a professional pitch

Once an entrepreneur has created and developed a new product and created a promotional campaign for it, they need to pitch the product to potential investors or businesses. A pitch is a verbal and visual presentation of a business proposal to get backing and support for the proposal. It needs to convince investors or business managers that the product is worth going ahead with and investing time and money in. It is therefore important to plan a pitch well (Figure 3.17).

A business/entrepreneur may have a number of different product proposals competing for time and money. Investors and business managers therefore have to weigh up the cost of producing and marketing each of the proposals against the benefits it could generate, such as increased sales or gaining competitive advantage. They have to decide where to best spend their time and money.

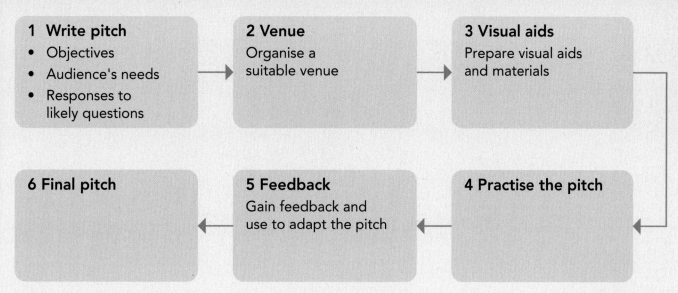

Figure 3.17: What are the stages in planning a pitch?

Pitch objectives

The objectives of the pitch are what the entrepreneur or business wants to achieve from it. The objectives also provide a guide for creating the pitch and evaluating its success. The two main objectives of the pitch are to:

- inform the audience

- persuade the audience.

Inform the audience

This is the entrepreneur's opportunity to fully explain their product proposal, present the essential data from the **market research** and outline the key points from the promotional campaign (Figure 3.18).

Persuade the audience

The entrepreneur needs to give convincing reasons for backing the product financially. A good pitch needs to make the audience listen and get them enthusiastic about the product. As a business or investor may have a number of different product proposals competing for their time and money, the pitch has to stand out and persuade them to invest.

The presenter needs to use a range of skills, techniques and methods to make the pitch interesting and engaging. They need to demonstrate a thorough knowledge of the product and be able to address any questions that the audience has.

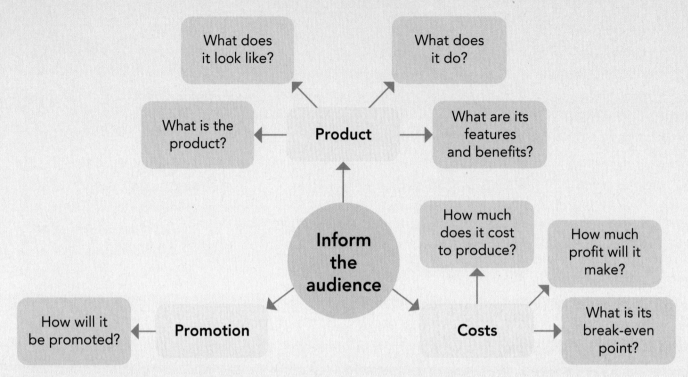

Figure 3.18: What information does the audience need to know to assess the business proposal?

Think about TV shows, such as *Dragons' Den,* where people pitch business proposals. Why do some entrepreneurs get investment and others get nothing? The successful entrepreneurs not only have a good product but also give a pitch that persuades the Dragons to invest in them.

Over to you!   1

There are many examples of business-style pitches on reality TV shows, such as *Dragons' Den* or *Shark Tank*. On YouTube, search for the clip 'BEST PITCHES: Levi Roots' Reggae Reggae pitch lures Peter Jones! Dragons' Den'.

1 How does the pitch meet the objective of informing the audience?

2 Were there any questions that Levi Roots could not answer? If so, what were they?

3 Do you think Levi was persuasive in his pitch? Explain why.

Stretch

4 Recommend two ways in which Levi Roots could have improved his pitch to the Dragons, and explain how your recommendations could have made his pitch better.

The audience

When developing a pitch for a new business proposal, an entrepreneur should ask themselves: 'Who am I pitching to?' Knowing the audience means the pitch is tailored to the audience (e.g. it is delivered at the right level using appropriate language and catering to the audience's interests).

Who is the expected audience?

To ensure the pitch hits the right notes with the audience, it is important to research the audience before the pitch and find out who they are and what their needs are. Is the pitch addressed at colleagues who work within a business (e.g. managers) or external people (e.g. bank manager, investors or customers)?

What are their needs and interests?

The information that is of interest to the audience will vary depending on who they are. For example, an investor will be particularly interested in the costs and whether the product makes a profit/breaks even. They want to know how the business will make them money. A customer is less interested in whether the business is profitable but more interested in how the product is beneficial to them.

Accessibility of content

The tone and language of the pitch are likely to be different depending on the audience's background and knowledge. Bear in mind that the audience may not be experts in the field. They may not have any technical knowledge or expertise in a particular area so it is important to avoid using jargon, acronyms or technical language that they may not understand or that may confuse them.

The presenter needs to also bear in mind any specific accessibility needs of the audience. For example:

- when talking, the presenter should speak clearly and not too fast. They should use simple language so that the whole audience, especially those that do not hear well, can understand the information that the presenter is delivering.

- when using visual and audio material, the presenter should make sure that text and visuals on slides are large enough to read even from the back of the room. They should use suitable backgrounds and text colours so that the whole audience can see them.

- moving text or images can be distracting and can make some people feel ill. So the presenter should consider whether slide transitions are necessary and whether will they make the information easier to understand.

- handouts of slides in large print or braille are helpful for people with visual impairment.

Over to you! 2

Identify and explain the needs of the following audiences:

a   Angela – a financial investor. She has hearing loss and wears a hearing aid.

b   Ibrahim – a marketing executive at the technology company you work for.

c   Emma – a social media influencer who is interested in featuring the product on her channel.

d   Cameron – a company executive who has to sign off on the project before it can be started. He will need to go away and consult with the other executives.

Let's get practical! 1

Your manager at the technology company you work for has asked you to begin preparing a pitch for your idea to the directors of the company. The five directors are all experienced business people. They have different areas of expertise, from sales and marketing to finance. Only one of them has any technical knowledge about mobile phones. One of the directors has a minor visual impairment and struggles to see objects in the distance.

1   Identify two objectives for the pitch for your new mobile phone (bearing in mind that this is a new product on the market).

2   Outline key factors you will need to consider to make sure the pitch meets the whole audience's needs. Your outline should include who the audience is, their likely expertise and what they are looking to get out of the new product.

*Tip: What might they be interested in (**financial viability**, suitability of promotion methods, etc.)? How might this impact your pitch?*

Venue

Let's get started   2

Look at the two images below. Which one would be the most appropriate for a pitch to small business investors? Why do you think this?

Figure 3.19: Potential venues for a pitch

It is important to check out the venue before the pitch to make sure that it is suitable and has what you need (Figure 3.20). Once the venue has been chosen, it needs to be booked and prepared for the pitch.

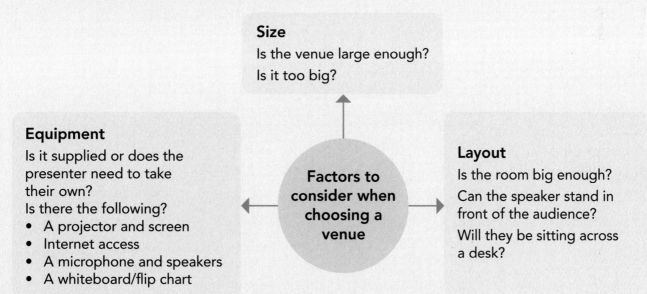

Size
Is the venue large enough?
Is it too big?

Factors to consider when choosing a venue

Equipment
Is it supplied or does the presenter need to take their own?
Is there the following?
- A projector and screen
- Internet access
- A microphone and speakers
- A whiteboard/flip chart

Layout
Is the room big enough?
Can the speaker stand in front of the audience?
Will they be sitting across a desk?

Figure 3.20: When choosing a venue for the pitch, what does a business need to consider?

Media and materials

A well-structured pitch will include a range of audio and visual materials and mediums (Table 3.13) to showcase the product.

Table 3.13: Mediums and materials that can be used within a pitch

Material/medium	Description and benefits
Presentation software	• Allows you to pull out the key points of the pitch as a slide slow • Presents a more professional pitch than a flip chart or whiteboard • Examples include: Microsoft PowerPoint, Google Slides and Prezi, with a range of animations and features
Prompt cards	• Small cards on which to write bullet-point reminders • Help ensure that the presenter covers the key points and does not forget anything • Can be looked at during the presentation with just a glance
Handouts/leaflets	• Takeaway notes covering the finer detail that is not included in the presentation because of time constraints (e.g. specific product details) • Can cover the information in detail • The audience can take them away to consider the proposal in more depth
Mock-ups	• An early draft of the promotional materials that the entrepreneur is planning on using to raise awareness or promote the product • Shows the audience what the campaign will look like • A visual way of showing the audience a promotional advertisement rather than just describing it
Videos/audio files	• Video or audio samples of advertisements or jingles for the audience to listen to • Bring the pitch to life for the audience
Prototype	• An early version of the product • Can serve as a useful **visual aid** in the pitch • The audience gets a chance to see and the inspect the product

Over to you!   3

1   For each of the materials/medium options in Table 3.13, suggest one limitation to using it in a professional pitch.

Stretch

2   Explain the consequences of not choosing appropriate materials/mediums in a professional pitch.

Let's get practical! 2

Part 1

Your manager wants to start getting things ready for your pitch to the directors of the technology company. So that she can book an appropriate venue, she has asked you to provide her with an outline of your needs for the pitch.

1   Identify the potential mediums and materials you will need in order to deliver a professional pitch to the company directors.

2   Justify your choice of medium and materials for the pitch.

Part 2

Your manager has found a possible venue for your pitch. She has asked you to consider the venue. She has also been informed that the finance director has recently had surgery and cannot drive to the venue so will need to get there using public transport.

3   Write a brief email to your manager, Samantha, outlining the venue requirements so she can assess whether the possible location is suitable. Include information on your requirements for:

   a   size of the venue (see Let's get practical! 1 for details about who will be attending)

   b   location of the venue

   c   accessibility considerations

   d   layout of the venue.

Personal appearance

If the entrepreneur looks the part they will feel more confident and the audience will have more confidence in both them and their pitch. A neat, well-presented entrepreneur can achieve a stronger more professional first impression than someone who has not taken the time to comb their hair or put on a smart pair of shoes for example. It is therefore important that the entrepreneur is clean and well presented, and that they wear clothes that are suitable for a business meeting. Their clothes should be clean and free of creases to avoid any unnecessary distractions from the pitch itself.

Good personal presentation goes beyond just looking smart and professional. It also includes a professional attitude, confidence and good communication skills and body language (see Section 3.2).

Structure of the pitch

Let's get started   3

What would you include in a pitch to get investment for a new product or service? Create a mind map of your ideas.

Having identified the objectives and the audience, arranged the venue, created the pitch materials and got the entrepreneur looking the part, the next step to consider is the structure of the pitch.

The pitch needs to be clearly structured so that it delivers the key information in a clear and logical way that engages with the audience and achieves the objectives. A pitch has three main parts (Table 3.14).

Your product proposal   1

Things to remember when pitching

As there is so much to remember and cover in a pitch, it is easy to forget things. Some key things to remember include:

- **The competition** – looking at the competition gives a complete picture of the market.

- **Avoid jargon, acronyms and abbreviations** – the audience are not necessarily industry experts and may find the pitch difficult to follow if it contains them.

- **Try not to read the pitch** – a pitch is meant to address an audience. The presenter cannot address the audience if their head is in their notes. Preparing and practising the pitch will ensure that the entrepreneur is more confident and familiar with their pitch so that they can use their notes as prompts rather than reading from them.

- **Know the facts inside out** – this will mean that the entrepreneur is well prepared to answer any questions thoroughly and confidently.

Table 3.14: The structure of a pitch

Element	Description

Introduction	• The entrepreneur should:
	  • introduce themselves and outline their experience and background to give the audience confidence in their knowledge and expertise
	  • introduce the product proposal clearly and briefly
	  • outline what they are going to cover in the pitch
	• First impressions are important so the introduction will set the tone for the rest of the pitch. It is therefore important to start confidently

Content presented logically (supported by visual aids)	• The content should be arranged in a logical way following the order in which the entrepreneur has developed the proposal.
	  • Customer needs and customer profile identified by market research
	  • The product and how it meets the customer needs, including its features and benefits
	  • Description of the competitors and why the proposed product will be more successful
	  • Feedback on the product from target customers
	  • Pricing
	  • Branding, promotional campaign – materials, methods, timescale and key milestones
	• The entrepreneur should work through the content in order, to make sure that they do not forget anything. Prompt cards will help to keep them on track
	• They might want to use a structure for their main content so that they deliver it in order. For example:
	  • What is the purpose of the product?
	  • Why is it needed?
	  • How does it meet customer needs?
	  • How will the product be promoted so customers know it meets their needs?
	  • What is the timeframe for the development and promotion of the product?
	• The entrepreneur should use visual aids and mediums to support the main content, engage the audience and bring the product to life

Conclusion	• A summary of the key points in the main content • This is what the audience is likely to remember the most so it needs to stand out • Outline what the entrepreneur wants from the audience (e.g. investment) • The presenter should thank the audience for taking the time to listen, and they should ask if there are any questions • The entrepreneur should have prepared answers to likely questions on the product and how it meets consumer needs

Use of visual aids

Visual aids are a key part of any pitch. They not only help to engage the audience, but they also show the audience what the product and promotional materials will look like. They are essential when trying to convince an audience to invest in the proposal. Table 3.15 outlines the different visual aids that can be used in a pitch.

Visual aids should be clear, simple and consistent, so that the audience can see and understand what is being presented. Too much clutter or an overly complicated graphic can sometimes mean the message is lost.

Table 3.15: Visual aids and how they can be used in a pitch. You will not be assessed on this content but may find it useful

Visual aid	How it can be used in a pitch
Slides	• Can be used to make the pitch more visually appealing and engaging for the audience • Keep text and slides to a minimum to avoid confusing or overwhelming the audience • Make one clear point on a slide and use your notes to talk about it. • Use slide designs, animations, fonts, photographs and graphics to illustrate the points and make the slides stand out, but do not overdo it! Sometimes, less is more • Use slide animations to reveal information step by step so that the audience is not given too much information at once
Videos/audio files	• Video or audio samples of advertisements or jingles can bring the pitch to life and show examples of promotional materials
Prototype of product proposal	• Gives the audience a chance to see and inspect the product • Makes the proposal more tangible and real in the minds of the audience
Examples of competitor products	• Gives the audience a chance to see and inspect competitor products • Can compare competitor products to the product that is being proposed
Examples of promotional materials	• Shows the types of promotional materials that will be used and what they look like • Shows the product branding, such as the company's logo
Images	• Images of the product, mock-ups of the promotional materials or even just the company logo add a professional element to a presentation • Specific points can be emphasised by using a picture
Charts and graphs	• Market research and financial information is often better presented as a visual graph or chart (e.g. market share) • It is easier to see percentage shares and trends in graph form

Over to you!   4

If you could only use two visual aids in a promotional pitch, which ones would you choose? Why? What are the advantages and disadvantages of the visual aids you have chosen?

How to anticipate potential questions and plan responses

Even the most rehearsed and practised pitch could still leave unanswered questions at the end of a presentation. Preparing for these is a vital part of the planning process. If an entrepreneur cannot answer an investor's questions, not only will they feel flustered and look unprofessional, but also their pitch will be less credible or less successful.

So it is important to research and prepare for the most likely types of questions. But how does a presenter do this? Here are some suggestions of areas to prepare.

- **Anticipate what different audiences want to know about the proposal:**

  - customers are going to want to know about the product and how it benefits them

  - investors will want to know about price, sales, profit and competitive advantage and how the entrepreneur plans to market the product or service. For example, who are the competitors for this product or service? What will give your product or service a competitive advantage?

  For each of the audience's particular interests, the entrepreneur needs to be prepared to explain how the proposal meets them.

- **Specific information and details** – what if the audience were so focused on one part of the presentation that they missed elements immediately after it? The presenter must know their pitch well enough to recall specific points on demand.

- **Commonly asked questions** – there are some pretty standard questions that the audience are likely to ask. The entrepreneur should research the most commonly asked questions for business pitches and prepare detailed answers relating to their specific product or service. For example, if there is a question about brand reputation, explain how the proposed product enhances or improves the brand's reputation.

- **Make notes** – making notes of anticipated questions and answers on prompt cards will ensure that the entrepreneur has thoughtful and sensible answers and is able to respond in a confident and professional manner.

- Prepare an immediate response for questions that you cannot answer – for example, 'Good question, I need to look into that and I will get back to you shortly.'

Over to you!   5

What questions might an investor have for an entrepreneur at the end of a pitch? Identify three points that you think an investor might want clarification on at the end of a promotional pitch. Write three questions that they might ask the entrepreneur to clarify these points.

Let's get practical!   3

Your manager has been very impressed with the development of your pitch so far and believes that the mobile phone proposal is ready to be pitched to the directors. She has asked you to:

a   identify and justify three visual aids that you plan on using for the pitch so that she can start getting them made

b   provide a brief outline of the pitch's contents for her to review (product design, branding, pricing, the proposed promotional campaign and any other relevant information)

c   anticipate three questions the directors might have when the pitch is over. You do not need to have an answer for the questions.

3.2 Use and development of personal and presentation skills

Let's get started **4**

How do you think each of the people in the photos is feeling?
Why do you think that? What is their body language communicating?

Figure 3.21: What does body language tell you about the way these people are feeling?

How the entrepreneur communicates with the audience will impact on how the audience feels about the pitch. It is therefore important to get it right. The saying 'you only get one chance to make a good first impression' has never meant more than in a proposal pitch. Audiences will judge the validity of the entire proposal based on how well the entrepreneur is able to deliver the information and whether they deliver it in a professional manner.

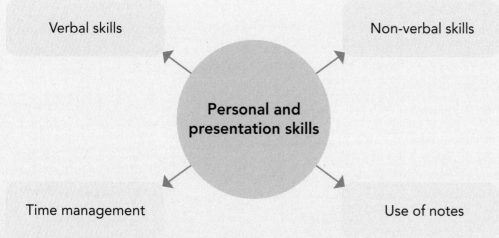

Figure 3.22: What are personal and presentation skills?

Verbal skills

Good verbal communication is vital when delivering a proposal pitch to ensure that the pitch has maximum impact. It is crucial to make sure the presenter delivers information clearly so that it can be heard and uses appropriate language so that it can be understood. As outlined in Table 3.16, **verbal skills** are more than just speaking.

Strong, verbal communication is a difficult skill to master and takes a lot of practice. Verbal communication skills are not only needed for pitching a product proposal. They are also essential in everyday life for communicating with friends, making appointments or arrangements and for working effectively with colleagues or team members.

Table 3.16: Verbal skills

Verbal skill	Description
Clarity	• Saying words and phrases clearly • It is important to speak with clarity to make sure that the information is communicated correctly • Avoid using slang and jargon • Make sure the audience can understand every word that is said • The audience does not want to have to ask a presenter to repeat something because they did not understand it

Tone of voice	• How something is said – the tone can signal whether the presenter is happy, sad or passionate about a product/idea
	• It needs to be appropriate and engaging, e.g.
	  • a single tone all the way through may make the pitch dull and boring
	  • a faster rate (but not too fast) will make the tone of voice seem more exciting
	• Alternating the tone of voice and pitch can emphasise that something is important or interesting and can draw an audience into the presentation

Voice projection	• Using the voice powerfully and clearly to deliver a presentation or speech • Good projection will ensure that the whole audience can hear the presentation
Formal/informal language	• **Informal language** is most often used with people with whom we have a personal or well-established working relationship, e.g. in everyday conversations, personal emails and on social media • **Formal language** is used when communicating with people we do not know very well or in a professional situation (managers, directors, etc.), e.g. in business emails or presentations • When trying to make a good impression, use formal language. For example, avoid slang or regional terms ('trainers' not 'kicks')

Speaking pace	• Speaking too slowly may:
	  • cause the audience to lose interest in the pitch
	  • mean the pitch runs over time if there is a time limit
	• Speaking too quickly (e.g. at normal conversation speed) may lose some of the audience where the pitch goes into more detail

Over to you!   6

Use your phone or a computer to record yourself reading a page from your favourite book or a story from the news and play it back. Or read the page out loud to family or friends. What do you think you could improve about your verbal skills based on this recording?

Non-verbal skills

Non-verbal communication, or body language, communicates how people feel even though they may not be conscious of the message that their body language is giving.

When trying to convince an audience of investors that the proposal is worth investing in, the entrepreneur's verbal skills can provide the information the audience needs, but their **non-verbal skills** also tell the audience a lot about the entrepreneur. Confidence and authority are displayed more by what a person does than what they say. So it is important to practise not only verbal but also non-verbal communication skills.

Non-verbal communication includes how you stand, eye contact, gestures and facial expressions. Positive body language can help to build a good relationship with the audience in a pitch and also more generally with people in everyday life (Table 3.17).

Table 3.17: The importance of non-verbal skills. You will not be assessed on this content but may find it useful

Non-verbal skills	Why is it important?	Positive body language	Negative body language
Eye contact	Eye contact makes the audience think they are being addressed directly It draws them in and makes them feel part of the pitch	Looking at each member of the audience Making eye contact when turning from the presentation to look at the audience	Avoiding eye contact altogether Looking at the floor or outside of the immediate space Staring at the audience
Gestures	Gestures enhance the points a speaker is making They can help to emphasise key points and show confidence	Expressive arm and hand movements Pointing at key elements of the presentation, the visual aids, etc.	Fidgeting Arms folded or permanently fixed behind the back
Posture and position	Positive posture can help a speaker to feel calm and it shows the audience they are in control	Standing up straight, leaning forward slightly Facing the audience Giving the audience personal space	Slouched Turned away from the audience Too close or too far away

Table 3.17: Continued

Non-verbal skills	Why is it important?	Positive body language	Negative body language
Facial expressions	Facial expressions can tell an audience a lot about your feelings and attitudes Your face communicates to the audience more than any other part of the body. If you do not like something, your face will say it before you have expressed a verbal opinion	Relaxed and smiling	Furrowed brow Rolling eyes at questions
Confidence	Confidence is important as it makes the audience believes in you and what you are presenting If you are confident in your product, that confidence will be transferred to the audience	Standing confidently, upright and facing the audience Calm facial expressions	Poor hand control (fidgeting or pointing directly at someone in the audience) Slumped posture Frowning
Persuasiveness	Persuasiveness will help to change the audience's mind if they are unsure It will convince the audience to back your product over another one	Enthusiastic hand and arm movements Good eye contact, giving the audience your full attention Listening actively to the audience	Losing eye contact with the audience Frequently checking notes to find any answers to questions Aggressive and arrogant body language

An entrepreneur can demonstrate persuasiveness through verbal skills as well non-verbal skills. For example by delivering a confident and engaging pitch, answering questions effectively, and by providing counter-arguments and solutions (without being aggressive).

Use of notes, cues and pitch script

Some people can remember a pitch or a speech without any notes or prompts while others need more support.

Notes

As there is a lot of information to deliver, pitch notes are a really useful way to avoid missing any key points, facts, figures and important features of a product.

Presenters should not use notes during the pitch itself as there is the temptation to read from them and lose eye contact with the audience. However, they are useful if a question from the audience requires more detailed information on facts, figures or details, such as actual figures from the market research.

Prompt cards and cues

Prompt cards are small cards that the presenter can hold in their hand and glance at during the presentation. This helps the presenter to maintain eye contact with their audience. Prompt cards are easy to make and can be used for:

- headline points that the entrepreneur uses as prompts for delivery, or something that the entrepreneur needs to highlight (cues), e.g. showing a slide with the logo or a chart

- summarising a slide, argument, fact or figure from the presentation

- additional information that the entrepreneur wants to share which is not on a slide

- a checklist of points to cover.

Pitch script

This is a line-by-line written text of the pitch and presentation slides. It should be prepared, practised and summarised on prompt cards. Like notes, a script is not something the audience should see. It is important not to read it out or memorise it word for word otherwise the pitch will lack a natural flow and tone.

Time management

Investors, managers and business backers are busy people. They will have taken time out of their schedule to attend the pitch and may be seeing a number of other pitches in a short timeframe. Therefore, it is vital that the pitch does not overrun or have to be cut short and misses out essential information. Time management of pitches is something that entrepreneurs have to practise.

Figure 3.23 shows the elements of good time management:

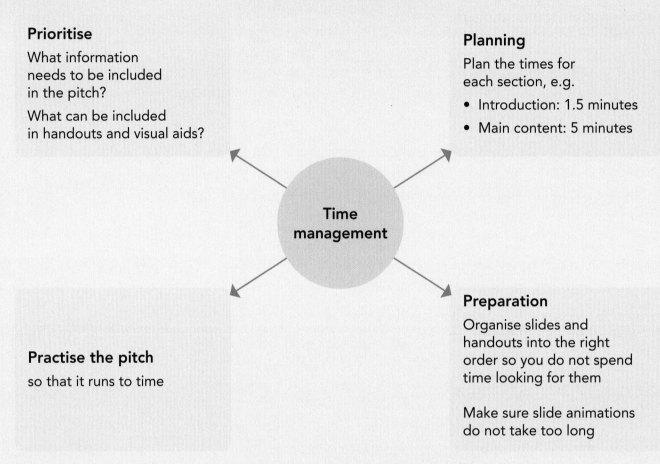

Prioritise

What information needs to be included in the pitch?

What can be included in handouts and visual aids?

Planning

Plan the times for each section, e.g.

- Introduction: 1.5 minutes
- Main content: 5 minutes

Time management

Practise the pitch

so that it runs to time

Preparation

Organise slides and handouts into the right order so you do not spend time looking for them

Make sure slide animations do not take too long

Figure 3.23: How an entrepreneur can ensure that they use their pitch time effectively

3.3 Benefits of using a practice pitch

Let's get started   5

Create a spider diagram of the reasons why it might be important to practise a pitch. Suggest one possible consequence of not practising a pitch. Explain your point.

An entrepreneur will typically only get one chance at impressing an investor or audience with their pitch. Even with thorough planning, there is still a risk that the presentation may not deliver what the entrepreneur needs it to. Most entrepreneurs are so involved and familiar with their products that they may not consider that the audience might not understand some of the pitch or the appeal of the product. A practice pitch is like a dress rehearsal in a play – it gives the entrepreneur a chance to test it out.

The practice pitch is delivered in front of just a few people to get some idea of how well it all works together. It allows the entrepreneur to see whether it delivers the required information, with the right level of detail and within the required timeframe. While this is time-consuming and not the 'real' pitch, it is an essential and valuable process as practice makes perfect. A practice run also helps the presenter to feel calmer and more confident before delivering the actual pitch.

Support peers

While friends, family or even colleagues may be aware of the business idea, they may not know the product as well as the entrepreneur, which makes them the perfect people to practise the pitch on. Likewise in a business, colleagues are often willing to be the 'audience'.

Peers can listen and pay attention to the pitch and make notes on how well they understood the concepts within the pitch and whether the information was covered with the right level of detail. They can also give feedback on verbal and non-verbal skills. They may even have questions that the presenter had not anticipated.

Constructive feedback

Feedback is a valuable part of any product development. However, feedback is only of use to an entrepreneur or business manager if it is constructive. For example, if a customer gives feedback that they do not like the food at a restaurant, then this is feedback but it is not very useful or constructive because it does not explain:

- what they do like about the restaurant
- why they do not like the food
- what the restaurant could do to improve the food.

Constructive feedback allows a business/entrepreneur to understand more fully what the problem is and how they can make changes to improve the product or service.

So, for example, if the customer had commented that they did not like the food because it was cold when it arrived, then the restaurant knows how to improve its product or service.

Likewise, when providing feedback to peers on their pitch, constructive feedback is supportive and helps to identify solutions. When offering constructive feedback:

- **Balance the positive with the negative** – people are more willing to take constructive feedback if they know what they did well, rather than just what they did not do well

- **Be specific** – what specifically did not work? The more specific the feedback, the more successfully it can be acted upon

- **Do not make it personal** – criticism is difficult to take. Adding personal elements (such as commenting on their choice of tie) makes them less likely to take the feedback on board

- **Be timely** – make sure the feedback is offered in a timely fashion. Feedback needs to be given while the entrepreneur still has time to make changes.

A good way of approaching constructive feedback is to start with the positives before moving on to the negatives and finally looking at suggested improvements.

Over to you!   7

1   Find a video of an entrepreneur's pitch, like the one you have seen in Section 3.1, but for a pitch that was not successful. Give constructive feedback on the pitch.

2   Can you identify why one was successful and the other wasn't? Suggest the key differences between the pitches.

Respond to feedback offered by peers

Feedback is a very useful tool in helping to improve a pitch. Presenters should consider all the points that their peers have raised and decide whether they are valid. The presenter/pitcher may not agree with them all, but if they are valid, they should try to address them and implement them in the pitch. For example, if the feedback was that:

- the introduction was too long, then the presenter/entrepreneur might consider shortening the introduction and deciding whether all of the information that they had included is necessary

- the audience did not understand the term 'customer profile', the presenter might decide not to change it as the audience for the actual pitch are business professionals and directors, who will be familiar with the term.

Over to you!   8

Your boss has asked you to watch a colleague's practice pitch and provide feedback to them. Design a feedback form that will allow you to give them thorough feedback. It should allow for feedback on performance as well as the content of the pitch itself. The form should include feedback on:

a   overall structure and quality of the content of the pitch

b   use of visual aids

c   use of other supporting materials and quality of them

d   verbal and non-verbal skills

e   use of notes

f   time management

g   personal appearance.

There should also be space for a response from the presenter on how they will respond to the feedback.

Review your own practice pitch

A practice pitch is a significant part of preparation for delivering a pitch. Like a dress rehearsal in a play, a practice pitch allows a presenter to identify any features that they want to improve upon. It could be anything from content they want to emphasise, to habits they did not realise they had but want to keep an eye on during a presentation.

An honest and detailed review of a practice pitch can help a presenter develop their pitch and improve their chances of success in the final presentation.

Over to you!   9

You should by now have created an outline practice pitch for your assessment.

1   Using the camera on a phone, or standing in front of a mirror, deliver your practice pitch and use the form you designed in Over to you! 8 to review your own performance.

2   Make suggestions for improvements to your practice pitch.

3   Annotate your handouts and notes to show how you will make the changes and improve on your practice pitch.

3.4 Deliver a professional pitch

Let's get started   6

Acting on feedback is essential for delivering the final, professional pitch. Using the feedback you have been given for your practice pitch, identify three things you can improve upon for the final pitch.

Now that the entrepreneur has completed the development of their product or service, it is time to deliver the pitch. They have to bring everything together – from undertaking the initial market research and developing the product/service idea through to producing it and marketing it.

Preparing	**Practising**	**Knowing the content**
Set SMART objectives Know who the audience is Create visual aids Write the pitch	Practise the pitch Amend pitch based on feedback	Know the content in detail to give a confident pitch
Timing	**Responding to questions**	**Memorising**
Plan the timings Practise so that the pitch runs to time Prioritise the information that needs to be delivered	Anticipate questions and plan responses	Memorise the key aspects of the pitch (key words, timing) to reduce the need for reference to speaker notes

Figure 3.24: What skills are required to deliver a successful pitch?

Your product proposal   2

Hints and tips for delivering a professional pitch

A checklist is a useful tool when preparing to deliver a pitch. The checklist could include:

- Practise the pitch

- Anticipate likely questions and prepare responses

- Think about the lessons learnt from the practice pitch

- Arrive at the pitch venue with plenty of time to set up and organise the layout

- Check personal appearance to make sure the presenter looks smart and professional

- Make sure that all handouts, materials, prototypes and other resources are ready well before the presentation begins so that there is sufficient time to check them

- Deliver the pitch using a logical structure, and remember to fully explain:

    - the opportunity that exists – the gap in the market, the competition and how the product will take advantage of these

    - the competition – who they are and how the product on offer is better or different

- Engage the audience by:

    - maintaining eye contact

    - keeping the content relevant to their background and interests

- Avoid any bad habits, such as fidgeting and over-use of notes

- Watch the clock. Timing is important and the pitch needs to be completed within the time allowed

- Invite the audience to ask questions, and respond in a calm and thoughtful way. If the presenter does not know the answer, explain that they will find out and get back to the person who asked the question.

Let's get practical!   **4**

You are now ready to deliver your pitch to the directors of the company. Create a checklist for the final pitch, making sure all of the necessary planning and preparation has been done.

Review your learning

Test your knowledge

1. State the two main objectives for a professional pitch.

2. Outline two types of medium or materials that could be used to deliver a pitch and explain how they support delivery of a professional pitch.

3. Explain why an entrepreneur needs to consider the audience in a pitch.

4. Why are practice pitches important to the successful delivery of a professional pitch?

5. Explain how constructive feedback from a practice pitch can be used to prepare for a final pitch.

What have you learnt?

	See section
• Considerations when planning a professional pitch.	3.1
• How to use and development of personal and presentation skills.	3.2
• Benefits of using a practice pitch.	3.3
• How to deliver a professional pitch.	3.4

Review a brand proposal, promotional campaign and professional pitch

Let's get started

What was the last film that you saw? What did you like about it? What did you dislike about it? What would you have improved about it? Write a list summarising the positives and negatives of the film and suggest how you would improve it.

What will you learn?

- How to review a brand using a range of sources.
- How to review a professional pitch to an external audience.

4.1 Review a brand using a range of sources

A review is a judgement or formal assessment of a product, service or piece of work against its objectives or **aims**. A review involves not only taking on board feedback from others, such as customers and peers, but also self-assessment. This ensures that the review is balanced and considers different viewpoints and experience.

Conducting a review of their brand, product and pitch allows an entrepreneur to understand whether they have met their objectives, what is good and more importantly what needs to be improved and how to improve it. It also allows them to assess the product and brand against:

- their own goals
- the goals of the business/investors
- the competition
- customer expectations.

The entrepreneur or business can use the review to make changes if necessary.

Once an entrepreneur or business has created a product, a brand and a promotional campaign for the brand using different promotional materials, they need to review them by looking at the different elements as shown in Figure 3.25.

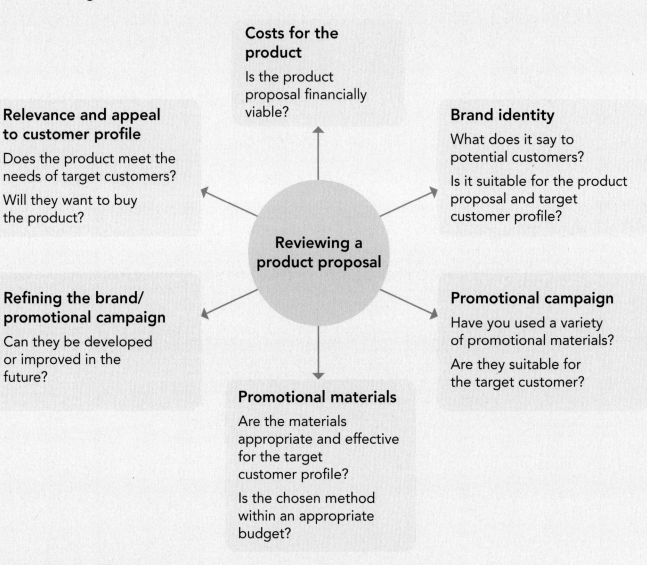

Costs for the product

Is the product proposal financially viable?

Relevance and appeal to customer profile

Does the product meet the needs of target customers?

Will they want to buy the product?

Brand identity

What does it say to potential customers?

Is it suitable for the product proposal and target customer profile?

Reviewing a product proposal

Refining the brand/ promotional campaign

Can they be developed or improved in the future?

Promotional campaign

Have you used a variety of promotional materials?

Are they suitable for the target customer?

Promotional materials

Are the materials appropriate and effective for the target customer profile?

Is the chosen method within an appropriate budget?

Figure 3.25: The different elements to consider when reviewing a product proposal

Self-assessment

Self-assessment is when the entrepreneur assesses their own performance, skills and work in relation to their brand proposal, promotional campaign and professional pitch. It can help the entrepreneur to:

- reflect on their work, knowledge and understanding
- identify their own personal strengths and weaknesses

- identify the strengths and weaknesses of the product proposal (e.g. the brand and promotional campaign) and the pitch

- identify areas for self-improvement (e.g. presentation skills, Section 3.2)

- identify aspects of the brand, promotional campaign or pitch that require improvement.

Good self-assessment requires openness and honesty.

Feedback from others

Constructive feedback (see Section 3.3) from a variety of sources ensures that the review is balanced and considers different opinions and experience. Figure 3.26 shows the different sources of feedback from others:

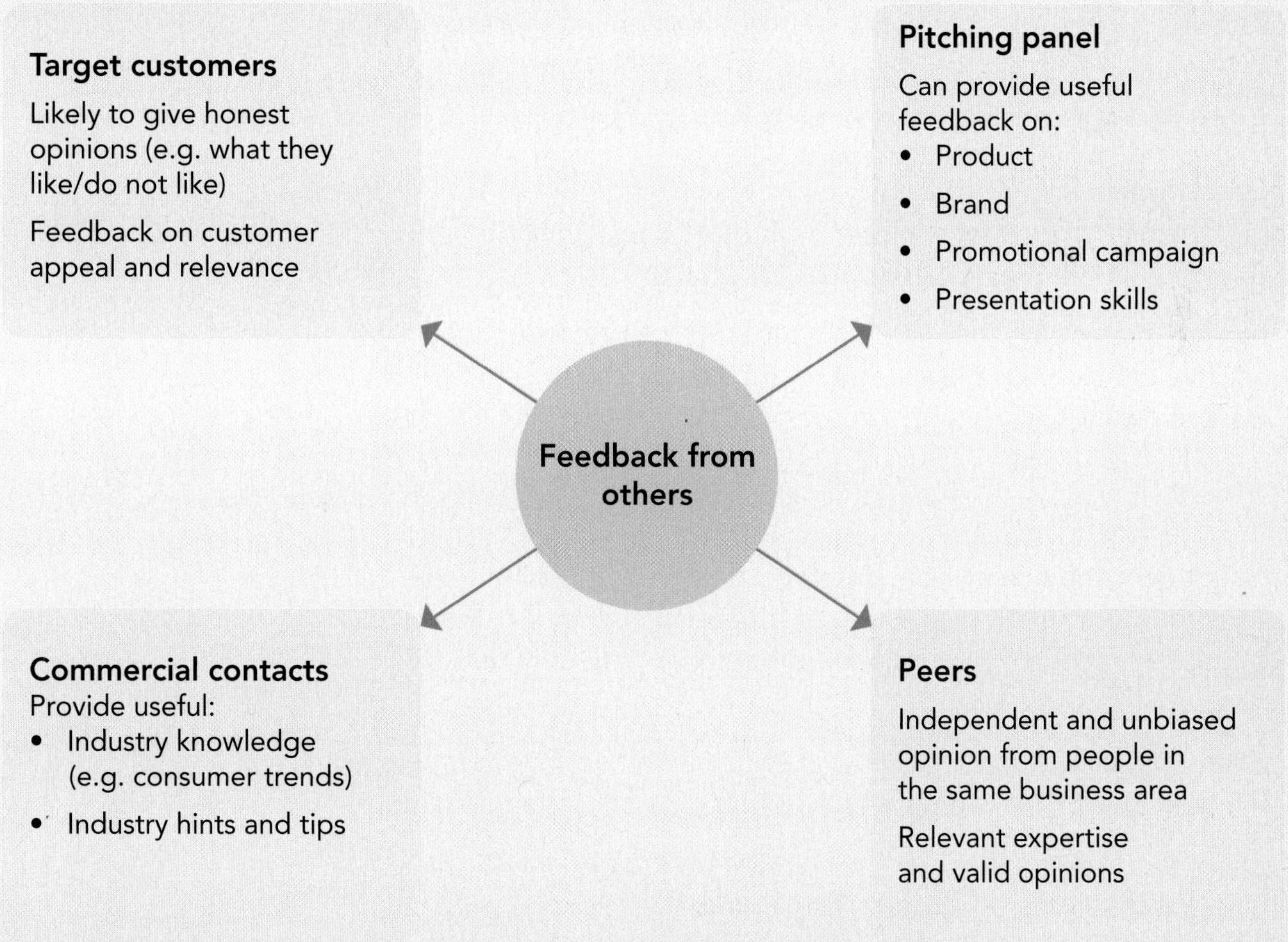

Target customers

Likely to give honest opinions (e.g. what they like/do not like)

Feedback on customer appeal and relevance

Pitching panel

Can provide useful feedback on:
- Product
- Brand
- Promotional campaign
- Presentation skills

Feedback from others

Commercial contacts
Provide useful:
- Industry knowledge (e.g. consumer trends)
- Industry hints and tips

Peers

Independent and unbiased opinion from people in the same business area

Relevant expertise and valid opinions

Figure 3.26: Where can you get feedback from?

Other sources of evidence for reviewing the product proposal

An entrepreneur may also want to review the whole product proposal against the:

- **financial predictions** that they set when designing the product proposal and assessing its financial viability (see Unit R068, Section 4.3) to ensure that:
  - it is still likely to **break even** and make a profit
  - costs and pricing decisions are still appropriate
- **competitor analysis** that they carried out as part of the brand development (see Section 1.4). This will help them to review the brand's strengths, weaknesses and USP against the competition and assess how their product proposal differs from that of the competition.

Lessons learnt from practice and professional pitch

Feedback from a practice pitch will allow an entrepreneur to learn lessons and understand what went well and what areas need improvement. For example, in the practice pitch they may have:

- spoken too quickly, making it difficult for the audience to follow. So they can practise delivering the pitch more slowly before the professional pitch
- used too much technical language that needs further explanation in the professional pitch.

Feedback from the practice pitch is also valuable as it can help the entrepreneur to further develop the product proposal and **refine** the product, brand and promotional campaign (see Section 3.3). Feedback could come from:

- asking the audience for either written or verbal feedback at the end of the pitch (which the entrepreneur can analyse after the pitch)
- following up with the audience after the pitch by email or in person (e.g. a phone call).

If the pitch was recorded, listening to it along with any audience questions can help to identify missing components. So, if the audience ask questions in the practice that could be answered in the pitch, you can add information to the final draft.

> **Let's get practical!** 1
>
> You have completed a professional pitch as part of your assessment for this unit. Review your pitch by:
>
> a conducting a brief self-assessment of your performance. Identify the strengths and weaknesses of the pitch
>
> b reading the feedback given to you by the audience. Identify two points that were positive and two areas to work on
>
> c comparing the feedback given by the audience to your own self-assessment. How is the feedback similar to your own self-assessment? How does it differ?

Future developments and refinement

Businesses are continuously developing and improving their products to meet customers' changing demands and to differentiate themselves from the competition. For example, mobile phone manufacturers are constantly updating their products to include new features and to use the latest technology so that they meet customers' needs.

The most successful businesses value customer feedback. They use it to shape the products or services they offer in order to meet customers' needs. The success of a product will depend on how well it meets customers' needs. Feedback from target customers might identify opportunities to develop or refine the product proposal such as:

- improving the product's performance by identifying the performance factors that are important to the target customer

- improving the user-friendliness of the product if customers are finding it difficult to use or understand

- reducing the costs by removing features that customers do not need

- creating promotional materials with more impact for the target customer

- adapting the brand identity (logo, website content, social media posts) to better suit the target customer.

Case study

Starbucks – Responding to customer feedback

Starbucks has launched many successful products over the years and developed a number of its products as a result of customer feedback. In 2008, Howard Schultz introduced the 'My Starbucks idea'. This is a way for Starbucks to get feedback from its customers. On its website the company asks customers to provide feedback or suggestions for new products or improvements to existing products. The idea is then shared with the community of customers and website users, who 'upvote' (agree with) the suggestion or idea if they like it. Starbucks collects the valuable data and makes changes to its products and services based on customers' needs.

Figure 3.27: Starbucks developed its hazelnut macchiato and mocha coconut frappuccino in response to customer feedback

As a result of the feedback, Starbucks has developed and refined its brand, products and services. For example, it has:

- introduced new products, such as cake-pops for those with a smaller appetite who want a treat

- introduced new services, such as free wi-fi for customers drinking in

- developed and refined its products, such as developing its coffee ranges to include new flavours, e.g. a hazelnut macchiato and mocha coconut frappuccino.

Starbucks has put in place 277 ideas since 'My Starbucks idea' was first introduced in 2008, meaning that feedback has had a significant impact on how the business operates.

Check your understanding

1   Suggest two benefits to Starbucks from making these changes based on customer feedback.

2   Suggest two limitations or drawbacks for Starbucks on making changes based on feedback.

3   Suggest how the customer benefits from being able to provide feedback to a company in this way.

Over to you!   1

Research two other examples of businesses that have adapted their products and services as a result of customer feedback.

1   How did they adapt their products/services?

2   What were the likely benefits to the business from the changes to its products and services?

Case study

FloraPhone (Part 1)

Michaela has developed a new mobile phone case – FloraPhone. Typical mobile phone cases are made from plastics, rubber and other materials that are difficult to recycle. The FloraPhone is a mobile phone case for both Android and Apple devices that is made from plant-based plastics, so it is biodegradable. This will reduce the amount of waste plastic that could end up in our oceans and landfill.

Market research

For her **primary market research**, Michaela first carried out a simple market research survey to find out what people thought about an environmentally friendly phone case and whether they liked her design ideas.

She decided to use a survey as her main primary source because it lets people express their opinions, so she was able to ask specific questions about the design. The survey asked about age, gender, occupation and income. It also asked if people would be willing to switch to an environmentally friendly product. To keep costs down and gather the data quickly, Michaela used convenience **sampling** (see Unit R068, Section 1.1).

From her research, Michaela found that:

- her idea was most popular with males and females between the ages of 16 and 24 from a middle to high income bracket.

- 65 percent of the people surveyed owned an iPhone, with 35 percent owning an Android device.

- 76 percent of 16–24 year olds who were surveyed watch streaming platforms and satellite TV.

- very few of this age group (16 percent) read newspapers or magazines.

Continued

Michaela also conducted a competitor analysis (see Section 1.4), looking at similar products on sale and her USP against other businesses. The competitor analysis helped to find the main competitors, but it also identified the popular styles of phone case. She found two similar mobile phone case products:

- SafeCase – a popular brand of durable case. The company is well known in the industry for modern designs and colours, but its cases are among the more expensive options for customers.

- EcoCase – an eco-friendly product. The main USP is that it is an eco-friendly product, and EcoCase is one of the few suppliers to offer this option. The products are limited in their colour choices and only cater to a small number of phone models.

Most of the competitor products had subtle designs on them and were black, purple or red, suggesting these colours are the most popular among the customers for these brands.

Michaela's third method of research was a **focus group** to gather some qualitative research (see Table 2.4 in Unit R068). Potential customers were asked questions about what they are looking for in a mobile phone case, but also what they felt was missing. From this research, Michaela found that durability was important, but that the eco-friendly idea was also very popular because people change their phones so often.

Michaela also had to consider the external environment to ensure that she was releasing the product at the right time. Even though it has been a tough year in terms of the economy, things have started picking up on the high street recently, making now the ideal time to release her new product into the market.

She collated the key **findings** from her primary and **secondary market research** in a summary table. Based on her research, she has decided to target fashion conscious, environmentally aware customers between the ages of 16 and 24, with a middle to high level of disposable income. Despite a lack of experience in the industry, Michaela hopes that good design and sustainability of the case will be real strengths.

Product design and development

Michaela created both a mind map of key features and a mood board of colours and designs to help with design ideas. She also sketched four design concepts for the phone case and decided on one final design that she felt met the research findings.

Her **design mix** includes a balance of all elements, with **aesthetics** and **function** being key. A motif shows the eco-friendly nature of the product, while the eco-friendly plastic she is using is very durable.

Continued

As a result of verbal feedback from a focus group on a prototype case, she has decided to change the product design so that it looks more natural and eco-friendly. She has added a green-coloured case to the current range of colours with a plant motif to reflect the eco-friendly nature of the product. Michaela's market research identified the iPhone as being the most popular model, so her initial product idea will be for the most recent iPhone release.

After reviewing and assessing the revised product design herself, Michaela decided that it now meets the needs of the customers identified in her market research and offers a good range of colour options. The iPhone is the top brand in the market right now and Michaela feels her product has the best chance to gain market share by targeting these customers. However, while her environmental sustainability USP sets her apart from most of the competition, her product is not the only eco-friendly mobile phone case on the market. Also, while her research supports her decision to focus on the iPhone market, she is a little concerned about losing potential custom from users of other brands.

Financial viability

The plant-based plastic Michaela is using is a little more expensive than usual production materials, and because she is including an embossed motif it means the variable cost is slightly higher. Michaela is predicting a variable cost of £7 per unit. She has also calculated total **fixed costs** of £45 000. This includes factory rent, **utilities** and the salaries of a small team of staff to help with production and packaging.

As Michaela is producing a high-quality product aimed at higher income earners, she has decided to use **price skimming** and sell each case for £20. She is confident that her USP will generate the sales she needs. With this strategy, Michaela estimates she will sell between 3000 and 3500 cases in the first year, making her total **variable costs** £24 500 if she hits her top figure of selling 3500 units.

Initial **break-even** calculations placed the break-even point too high, so Michaela had to make some changes to her plans. She sourced a cheaper machine to manufacture the products and decided to produce them herself initially to reduce the fixed costs. With these changes, she reduced her annual fixed costs to £28 000. If Michaela achieves her higher sales number, this will generate a pre-tax profit of £17 500.

Brand

Michaela is developing an exciting brand personality in the environmentally friendly but fashionable phone case, and she is aiming the product at younger (16–24 year old) customers. Her company logo uses popular colours and will be printed on the inside of the case.

Continued

From the market research, Michaela has identified black and purple as the most popular colours. She has chosen to have the company logo printed inside the case because Michaela wants the company logo to be seen by her customers, but not to take away from the embossed motif on the case itself.

As the target market is young and trendy teenagers to young adults, Michaela has decided that a strapline for her advertising 'the green approach' is the most appropriate method of getting the message across to the market.

Promotional campaign and materials

Michaela has set herself an objective of achieving sales of 3000 units by the end of the first year, and she aims to expand into other phone models in the second year. To achieve this, she has offered free samples of her products to some social media influencers and will post information, adverts and pictures on various social media platforms as part of a social media campaign. She will also include adverts on billboards at bus stops. She plans to run the launch campaign for six months. She has chosen to use billboards and social media influencers to keep the promotion costs down and target her chosen market.

Michaela has set herself the following key performance indicators for the six-month campaign to judge its success:

- an average daily sales rate of 50 units

- engage with customers, achieving 2000 social media contacts (subscribers) across the different social media platforms that she used

- get her phone cases sold by two leading shops.

Check your understanding

Review Michaela's business proposal for FloraPhone.

1   Explain one strength and one weakness of Michaela's:

    a   product design

    b   brand identity and personality

    c   promotional materials

    d   promotional campaign.

2   Suggest two improvements Michaela could make to her proposal.

3   Do you think her proposal will be successful? Explain your answer.

Your product proposal   1

Reviewing the overall success of your business proposal

When carrying out a review of your business proposal, remember to:

- refer to the original aims of your product based on market research

- look at the costs for your product and assess whether it is **financially viable** (Unit R068, Sections 4.1, 4.3)

- identify the strengths, weaknesses and areas for improvement in your proposal and pitch (Section 4.1)

- evaluate the suitability of the methods of promotion, the promotional materials you have used and the brand personality in relation to your product (Sections 1.1, 2.1)

- assess the likely success of your proposal

- recommend improvements based on the areas of weakness and development that you have identified.

4.2 Review a professional pitch to an external audience

Delivering an effective pitch is a skill that takes practice to perfect. It is therefore important to review a pitch to understand what went well and what improvements you could make for future pitches.

Your product proposal   2

Reviewing your pitch

Section 4.1 covers the different types and sources of feedback that you can use to review a pitch, including self-assessment and feedback from others. Figure 3.28 outlines key points to consider when reviewing your pitch.

Did it meet the objectives?
- Did it inform the audience?
- Did it persuade the audience?

Answering questions
- Did the presenter anticipate the key questions?
- Did the answers show knowledge, confidence and accuracy?

What went well?
- What did the audience respond well to?
- Did the presenter cover all they needed to in the time allowed?

Reviewing a pitch

Professionalism
- Was the pitch delivered confidently and in good time?
- Did the presenter look professional and appear confident?

What could have been improved?
- Could the information have been clearer?
- Was the USP clear?
- Did the pitch address the competition?

Non-verbal communication skills
- Were the visual aids impactful and informative?
- Was the presenter's body language positive?

Verbal communication skills
- Was the message communicated clearly?
- Were the format, content and language of the pitch appropriate?
- Was the pitch at the right level to engage the audience?

Figure 3.28: What key points should you consider when reviewing your pitch?

Over to you! 2

Look back to Section 3.1 and watch the video clip of Levi Roots' pitch on *Dragons' Den* again.

1 Identify three things that went well during his pitch.

2 Identify three things that he did not do so well.

3 Suggest two improvements he could make to his pitch.

Let's get practical! 2

Feedback and reviews are useful, but sometimes it can be difficult to get feedback from audiences as they do not know what to focus their comments on.

Using the feedback form you designed in Section 3.3, Over to you! 8, provide Levi with constructive feedback on how he could improve his pitch to the Dragons.

Tip: Think about how your feedback will improve the pitch.

Case study

FloraPhone (Part 2)

Michaela has considered the feedback from peers and consumers. She is now ready to start planning, preparing and developing her pitch to potential investors.

Pitch planning

As a new business, Michaela needs financial investment to develop, manufacture and market her new phone case. Her pitch objectives reflect this.

- Inform the audience of the product, highlighting the eco-friendly USP.

- Inform the audience of the research results and product development.

- Persuade the audience to invest in the product.

Michaela has invited a panel of four potential investors and two potential stockists to the pitch, aiming to persuade the investors to provide financial backing and the stockist to place her product in their shops. The investors and stockists will be travelling by car from across the UK.

Continued

As the panel is quite small, Michaela has booked a meeting room at a local hotel. There is parking outside the hotel, and a conference table and refreshments will be provided with the meeting room. She has asked if the hotel can make a projector available. For the pitch itself, she has created a PowerPoint presentation and two handouts – one containing a summary of the collated market research findings and another with financial information on it.

Practice pitch

Before carrying out the pitch in front of the investors and stockists, Michaela pitched the idea to her friends and partner, who gave her feedback. The practice pitch included the same PowerPoint and handouts that the potential investors will be receiving. However, she was not prepared for some of the questions that her friends asked her and struggled to answer them.

Practice pitch feedback and action plan

The audience for Michaela's practice pitch were impressed with her product idea and the research she had done to support the product. They also felt the pitch content had been delivery clearly and in a logical order. However, they felt that some of the language she used to explain the eco-friendly plastic she would be using got a little too technical. They fed back that she should change it so the investors and stockists do not get confused by the science. They also suggested that, while the images of the products on the PowerPoint were useful, an actual prototype product that they could see and hold would have been nice and would have added something extra to the pitch.

Going forward, Michaela decided to take on board their feedback about the prototype. She had a prototype of each colour phone case made up for the investors to look at and try out. However, she decided to keep most of the technical language. She felt it supported her USP and emphasised to the investors that the product was truly eco-friendly.

She also carried out a self-assessment and decided to practise her verbal skills so that she felt more confident delivering the pitch. She prepared answers to the questions she could not answer and researched other questions that she might be asked.

The final pitch

The final pitch took place in the hotel meeting room, with the prototype products included as a visual aid. Michaela felt much more confident presenting having practised the pitch several times. However, she had some technical issues getting the projector to work, which delayed the start of the presentation. The presentation did include much of the technical language about the eco-friendly plastic, but for clarity she included further explanations of the technical terms in the handout.

Continued

At the end of the pitch, the investors asked questions about her costs and financial viability, which she answered well. However, despite lots of preparation, she had to refer to her notes to answer a question on the USP of the nearest competitor, EcoCase.

Check your understanding

1   Was Michaela's choice of venue and presentation support materials appropriate and suitable for the target audience? Explain your answer.

2   How did Michaela respond to the feedback from her practice pitch? Was her response adequate? Explain your answer.

3   Explain how the practice pitch helped Michaela prepare for the pitch to the investors and stockists.

Review your learning

Test your knowledge

1   What is a review?

2   Why is it important to carry out a review of a business proposal?

3   Explain one method that an entrepreneur can use to review a promotional campaign.

4   Explain why it is important to compare the outcomes of the pitch with the initial objectives.

What have you learnt?

	See section
• How to review a brand using a range of sources.	4.1
• How to review a professional pitch to an external audience.	4.2

Glossary

4Ps: The 4Ps is a reference to the marketing mix elements of product, place, promotion and price. The four elements make up the marketing mix for a product.

Accountant: A professional who prepares and analyses financial records and accounts.

Accounts: A statement of the financial position of a business. The accounts may show the profit/loss made by the business over a period of time and/or the value of the things it owns and its debts.

Added value: The difference between the cost of the materials used to produce a product and the selling price.

Advertising: A promotion technique to inform and attract customers to buy a specific product.

Aesthetics: How a product appeals to customers' senses.

The swimwear needs to have good aesthetics so that it looks fashionable and attractive.

Aim: A target or goal.

Biased: A tendency to favour one thing or person over another.

Convenience sampling reduces possible bias in the findings because it does not target specific groups.

Blog: Where a blogger (the author) writes regularly about a product or topic that will be of interest to followers.

Brand: A name, sign, symbol or slogan that is linked to a specific product or service that makes it stand out from the competition.

Brand association: When a brand is linked with positive or negative qualities or memories.

Brand identity: A set of elements created and used by a business to present the desired image of the company to customers.

Brand image: The perception that customers have of the brand. It is based on their experience with the brand or their beliefs about what the brand stands for.

Brand personality: Human characteristics associated with a brand name (e.g. exciting, rugged, sincere, competent).

Branding methods: The activities undertaken by a business to build a brand for their product or service (e.g. creating a brand name, jingles, straplines).

Break even: To earn sufficient revenue to cover all costs.

Break-even level of sales: The level of sales at which the total costs are equal to the total revenue generated.

Break-even point: The point at which a business is not making a profit or a loss. The total costs are equal to the total revenue generated.

Break-even quantity: The number of units that the business needs to sell to break even.

Budget: A prediction of income and expenditure over a period of time.

Business: An organisation that provides goods and services to satisfy customer needs.

Business angel: An experienced business owner who offers capital to support entrepreneurs to start or expand a business.

Business cycle: A series of events that the economy goes through, from economic booms (peaks) to recessions (troughs).

Capital: A sum of money owned by a business or used in a business for start-up or one-off expansion/investment.

The entrepreneur used their own savings to invest capital into their new business.

Cash: The physical money (notes and coins) that a business holds within the business and its bank account so that it is readily available to pay any debts or expenses.

The business had enough cash to pay all of its bills.

Celebrity endorsement: Using a celebrity's popularity or social status to sell a brand.

Chamber of Commerce: An organisation that promotes the interests of local business owners and entrepreneurs within a local area.

Characteristics: Qualities or features that determine an individual's personality.

Characteristics of target customers include their gender, age and lifestyle.

Charity: A not-for-profit organisation that raises money to support a specific cause.

Closed questions: Questions where the answer is limited to specific options, such as 'yes' or 'no', or selecting from fixed responses given in a multiple-choice list.

Commercial contacts: Other businesses that the entrepreneur deals with, such as suppliers and retailers, which the entrepreneur can call upon for feedback and advice.

Competitive pricing: A pricing strategy where prices are set in line with competitors' prices.

Competitor analysis: A study of a business's competition carried out by researching competitors' strengths and weaknesses.

Competitors: Other businesses that offer goods and services similar to those offered by the entrepreneur's business. The other business will try to meet the needs and wants of the same customers as those that the entrepreneur is targeting.

Constructive feedback: Supportive feedback that helps to improve weaknesses. It contains both positive and negative feedback.

The customer provided the restaurant with constructive feedback which explained what they liked about the restaurant, why they did not like the food, and suggestions about what the restaurant could do to improve the food.

Contingency plan: A strategy that a business/entrepreneur puts in place in case an unexpected event or situation occurs.

The school put in place a contingency plan so that if a pandemic occurs, lessons can still take place online.

Copyright: The legal right given to a person to protect their work for a period of years. It stops others from using or copying their work without permission. Copyright can apply to a design, a piece of music or other creative work, etc.

Costs: The money that a business has to pay out to run the business. That is, the expenses that a business incurs to produce and sell its goods and services.

Crowdfunding: A way of raising capital from a large number of people who each contribute a portion of the amount required. Usually the money is generated by advertising the business idea on a crowdfunding website to attract 'sponsors' to offer money.

Customer perception: How customers feel about a business's products and brand as a result of their experiences and interactions with the business.

Customer profile: The main characteristics of a customer or group of customers.

Data: Facts and figures that have been collected through research.

Demographic: Statistical data about the population of a country or region, or a specific sector, such as age, gender and income.

Design mix: The three elements that you need to consider when designing a new product: function, aesthetics and economic manufacture.

Differentiation: Making a brand stand out from the competition.

Dividend: A share of the profits that a company pays out to its shareholders.

E-commerce: This stands for electronic commerce and it is the buying and selling of goods and services over the internet.

Economic boom: A period of time when the economy is growing. Sales are high, unemployment is low and household incomes are rising.

Economic conditions: The state of the economy, e.g. what is the unemployment rate? What is the rate of inflation? Are incomes rising or falling?

Economy: All activities in a country concerning the making, selling and use of goods and services, measured by the level of GDP. (*See* **gross domestic product**)

Entrepreneur: An individual who sets up a new business providing a good or service that people are willing to buy to satisfy their needs. The entrepreneur bears the risk and receives the rewards of the business.

Extension strategy: A strategy used by an entrepreneur to stimulate more sales of a product when it is reaching the end of the product lifecycle.

External environment: Factors or forces outside of the business's control that are not within the business. For example, economic, ethical and technological factors that can change and have an impact on the business's operations.

Facilitator: A person who coordinates a focus group by asking questions and directing the conversation.

Feedback: A critique or information provided in response to a draft or initial idea.

Finalise: Complete a finished version of something (i.e. your design).

Financial viability: Whether a business or product is able to make sufficient (enough) sales and earn sufficient revenue to cover its costs and at least break even.

Financially viable: Able to generate enough income to cover the costs incurred to run the business.

The business was financially viable because its revenue covered its costs and it made a profit.

Findings: Information (data) that has been collected through research.

Fixed costs: Costs that do not change regardless of the level of output of the business.

The business's fixed costs included rent, electricity and gas bills, and advertising, and they were not affected when the level of output reduced.

Focus group: A group of people that meet to discuss their views on specific products or topics.

The focus group met face-to-face to discuss their opinions and views on a new range of biscuits.

Footfall: The number of people that are in, or walk past, a specific location.

Forecast: A prediction or estimate of what might happen in the future.

The business's sales forecast was accurate so it sold the number of products it had estimated.

Formal language: Used in professional situations or with people that we do not know well. Grammar is more complex and sentences are usually longer.

Franchise: An arrangement where one business allows another business to operate under its brand name or business format, usually in return for a fee.

Many fast-food restaurants, such as Subway and Burger King, operate as franchise businesses whereby the owner of the original business sells the right to operate under a well-known brand.

Franchisee: The business that has bought the right to operate under the franchise's brand name.

The franchisee paid Subway a fee to operate their business under the Subway brand.

Franchisor: The business that owns the franchise and grants a licence to the franchisee to use the brand/business format. Subway is an example of a franchisor that allows other businesses/entrepreneurs to open and run a business using the Subway brand name in return for a fee.

Function: How a product 'works' or what it 'does'.

The function of the shopping bag is to carry all of the items that the shopper has bought. It needs to be lightweight but also strong, so that it does not break if heavy items are placed inside.

Gantt chart: A visual planning tool that shows the start date, completion date and duration of each activity/task in a project, such as a promotional plan.

Gap in the market: An opportunity to provide a good or service which is currently not offered by other businesses in the market.

Global business: A business that operates in several countries across the world. The operations will include manufacturing and distribution facilities in different countries.

Goods: Items that businesses make and sell to satisfy customers' needs. Goods are often physical products.

Grants: Capital given to the business by the government or charities to start up or expand a business. Grants do not usually have to be repaid.

Gross domestic product (GDP): The total value of goods and services produced in a country.

Income: The money that a person earns. The amount varies depending on the type of job that they do.

Influencer: A person who can affect consumers' buying decisions. Influencers are commonly used in social media marketing and produce content (blogs, vlogs) recommending or outlining the features of a product or service to influence the buying decisions of others.

Informal language: Used when talking with or writing to people we know well. It is more casual or familiar language in terms of the tone and structure.

Inheritance: A sum of money or an object/property that a person is left (bequeathed) when a close friend or relative dies.

Insurance: Insurance offers protection to the entrepreneur against a potential financial loss. The insurance provider guarantees to provide the entrepreneur with financial compensation/payment in the event that an insured event, such as a fire or flood, occurs which causes the entrepreneur to suffer financial loss.

Interview: A structured conversation between the interviewer and one or more interviewees. The interviewer will ask a series of questions that the interviewee(s) answer(s). The interview could be carried out face-to-face or over the telephone or online.

Key performance indicator (KPI): A measurable value used in a business project or campaign to track progress towards and achievement of objectives.

The business set a KPI to increase the number of visitors to its website by 10 percent over the next six months.

Level of output: The number of units/products produced by a business.

Liability: Being responsible for something, such as paying a debt. The liability may arise as a result of signing a contract or it may be a legal responsibility, such as ensuring safe working conditions for employees.

Limited liability: If the business fails or gets into debt, the owner of the business can only lose the amount that they originally invested. They cannot be forced to sell their personal possessions to pay for the business's debts.

The shareholders of the private limited company lost the amount of money they had invested in shares, but they were not responsible for all of the debts of the business because it had limited liability.

Limited liability partnership: A business that is jointly owned and controlled by two or more people who benefit from limited liability. (*See* **limited liability**)

Logo: A symbol or picture that represents the business. It should be easy to recognise.

Loss: The amount of money that a business/entrepreneur loses. It is the opposite of a profit.

The business suffered a loss because its total revenue was less than the money it had spent (e.g. costs).

Manufacturing: The process of making or producing a product.

Market presence: The existence of a product, service or brand in the market and how well known and available it is.

The new product had a good market presence.

Market research: Activities to gather information about the needs and preferences of the target customers.

Market segmentation: The process of dividing up a market for a specific product into different groups, or segments, according to different characteristics, such as age, gender, occupation and lifestyle. This allows a business to target relevant customers.

Market share: The proportion of the total sales in a market made by a specific product or business. Market share is often expressed as a percentage.

The toy company increased market share by gaining sales from its competitors.

Marketing mix: The marketing mix is the four elements that the entrepreneur must use to promote its business or product. The four elements are: product, place, promotion and price.

Mass market: A good or service that appeals to nearly everyone. The market for the good or service is not segmented.

Mental health: How well an individual is in terms of their emotions, thoughts and feelings, and their ability to solve problems, work productively and cope with everyday life. It is part of overall well-being.

Minimise: Reduce as far as possible.

The business's strong brand reputation minimised the risk that customers would choose to buy a competitor's product instead.

Modifications: Changes made to a product to improve it.

Customer feedback showed that the product was too big to handle easily, so the entrepreneur made modifications to make it smaller.

Negotiation: A discussion aimed at reaching an agreement. Each person (known as a 'party') in the discussion may need to change what they want in order to reach an overall agreement.

Non-verbal skills: The way in which people communicate using body language, eye contact, facial expressions and gestures.

Objective: A measurable goal or target.

The objectives of the promotional campaign for the new product were to raise awareness of the product with potential customers, and make the product stand out from competitors' products.

Open questions: Questions that encourage people to respond using their own words, such as giving their views, reasons or opinions.

Partnership: A business that is jointly owned and controlled by two or more people. The partners generally have unlimited liability.

Partnership agreement: A contract prepared by the partners when they set up a business as a partnership. The contract will outline how profits/losses are to be shared, the amount of capital invested by each partner, information about how the partnership operates and the role of each partner. A partnership agreement is also known as a deed of partnership.

Patent: A patent gives a product's inventor/creator the legal right to stop other people making, using or selling their invention.

Physical health: The state of the physical body and how well it is functioning. Together with mental health this is part of overall well-being.

Pitch: A presentation designed to persuade an audience to invest in a business idea.

Pitching panel: A group of people who volunteer their time and expertise to offer advice to entrepreneurs about their pitches.

Podcast: A recording of someone discussing a specific product, business or topic on the internet. Podcasts can be downloaded as audio files.

Press/media release: A summary of a news story that is sent to journalists or radio and TV stations in the hope that they will publish or cover the story, which will generate free publicity for a business.

Price penetration: A pricing strategy in which products are launched with a low price. This price will increase over time as sales increase.

Price skimming: A pricing strategy that involves products being launched with a high price. This price will then reduce over time.

Pricing strategy: The method that businesses use to set a selling price for a product or service.

Primary market research: Data that is collected first-hand, i.e. the researcher collects the data themselves rather than relying on data that has been collected from previous research.

Private limited company: A business that is owned by shareholders. Each shareholder receives a proportion of the profits that the company makes based on the number of shares that the shareholder purchased.

Product lifecycle: A model which shows the stages that a product goes through from when it was created to when it is withdrawn from the market.

Profit: The amount of money that a business or entrepreneur makes. It is calculated by subtracting the money it has spent (e.g. costs to produce a product and operate the business) from its total income.

After a year of trading, Josh had sold enough T-shirts to cover his costs and make a profit.

Promotion: Activities and methods that businesses carry out to make potential customers aware of products and services.

Promotional campaign: The use of various advertising mediums and promotional techniques to promote the benefits of a product, service or brand to consumers and potential customers.

Proposal: A formal document created to convince an investor to invest in a business idea or product.

Prototype: An original or sample version of a product that is then modified to arrive at the design that a business sells to customers.

Psychological pricing: A pricing strategy to make products appear cheaper and more affordable by avoiding round numbers, e.g. £9.99 rather than £10.00.

Public relations: Promoting the company's reputation and building a beneficial relationship/positive image between a business and the public.

Qualitative data: Data expressed as opinions and views.

The qualitative data detailed what customers liked about the new baked beans they had bought.

Quantitative data: Data expressed as numbers or facts.

The quantitative data showed the number of people who bought a can of baked beans last week.

Questionnaire: A set of questions written to collect information from a group of people to meet a specific aim or purpose. The questions may be open and/or closed. A questionnaire may be part of a wider survey.

Raw materials: The materials, ingredients and resources used to produce a product.

Recession: A period of time when the economy is shrinking. Sales are low, unemployment is high and household incomes are likely to be falling.

Refine: Make minor changes to a proposal, campaign or pitch to improve the clarity or remove unwanted elements.

The entrepreneur refined their pitch by including more visual aids.

Reliability: How likely information (data) is to be accurate.

Respondents: The people completing a questionnaire or survey.

Revenue: The money that a business receives from selling its goods or services.

Josh made £1500 in revenue from selling 100 T-shirts at £15.

Review: A formal assessment of a product, service or piece of work against its aims. The findings of the review can be used to make improvements.

Reward: The benefit that the entrepreneur gets from taking the risk to start the business.

Risk: The chance that an action will have an adverse (negative) outcome. Starting a new business is a risk as it is not guaranteed to be a success.

Royalty fee: The share of the profits made by a franchisee that is paid each year to the franchisor. (*See* **franchisee** and **franchisor**)

Salaries: Payments to employees which do not vary according to the number of hours worked or their output. A salary is usually an annual amount which is divided into 12 equal monthly instalments that the employee receives for their work each month. Salaries are an example of a fixed cost.

Stefan's annual salary was £24 000, so at the end of every month he received a monthly salary of £2000.

Sample: The people chosen to take part in primary research.

Sampling: Choosing groups of individuals to represent the whole population or a sector of it.

Secondary market research: Data from sources that has been collected before.

The entrepreneur used government statistics when carrying out secondary research to find out the number of people living in a particular area.

Segment: A section of a market that contains specific groups of people.

Car manufacturers divide their market to target different models at different market segments, e.g. compact cars for those living in cities.

Self-assessment: The evaluation of your own ideas, design and performance.

The entrepreneur used self-assessment and feedback to review their pitch.

Self-satisfaction: When a person is pleased with themselves and their achievements.

Services: A non-physical task (e.g. teaching new skills to a group of trainees) that a business carries out to provide a benefit to the customer or meet customers' needs.

Shareholder: An individual who owns shares in a company. They become an owner by buying a share in the business.

SMS text message: Short Messaging Service is a messaging service used on mobile phones to send text-only messages to other mobile phones.

Social entrepreneur: An entrepreneur who establishes a business with the aim of solving a social or community-based problem. (*See* **entrepreneur**)

Sole trader: A business that is owned and controlled by one person.

A sole trader, such as a hairdresser or plumber, runs a business as an individual and is self-employed.

Solicitor: A professional who advises on legal matters relating to running a small business or a personal matter such as buying a house or managing divorce proceedings.

Sponsorship: Where a business offers financial support to an event, sports team or charity organisation in return for free advertising (e.g. sponsoring a sports team in return for the business's logo being printed on the team's shirts).

Start-up business: A new business that has just started to trade.

Strapline: A short, easy-to-remember phrase that summarises what a brand stands for. It can support a company's brand position. For example, 'Every little helps' by Tesco highlights their competitive pricing position.

Survey: The process of collecting, analysing and understanding the data collected from a group of people. A survey may include a questionnaire but is 'wider' than just a questionnaire.

Sustainable: Not depleting natural resources or upsetting the ecological balance. For example, cutting down forests for wood or to make way for livestock farming.

Target market: The customers that a business aims its products at.

The target market for toys is likely to be children.

Tax return: A document that a business submits to Her Majesty's Revenue and Customs (HMRC – the government department responsible for tax) each year showing its income and outgoings. It can be completed online. The tax return has a calculation showing how much tax is due. It is a legal requirement to submit a tax return.

Total costs: All of the costs that the business incurs for a particular level of output.

Unbiased: Not influenced by a person's own opinions.

Unique selling point (USP): A feature of a business's product, service or brand (e.g. a logo) that is the only one of its kind and distinctive. It makes the product or service stand out from those of competitors.

M&Ms' unique selling point that makes it stand out from its competitors is that 'the milk chocolate melts in your mouth, not in your hand'.

Unlimited liability: The owner of the business is liable for the total debts of the business. If the business fails or gets into debt, the owner may be forced to sell their personal possessions to repay the business's debts.

Utilities: Services such as gas, electricity, water, internet and telephone. A business requires these services to be able to operate.

Variable costs: Costs that vary in direct proportion to changes in the level of output.

The business's variable costs included the raw materials to make the product, and packaging.

Verbal skills: The use of language, words and tone of voice to share information with other people.

Visual aids: Items of a visual nature such as charts, graphs, images and videos, that support a presentation.

Vlog: Similar to a blog but using video. A vlogger (the author) produces visual information/video footage about a product or topic that will be of interest to followers. The footage is posted online.

Wages: A payment to employees which varies according to the number of hours worked or their output. A wage is an example of a variable cost.

The employees making the trainers are paid an hourly wage based on the number of hours they work. If they work fewer hours they are paid less, but if they work more hours they are paid more.

Well-being: The state of being healthy, happy and comfortable. Well-being can be physical or mental.

Work–life balance: The balance between the amount of time spent working and the amount of time spent on non-work activities.

Index